Forms of Hypocrisy in Early Modern England

This collection examines the widespread phenomenon of hypocrisy in literary, theological, political, and social circles in England during the years after the Reformation and up to the Restoration. Bringing together current critical work on early modern subjectivity, performance, print history, and private and public identities and space, the collection provides readers with a way into the complexity of the term, by offering an overview of different forms of hypocrisy, including educational practice, social transaction, dramatic technique, distorted worship, female deceit, print controversy, and the performance of demonic possession.

Lucia Nigri is Lecturer in Early Modern English Literature at the University of Salford, Manchester.

Naya Tsentourou is Lecturer in Early Modern Literature at the University of Exeter.

Routledge Studies in Renaissance Literature and Culture

For a full list of titles in this series, please visit www.routledge.com.

30 Imagining Arcadia in Renaissance Romance
Marsha S. Collins

31 Male-to-Female Crossdressing in Early Modern English Literature
Gender, Performance, and Queer Relations
Simone Chess

32 The Renaissance and the Postmodern
A Study in Comparative Critical Values
Thomas L. Martin and Duke Pesta

33 Enchantment and Dis-enchantment in Shakespeare and Early Modern Drama
Wonder, the Sacred, and the Supernatural
Edited by Nandini Das and Nick Davis

34 Twins in Early Modern English Drama and Shakespeare
Daisy Murray

35 Gender, Speech, and Audience Reception in Early Modern England
Katie Kalpin Smith

36 Women's Prophetic Writings in Seventeenth-Century Britain
Carme Font

37 Mendacity and the Figure of the Liar in Seventeenth-Century French Comedy
Emilia Wilton-Godberfforde

38 Forms of Hypocrisy in Early Modern England
Edited by Lucia Nigri and Naya Tsentourou

Forms of Hypocrisy in Early Modern England

Edited by Lucia Nigri
and Naya Tsentourou

Routledge
Taylor & Francis Group

NEW YORK AND LONDON

First published 2018
by Routledge
711 Third Avenue, New York, NY 10017

and by Routledge
2 Park Square, Milton Park, Abingdon, Oxon OX14 4RN

Routledge is an imprint of the Taylor & Francis Group,
an informa business

© 2018 Taylor & Francis

The right of the editors to be identified as the authors of the
editorial material, and of the authors for their individual
chapters, has been asserted in accordance with sections
77 and 78 of the Copyright, Designs and Patents Act 1988.

All rights reserved. No part of this book may be reprinted
or reproduced or utilised in any form or by any electronic,
mechanical, or other means, now known or hereafter invented,
including photocopying and recording, or in any information
storage or retrieval system, without permission in writing from
the publishers.

Trademark notice: Product or corporate names may be
trademarks or registered trademarks, and are used only for
identification and explanation without intent to infringe.

Library of Congress Cataloging-in-Publication Data
CIP date has been applied for.

ISBN: 978-1-138-29124-9 (hbk)
ISBN: 978-1-315-26556-8 (ebk)

Typeset in Sabon
by codeMantra

Contents

Bibliographical Note		vii
	Introduction	1
	LUCIA NIGRI AND NAYA TSENTOUROU	
1	Hypocrisy, Dissimulation, and Education for Civic Life in Pre-Revolutionary England	15
	MARKKU PELTONEN	
2	Trading in Gratitude: John Donne's Verse Epistles to His Patronesses	33
	SILVIA BIGLIAZZI	
3	Religious Hypocrisy in Performance: Roman Catholicism and The London Stage	57
	LUCIA NIGRI	
4	Flattery, Hypocrisy, and Identity in *Thomas of Woodstock*	72
	ROSSANA SEBELLIN	
5	"Come buy Lawn Sleeves": Linen and Material Hypocrisy in Milton's Antiprelatical Tracts	87
	NAYA TSENTOUROU	
6	"Much like the Picture of the Devill in a Play": Hypocrisy and Demonic Possession	101
	JACQUELINE PEARSON	

vi   *Contents*

7   Abject Hypocrisy: Gender, Religion, and the Self   119
    KATHARINE HODGKIN

8   Henry Hills and the Tailor's Wife: Adultery and
    Hypocrisy in the Archive   138
    MICHAEL DURRANT

    Notes on Contributors   157
    Index   161

Bibliographical Note

In this volume the authors have retained the spelling of the texts or editions from which they quote, but have modernised typography, substituting modern equivalents for obsolete characters and rationalising conventions such as u/v and i/j spelling.

Introduction

Lucia Nigri and Naya Tsentourou

The Circulation of Hypocrisy

In a play famously concerned with the epistemological distinction between what 'seems' and what 'is', Polonius warns Ophelia against accepting Hamlet's declarations of love. His paternal sermon ends in the following instructions:

> In few, Ophelia,
> Do not believe his vows, for they are brokers
> Not of that dye which their investments show,
> But mere implorators of unholy suits
> Breathing like sanctified and pious bonds
> The better to beguile. This is for all.
>
> (1.3.125–30)

The message in these lines is rather straightforward: Hamlet's personified vows are hypocritical because they assume an honest appearance in order to achieve immoral ends. For Polonius, Hamlet's encounters with Ophelia might come with promises of sincere affection but they ultimately target sexual gratification. While the gist of Polonius's authoritarian command is clear, the passage is complex in its blend of overlapping vocabularies (religious, financial, material, sexual) and in its unstable textual history, making multiple interpretations available all at once. If the vows are "breathing like sanctified and pious bonds" does that mean they are to be read as the bonds of holy matrimony? Do Hamlet's vows assume a reverential exterior, the personification tapping into the early modern period's widespread concern with religious hypocrisy? This reading would fit quite well with the vows acting as "mere implorators of unholy suits" ("suits" here referring to requests of devout supplicants), as well as with the duplicity of their clothing ("investments"), given contemporary controversies over clerical garments (Hwang 2016). But religious hypocrisy, or Hamlet's ungodly behaviour in his treatment of Ophelia, might not be what is at stake for Polonius. The "vows", alongside their personification as "brokers", "implorators", and "bonds" could be inviting a predominantly secular

2 *Lucia Nigri and Naya Tsentourou*

reading that underpins the language of financial transaction. Focusing on the commercial undertones of the passage Hamlet is presented as a dissembling trader, his vows mediating between bargains unprofitable to Ophelia. In keeping with the clothing metaphor – but in a sense wider than solely church vestments – the "dye which their investments show" suggests the materiality of their deception: Hamlet's vows come in an attire that both masks their true intentions and conceals the expected revenue. If we accept "the centrality of clothes as the material establishers of identity" in the Renaissance (Jones and Stallybrass 2000, 4), Polonius here is eager to expose the fraudulent nature of Hamlet under the metaphorical cloak of his vows. Coupled with his sarcastic twist on Ophelia's use of the term "fashion" (1.3.110) a few lines earlier (in response to Ophelia referring to Hamlet's manner of making his love known as "honourable fashion"; 1.3.109), the embodiment of hypocrisy in one's garments informs Polonius's convoluted speech. Moreover, as discourses of material transactions and financial exchange are never too far from discourses of sex, the term "brokers" (recorded in the *Oxford English Dictionary* as "an intermediary" both "in business" and "love affairs"; Proffitt 2016) frames Hamlet's deceitfulness as sexually driven, and his vows as prostituting words that seek to defile Ophelia with their "unholy suits" or corrupt desires.

Since the publication of the play, editorial choices, instead of clarifying, have added to the density of the metaphor. The sexual significance of the passage has been reinforced by editors, such as Oxford's G. R. Hibbard who, following Lewis Theobald's emendation in his *Shakespeare Restored* (1726), chooses to print "bawds" in place of "bonds" (Seary 1990, 72–3). While acknowledging the sexual implications of the words "bawds" and "brokers", the Arden editors, Ann Thompson and Neil Taylor, prefer to maintain "bonds" as more in line with what they perceive "as the main focus" of Polonius's speech: "the near-synonymous triplet of vows-suits-bonds" (2016, 230). "Dye", "implorators", and "beguile" also have a contested history, being in Judith Anderson's words "irreducibly duplicitous" and rendering any definite interpretations of the passage impossible (1998, 251).

Whether in Polonius's speech Hamlet's hypocrisy participates in sacred or profane debates of the period is hard to determine, but we might be missing a trick if we insist on trying to establish the exact context in which the metaphor belongs. "Sex, religion, clothing, and commerce intertwine" (ibid.); the concept that ties these discourses together and gives them all currency simultaneously is hypocrisy. The theme of hypocrisy permeates the extract as it circulates from religious to secular discourses, located in the exchanges between brokers and their targets. Considering that there is little evidence to suggest Hamlet is insincere in his affections for Ophelia, hypocrisy is everywhere and yet nowhere. Asking Ophelia to trust his paternal warning, Polonius

Introduction 3

projects hypocrisy on to Hamlet's speech acts, such as his vows. But it is Polonius who can be regarded as the ultimate "broker" in the play, who acts as a negotiator of both the couple's mutual understanding of their sentiment and the king's interpretation of Hamlet's madness/love. The evocation of Hamlet's "unholy suits" indeed serves his aim to convince Ophelia of a certainty he has no direct knowledge of, and of which he swiftly backtracks in Act 2 ('I feared he did but trifle / And meant to wrack thee – but beshrew my jealousy' (2.1.109–10).

The context that critics tend to ignore in trying to understand this passage and to unravel the contesting metaphors of hypocrisy is that of air and breath. Hypocrisy appears in this extract as flowing energy, akin to breath via which it is transmitted. The line "breathing like sanctified and pious bonds" captures the elemental nature of both breath and hypocrisy: both invisible yet present, both circulating between bodies, both originating in an internal state but identifiable by external symptoms. This is not the first time Polonius uses breathing when referring to spreading lies. Catechising Reynaldo about how to engage in espionage of Laertes, Polonius again uses "breath" to refer to hypocritical words, and to the spread of unsubstantiated rumours: "But breathe his faults so quaintly / That they may seem the taints of liberty" (2.1.31–2). Yet, the air might not be only metaphorically corrupt. If we follow Theobald's and Hibbard's choice of "bawds" instead of "bonds", the lines open up interesting questions about prostitution and pestilence, another central preoccupation of the play that dramatises the "foul and pestilent congregation of vapours" (2.2.268). The close proximity between metaphorical and literal understandings of hypocritical breathing, or between the "religious and climatological forms of corruption" (Mazzio 2009, 177), is further reinforced if we place the breathing "bawds"/"bonds" next to the opening of the following scene. A few lines later, scene 4 begins with Hamlet exclaiming "the air bites shrewdly; it is very cold" to which Horatio responds "it is nipping, and an eager air" (1.4.1–2). The insubstantial claims Polonius attributes to Hamlet only add to an already hostile atmospheric environment. However one highlights the significance of air and breathing in the construction of Polonius's conceit, we are not closer to define hypocrisy. Far from it, the passage becomes even more complex and slippery. And yet, thinking about hypocrisy as breathing opens up new directions into the exploration of a term as elusive as air; it urges us to consider hypocrisy as elemental and as a circulating energy that brings into dialogue competing discourses.

Approaching Hypocrisy: The Bible, Identity, and Practice

The current collection takes as its starting point the pervasiveness of hypocrisy in sixteenth- and seventeenth-century England and is interested in recovering and historicising some of its most notable material

4   *Lucia Nigri and Naya Tsentourou*

manifestations. Although our study acknowledges that hypocrisy, dissimulation, equivocation, lying, and similar duplicitous behaviours are not exclusive to the early modern period, we follow historians and literary scholars who have argued for "an early modern obsession with false identities" (Eliav-Feldon 2015, 1) and an unprecedented "intensity" of charges of hypocrisy in the period (Bailey 2015, 9, see also Zagorin 1990, Chapter 1). An admittedly basic test proves the hypothesis: an EEBO search of works in the sixteenth and seventeenth century featuring in their content the word "hypocrisy" in its variant spellings and forms returns 39,223 hits in 10,497 records. This is only an elementary indication of the widespread use of the term, but it highlights the extensive preoccupation with the phenomenon of hypocrisy, and the time and effort spent on its articulation.

In the vast majority of these works hypocrisy is associated with false religion, drawing on the biblical precedent of the archetypal hypocrites: the Pharisees. While the Pharisees have become a stock figure of hypocrisy, it is worth here to briefly look at their function in seventeenth-century texts in order to raise some preliminary questions about hypocrisy in the context of religion, identity, and social order. A case in point is Robert Ball, preacher in the County of Sussex, who published in 1635 a collection of six sermons under the title, *The Mirror of Pure Devotion: or, the Discovery of Hypocrisie*. The six sermons comprised of an exposition on the parable of the Pharisee and the Publican found in Luke: 18. In Luke's account, the parable was delivered by Jesus to his disciples describing two petitionary models: the Pharisaic one, characterised by arrogantly eloquent speech, condemnation of the fellow human being, and blind observation of the fast and tithes of the church, and the Publican's model, characterised by humility, intense devotional gesture, and acknowledgement of one's sins. The biblical moral of Jesus's story was that "every one that exalteth himself shall be abased; and that he that humbleth himself shall be exalted" (Luke: 18.14; King James Bible). Pride and confidence in one's assumed state of sinlessness would be condemned by God on Judgement Day, whereas the heartfelt expression of one's penitence would be celebrated. For Ball, the purpose of the parable, and therefore of his delivered and printed sermons, was twofold: "for this Parable was propounded not onely in *terrorem populi* ... for the terrour and confusion of hollow hypocrites ... but also in *consolationem sanctorum*, for the comfort and consolation of true Saints" (178). The tale served as a denunciation of hypocritical prayer and as a panegyric for honest devotion. Other than this collection of sermons there is very little known about Ball, but his published work fits neatly within this trend in religious pamphlet-writing to have hypocrisy "detected", "diplay'd", "unmasked", "discovered", "manifested" and "unvail'd". The Pharisaic model of petition and its insincerity were very frequently expounded upon in sermons and treatises of the early modern period,

Introduction 5

from William Tyndale's *An Expocition Uppon the v.vi.vii chapters of Matthew* (1533) to George Topham's *Pharisaism display'd, or Hypocrisie detected* (1690).

The Pharisee and the Publican parable was only one of the biblical texts that contributed to the association of the Pharisees with hypocrisy. The most prominent account of the New Testament that established the connection between the two terms was in Matthew 23. This passage follows Jesus casting the merchants and traders out of the temple of God in Jerusalem and then answering the questions of the religious authorities whose power he came to overturn. After exposing the Pharisees' ignorance of the true nature of the Law and of God's ways, Jesus addresses his disciples and the people, painting the portrait of the Pharisees as "an outstanding example of extrinsic religiosity" (Moberg 1987, 7). In successive accusations and with a damning tone, Jesus attacks their two-facedness:

> Woe unto you, scribes and Pharisees, hypocrites! for ye shut up the kingdom of heaven against men: for you neither go in yourselves, neither suffer ye them that are entering to go in... for you devour widows' houses, and for a pretence make long prayer... for you are like unto whited sepulchres, which indeed appear beautiful outward, but are within full of dead men's bones, and of all uncleanness.
> (Matthew 23: 13–27; King James Version)

The "pretence [of] long prayer" is also evident in Matthew 6, where hypocrisy is again identified as the opposite of devotion. Jesus urges the people to avoid the example of the hypocrites in prayer who "sound a trumpet", "pray standing", and are "of a sad countenance" (6: 2–16). The biblical designation of hypocrisy as an improper, or degenerated, prayer became a common trope in early modern writing, where the figure of the hypocrite featured very often as one who pretended to be devout. John Bate, for instance, remarked in his 1589 work, *The Portraiture of Hypocrisie*, that "if a man boast that he feareth God and liveth christian like ... not doing him honour in heart by obedience, to whom with lippes hee acknowledgeth subiection, is it not too too grosse hipocrisie?" (5) Almost a century later, Samuel Speed gave a more humorous account of the hypocrite, drawing heavily on the biblical examples of hypocrisy:

> When to the Church he comes, he there salutes
> One of the Pillars, and on knee confutes
> The Atheist, worshiping that God, in part,
> Whose Precepts never could affect his heart.
> He rises, looks about, and takes his seat.
> (1677, 31)

6 Lucia Nigri and Naya Tsentourou

Speed summarised the attributes of a hypocrite in one line: "hypocrites habit is Formality" (54), thus providing another example of a discourse of hypocrisy as embodied in devout exterior.

What exactly was the danger of hypocrisy that Jesus and early modern writers urged against? A closer examination of Matthew 23 might suggest that the danger of hypocrisy was of concern for the individual's moral state, yet it entailed an additional social dimension, which made hypocrisy a Christian's enemy and an enemy of Christianity. The Scribes and Pharisees personified the concealed gap between inward corruption and outward devotion, but in their function as religious authorities they jeopardised not only their own relationship to God, but also the physical and ideological state of their subordinates. By "shutting up the kingdom of heaven against men" and "devouring widows' houses", they constituted a threat to the wider devout and less privileged community that Jesus was primarily concerned with (Hogan 1999, 99). Bate's treatise expressed similar concerns:

> For if the hollownesse of their hearts were laid open, wee shoulde finde that they hate him, for like as malefactors coulde wish in heart there were no Judge, no order, no pollicie, no governement in the world, that they might comit mischiefe with more libertie: even so these, what copie soever their countenance carrieth, in mind they despise God, and if it were possible, woulde plucke him out of heaven.
>
> (Bate 1589, 5)

Whereas individual hatred against God might not have been a matter of public concern, the act of hypocrisy demonstrated a rejection of God as omnipresent and omniscient and a perpetuation of social inequality. By putting on a false exterior, the hypocrite for Bate became almost an anarchist figure, standing for a lawless, immoral, and disorderly life, where God was no longer capable of witnessing and judging human actions. For these writers, hypocrisy and order seemed engaged in a paradoxical relationship: hypocrisy needed order or, to borrow Speed's term, "formality" to be successful in hiding its interior state, yet hypocrisy subverted order by denying God's place in man's life and by encouraging an unjust social setting.

This dialectic relationship between order and hypocrisy is a clear manifestation of the tension of a turbulent epoch of increasing anxiety when the "ubiquity of hypocrisy", to use Markku Peltonen's words, is manifested through a wide range of strategies of subversion (political, religious, rhetorical) that destabilise social order while, paradoxically, preserving and restoring it. Cutting across many cultural fields, the widespread and thoroughly debated phenomenon of hypocrisy – which, according to Jacqueline Pearson's chapter in this volume, "may ... only be one part of a complex tangle of conscious and unconscious

Introduction 7

motivations" – functions in less rigid ways than those articulated by the Christian writers above. In the context of treatises on moral philosophy and political theory, for example, the motives and ramifications of hypocrisy address specific discourses on practical statecraft and political calculation (Strohm 2005), with the Machiavellian stock-figures that come to epitomise ambiguous and complex attitudes to power (Grant 1997, 3–7; Zagorin 1990, 6–13; see also Nigri's and Sebellin's chapters in this collection, which engage with discourses and practices related to deception and theatricality in the period between *ca.* 1500 and 1750).

Even for thinkers of civic life and rhetoric, hypocrisy was a productive force in shaping one's relation to their immediate and wider social circles, in the court and in the state, as demonstrated by the identification of practices of equivocation and dissimulation (Berensmeyer and Hadfield 2016; Herzig and Eliav-Feldon 2015; Zagorin 1990). Markku Peltonen's chapter on the analysis of rhetoric manuals and Silvia Bigliazzi's close examination of the expressive strategies John Donne developed in response to the pressures of the patronage system further explore relevant conduct and societal codes in the early modern period.

As the title suggests, the contributors explore different 'forms' of hypocrisy, and they investigate hypocrisy in its multiple institutionalised, public, or private practices. If hypocrisy as a phenomenon is as elusive and abstract as air, and as prevalent in the early modern era as in contemporary twenty-first-century post-truth politics, the study of the material forms it takes, together with a discourse of hypocritical identities and self-conscious acting, can prove methodologically the most effective in initiating a meaningful debate of its significance. Form, of course, can vary in its definitions, from referring to "shapes and arrangement of parts" to "prescribed methods of procedure" and "fixed order of words" (*OED*; Proffitt 2016), or from material objects and conditions to rhetoric and literary genres. In the followings chapters, forms of hypocrisy include conduct manuals, verse epistles, and expressions of politeness, the female body, clothing, and print accounts. What the chapters share is an interest in exploring how narratives of hypocrisy adopt these specific forms, how they come to be constructed and circulated in a period that witnessed an unprecedented rise in the scrutiny of the meanings of 'sincerity', and sought to contain religious and emotional fraud. Very often these forms are themselves unstable and that renders the attribution of intentions or agency problematic: they can come charged with a combination of religious and market ideologies (Tsentourou's chapter), they can be associated with femaleness (Hodgkin's chapter), or they can capitalise on print culture's blurry lines between assumed facts and fictions (Pearson's and Durrant's chapters). As in the example of Polonius, we understand that hypocrisy is the main idea, but we simply cannot tell for certain where he draws his examples from or what critique Shakespeare might be aiming at. The multivocality and multiformity of hypocritical discourses in this collection point to a similar problem. Uncovering any essential truth under the web of discourses and multi-layered forms is impossible, and this is where our collection departs from existing scholarship on hypocrisy as the volatile nature of the material discussed here undermines attempts to speak of fixed identities. While Jacques Bos argues that "the hypocrite tries to manipulate the semiotic system that theoretically makes it possible to recognise moral qualities" (2002, 75), our contributors are less eager to separate hypocrites from the systems they try to manipulate. This degree of autonomy on the part of the hypocrite is implicit in studies which explore the masking (literal or metaphorical) of individuals or groups of individuals as self-fashioning or accusations of hypocrisy as a mechanism for othering. In the context of religious disputes of the mid-seventeenth century for, instance, Peter Lake has shown that the visible holiness of the godly led their opponents to accuse them of hypocritical behaviour:

> Alienating their neighbours by their aggressively holier-than-thou self-image and rhetoric, the godly's pretensions to godliness and infractions of the norms of good neighbourhood and good fellowship positively invited the sort of inversionary libels and satires, the accusations of self-serving hypocrisy and faction.
>
> (1996, 160)

The difference from the ungodly was a prerequisite for the formation of the godly identity: "the one implied, indeed needed and in part created, the other" (ibid., 165). Hypocrisy in this respect was a label that simultaneously defined both the labelled and the 'labeller' and, in a similar vein, Mark Knights writes that "the notion that there was a real inner self, to which you could be sincere or hypocritical, seems an important step towards a modern notion of an autonomous self" (2011, 165). In his historical account, Lake underlines the construction of the self in the godly communities: "the ungodly then were the alter egos, the evil twins, of the godly" (1996, 164). Katharine Eisaman Maus, in her study of early modern inwardness, reaches similar conclusions: "the extravagant hypocrites of the religious polemics are the evil twins, as it were, of saints and martyrs. They personify the dark underside of a positive theology of interior conviction" (1995, 44). Hypocrisy thus becomes, for both Lake and Maus, a mechanism for self-identification and representation. More recently, Tobias B. Hug has also been interested in the self-representation of impostors in early modern England, or else in "the shaping of their identities and stories, understood as a cultural practice" (2009, 1) and, while drawing on the dialogic form of courtesy books, Jennifer Richards has paid close attention both to individual agency and social interactions in her study of Renaissance humanists and their use of the dialogue form (2003).

Introduction 9

While such scholarship has been valuable in understanding the multiple purposes that public or private hypocrisy could serve, it has treated the phenomenon of hypocrisy as originating in conscious acts of self-assertion. Our collection shifts the focus from the hypocrites to the wider responses they inspired and the materials that shaped and gave voice to these responses. While attentive to the implications of their respective case studies for the formation of individual and communal subjectivities, the contributors here are interested in the practice rather than the identity politics of hypocrisy. The term hypocrisy has been chosen for its multivalence and inclusivity, drawing on its original meanings of interpreting, judging, and answering. It has also been chosen to avoid the limitations of terms such as dissimulation or lying, which presuppose again a degree of agency on the part of the dissembler and a conscious act of concealment. The collection contributes to, and shares, the intellectual and methodological values that inform Ingo Berensmeyer and Andrew Hadfield's recent work on mendacity where systems of truth and falsehood are explored in their connection to historical and cultural change (2016). Though narrower in chronological scope, this volume is influenced by their approach and seeks to build on their findings towards establishing a field of 'hypocrisy studies'.

This book is also indebted to less censorious methodologies, such as Jenny Davidson's call "that hypocrisy [can] be treated as morally neutral" (2003, 5). Drawing on eighteenth-century literature, Davidson identifies the problem with current criticism on hypocrisy:

> we are consequently put in the position of having to choose between two unsatisfactory alternatives: a philosophical vocabulary that is inherently antagonistic to hypocrisy and a sociological vocabulary to which hypocrisy is so integral that it offers no way of speaking about hypocrisy (as it were) from the outside.
>
> (Ibid., 6)

By philosophical vocabulary Davidson refers to thinkers such as Augustine, Castiglione, Machiavelli, and Kant who either condemned hypocrisy or theorised it as a strategy (see also Berensmeyer and Hadfield 2016), while in the sociological vocabulary she enlists the work of Erving Goffman whose discussion of all human activity as performance allows little scope for seeing hypocrisy as anything other than acting. Commenting on misrepresentation, for instance, Goffman writes:

> Whether an honest performer wishes to convey the truth or whether a dishonest performer wishes to convey a falsehood, both must take care to enliven their performances with appropriate expressions that might discredit the impression being fostered, and take care lest the audience impute unintended meanings. Because of these shared

10 *Lucia Nigri and Naya Tsentourou*

dramatic contingencies, we can profitably study performances that are quite false in order to learn about ones that are quite honest.

(1990, 73)

Goffman here essentially breaks down any division between honest and false performances, rendering meaningful interpretations of hypocrisy impossible.

Forms of Hypocrisy

The alternative approach this book offers to such a contested and open-ended concept as hypocrisy is its focus on material forms. The volume's textual interest is in fact underpinned by a cultural and materialist approach where a range of texts are contextualised against the political, religious, and social background of reformation and post-reformation England both implicitly and explicitly. This thematic consistency allows the authors of the essays to examine a range of manifestations of hypocrisy both across and within genres, thus ensuring interdisciplinarity, while addressing, in its spatial and chronological scope, possible ways into the complexity of the term and into the cultural roots of conceptual issues relating to falsehood, truthfulness, and power.

In the following chapters, materiality is defined in a variety of ways, referring to bodies and objects as much as education, audiences, and readers, theatre, patronage, autobiography, and community. The essays offer close textual analysis of verse and prose writings as well as drama with an exploration of contemporaneous ideological anxieties stemming from the paradigm shift experienced in the period to present a reading of prevalent cultural, religious, and gender ideologies.

The first two chapters by Markku Peltonen and Silvia Bigliazzi open the discussion on hypocrisy by taking us back to the basics of the practice as they both investigate hypocrisy's relation to manners and its practical applications to everyday life in the early modern period.

In the first chapter, "Hypocrisy, Dissimulation, and Education for Civic Life in Pre-Revolutionary England", Markku Peltonen offers a new perspective on how rhetoric classes and manuals had a distinctive place in early modern grammar schools. Stemming from Peltonen's previous work on manners (2003), this contribution places his research in a wider framework of hypocritical behaviour in the period and demonstrates the importance of rhetoric and civil conversation in pre-revolutionary England when schoolboys were taught in the values of dissimulation, fraud, and hypocrisy as a way of participating, and exercising, political power.

This perspective establishes hypocrisy as a rhetorical trope, which figures prominently in the next chapter by Silvia Bigliazzi: "Trading in Gratitude: John Donne's Verse Epistles to His Patronesses". Here, classroom rhetoric

Introduction   11

gives way to courtly writing conventions and hypocrisy is exposed as a self-fashioning mechanism relied upon for power and social status. In Bigliazzi's contribution, a close reading of Donne's figurative and argumentative strategies contained within his verse epistles to his patronesses shows how gratitude and hypocrisy gave shape to a codified discourse of power- and identity-trade. Donne's intricate discursive practices negotiate praises and pleads for favours to his patronesses, thus offering a privileged insight into social negotiations shaping his relationship with them and his camouflaged desire to free himself from any obligation.

The following two chapters by Lucia Nigri and Rossana Sebellin engage with issues of theatricality, both in practical and ideological terms. In *Characters of Virtues and Vices* (1608), Joseph Hall describes the character of "The Hypocrite" as the "worst kind of player, by so much as he acts the better part" (1837, 104). This description, together with Earle's characterisation of the "Shee-precise Hypocrite" in 1628, is evidence of the popularity of both the term and the type in cultural discourses of early modern England. The Elizabethan and Jacobean stage confirms the 'attractiveness' of this character which persistently appears in comedies, history plays, and tragedies. The important thing is that there is a clear connection here between the drama and the prevailing social reality. The 'stage hypocrite' is a product only partly of theatrical tradition: he could and often did express the sense of deception and incoherence experienced in specific forms by members of the audiences who watched these plays and who very often associated this figure with clergy's behaviour.

Lucia Nigri's "Religious Hypocrisy in Performance: Roman Catholicism and The London Stage" investigates how, spurred on by anti-catholic feelings, representations of hypocrisy and early modern audience's expectations of stage hypocrites are dealt with during the most formative and productive decades of the early modern English stage, the 1590s–1610s. Shakespearean and non-Shakespearean plays use performance itself to illuminate the issue of hypocritical performance on a metatheatrical level and become distinctive *loci* where interpretations of hypocrisy are negotiated and where dramatists engage with the issue through stagecraft and related practices, such as garments.

The commercial stage and the dramatisation of hypocrisy in the period are also central to Rossana Sebellin's chapter, "Flattery, Hypocrisy and Identity in *Thomas of Woodstock*". Sebellin explores theatrical representations of hypocrisy in the anonymous early modern play, *Thomas of Woodstock*, also known as *King Richard II part 1*. The focus here is on the display of falseness and the double standards of behaviour between public display of bounty and virtue and the actual political cunning and imposture of the Court, which stand as strongly critical of the true nature of power as opposed to its public appearance. As Corbin and Sedge state in the Introduction to the Revels Plays edition, "the play

12 *Lucia Nigri and Naya Tsentourou*

as a whole allows its audience to look beneath the façade of 'establish-ment' ceremony and public relations iconography to examine the naked ambition and jockeying of power and influence which characterize the *realpolitik* and falsehood of stagecraft" (2002, 36–7).

The anxieties about the immoral nature of early modern spectacles is then addressed by Naya Tsentourou who examines the material culture of hypocrisy in Milton's polemical tracts. In her chapter, "'Come buy Lawn Sleeves': Linen and Material Hypocrisy in Milton's Antiprelatical Tracts", Tsentourou explores popular culture and Milton's prose in the context of 1640s anti-Laudian sentiment. Focusing on Milton's rhetori-cal strategy as one that blends texts with textiles, the chapter argues for a re-evaluation of Milton's references to the bishops' linen vestments as participating in a mercantile economy of embodiment.

Religious hypocrisy is further developed in Jacqueline Pearson's chapter, "'Much like the picture of the Devill in a play': Hypocrisy and Demonic Possession". Pearson examines a very effective assemblage of accounts of demonic possession and their ambivalent degree of authen-ticity. More than any other supernatural event, demonic possession in the early modern period raised conundrums about authenticity, hypoc-risy, and performance, since the only evidence was the performance of the alleged victim. The author's exploration of the motives they often conceal is both subtle and persuasive and she lays the basis for a dis-cussion on discourses of hypocrisy as part of the struggle between the established church and its critics.

Katharine Hodgkin's discussion of the outward and inward division of hypocrisy in "Abject Hypocrisy: Gender, Religion, and the Self" re-flects on the inward mobility of hypocrisy which changes from a charge directed at an external group (as seen in Nigri's, Tsentourou's, and Pearson's contributions to this collection) to an internal dilemma of recognising and reforming or managing a hypocrite. Looking at John Stachniewski's *The Persecutory Imagination* for its remarks on the anx-ieties induced in the Protestant mind by the idea of hypocrisy, Katharine Hodgkin's discussion of Protestant understandings of hypocrisy scru-tinises misogynistic associations of deceit with femaleness ("hypocrisy as a spiritual sin is closely entangled with the feminine, both as a set of shared quality ... and as a rhetorical trope which highlights the dis-continuity of the bosy's inside and outside through the metaphor of the painted woman", she argues). Gender and deceit are here explored in the context of spiritual autobiography where sexual and spiritual dishonesty are often intimately connected in the conscience of seventeenth-century Protestant believers. Sexual and spiritual untrustworthiness are figured as versions of one another.

The final chapter "Henry Hills and the Tailor's Wife: Adultery and Hypocrisy in the Archive" by Michael Durrant is a detailed account of the print culture of Restoration London, via a case study of one of its more colourfully protean figures. Life-writing, print culture, and dissimulation are the central concerns of this essay on the intriguing figure of Henry Hills, a seventeenth-century printer whose diverse biographical accounts betray the role of print in creating hypocritical narratives. The archival materials that remain to tell Hills' life story are peppered with dramatic scenes of dissimulation, domestic disruption, side-changing, and conspiracy, so much so that Hills emerges less as a tangible, or easily retrievable, historical figure, than he does a cultural emblem or metonym, encapsulating a number of complex politico-religious and cultural anxieties prevalent during his own lifetime and after. Durrant locates his discussion on "hypocrisy in the archive" not only in relation to debates around how we write early modern lives, but also in the context of a wider scholarly turn towards the "human personalities" (McDowell 2007) who utilised the technologies of early modern book production.

Works Cited

Anderson, Judith H. 1998. "Translating Investments: The Metaphoricity of Language, *2 Henry IV*, and *Hamlet*". *Texas Studies in Literature and Language* 40(3): 231–67.

Bailey, Michael D. 2015. "Superstition and Dissimulation: Discerning False Religion in the Fifteenth Century". In *Dissimulation and Deceit in Early Modern Europe*, edited by Tamar Herzig and Miriam Eliav-Feldon, 9–26. New York: Palgrave.

Ball, Robert. 1635. *The Mirror of Pure Devotion: or, the Discovery of Hypocrisie Delivered in Sixe Sermons*. London: Iohn Legatt.

Bate, John. 1589. *The Portraiture of Hypocrisie, Lively and Pithilie Pictured in Her Colours Wherein You May View the Ugliest and Most Prodigious Monster that England Hath Bredde*. London: Robert Robinson.

Berensmeyer, Ingo and Andrew Hadfield (eds). 2016. *Mendacity in Early Modern Literature and Culture*. London: Routledge.

Bos, Jacques. 2002. "The Hidden Self of the Hypocrite". In *On the Edge of Truth and Honesty: Principles and Strategies of Fraud and Deceit in the Early Modern Period*, edited by Toon van Houdt et al., 65–84. Leiden Boston: Brill.

Corbin, Peter, and Douglas Sedge. 2002. Introduction to *Thomas of Woodstock or Richard the Second, Part One*, by Anonymous, 1–46. Manchester: Manchester University Press (The Revels Plays).

Davidson, Jenny. 2003. *Hypocrisy and the Politics of Politeness: Manners and Morals from Locke to Austen*. Cambridge: Cambridge University Press.

Eliav-Feldon, Miriam. 2015. Introduction to *Dissimulation and Deceit in Early Modern Europe*, edited by Tamar Herzig and Miriam Eliav-Feldon, 1–8. New York: Palgrave.

Goffman, Erving. 1990. *The Presentation of Self in Everyday Life*. London: Penguin Books.

Grant, Ruth W. 1997. *Hypocrisy and Integrity: Machiavelli, Rousseau, and the Ethics of Politics*. Chicago, IL: The University of Chicago Press.

14   *Lucia Nigri and Naya Tsentourou*

Hall, Joseph. 1837. *The Works of Joseph Hall, with Some Account of His Life and Sufferings*. A new Edition, revised and corrected, vol. VI. Oxford: D. A. Talboys.

Herzig, Tamar, and Miriam Eliav-Feldon. 2015. *Dissimulation and Deceit in Early Modern Europe*. New York: Palgrave.

Hogan, Patrick Colm. 1999. "Christian Pharisees and the Scandalous Ethics of Jesus: Teaching Luke's Gospel at the End of a Millennium". *College Literature* 26(3): 95–114.

Hug, Tobias B. 2009. *Impostures in Early Modern England: Representations and Perceptions of Fraudulent Identities*. Manchester: Manchester University Press.

Hwang, Su-kyung. 2016. "From Priests' to Actors' Wardrobe: Controversial, Commercial, and Costumized Vestments". *Studies in Philology* 113(2): 282–305.

Jones, Ann Rosalind, and Peter Stallybrass. 2000. *Renaissance Clothing and the Materials of Memory*. Cambridge: Cambridge University Press.

King James Bible. 1613. *The Holy Bible Containing the Old Testament, and the New: Newly Translated out of the Original Tongues... by His Majesties Speciall Commandement*. London: Robert Parker.

Knights, Mark. 2011. *The Devil in Disguise: Deception, Delusion, and Fanaticism in the Early English Enlightenment*. Oxford: Oxford University Press.

Lake, Peter. 1996. "'A Charitable Christian Hatred': The Godly and Their Enemies in the 1630s". In *The Culture of English Puritanism, 1560–1700*, edited by Christopher Dunston and Jacqueline Eales, 145–83. Basingstoke: Palgrave.

Maus, Katharine Eisaman. 1995. *Inwardness and Theater in the English Renaissance*. Chicago, IL: The University of Chicago Press.

Mazzio, Carla. 2009. "*The* History of Air: *Hamlet* and the Trouble with Instruments". *South Central Review* 26(1): 153–96.

McDowell, Paula. 2007. "'On the Behalf of Printers': A Late Stuart Printer-Author and Her Causes". In *Agent of Change: Print Culture Studies after Elizabeth L. Eisenstein*, edited by Sabrina Alcorn Baron, Eric N. Lindquist, and Eleanor F. Shevlin, 125–39. Amherst, MA: University of Massachusetts Press.

Moberg, David O. 1987. "Holy Masquerade: Hypocrisy in Religion". *Review of Religious Research* 29: 3–24.

Peltonen, Markku. 2003. *The Duel in Early Modern England: Civility, Politeness, and Honour*. Cambridge: Cambridge University Press.

Proffitt, M. (ed.). 2016. *The Oxford English Dictionary Online*. Available online at www.oed.com (accessed 15 May 2016).

Richards, Jennifer. 2003. *Rhetoric and Courtliness in Early Modern Literature*. Cambridge: Cambridge University Press.

Seary, Peter. 1990. *Lewis Theobald and the Editing of Shakespeare*. Oxford: Clarendon Press.

Shakespeare, William. 2008. *Hamlet*. Edited by G.R Hibbard. Oxford: Oxford University Press.

Shakespeare, William. 2016. *Hamlet (The Arden Shakespeare)*. London: Bloomsbury.

Speed, Samuel. 1677. *Prison-pietie, or, Meditations Divine and Moral Digested into Poetical Heads*. London: J.C..

Strohm, Paul. 2005. *Politique: Languages of Statecraft between Chaucer and Shakespeare*. Conway Lectures in Medieval Studies. Notre Dame, Indiana: University of Notre Dame Press.

Zagorin, Perez. 1990. *Ways of Lying: Dissimulation, Persecution, and Conformity in Early Modern Europe*. Cambridge, MA: Harvard University Press.

1 Hypocrisy, Dissimulation, and Education for Civic Life in Pre-Revolutionary England

Markku Peltonen

I

The main purpose of this chapter is to explore the themes of hypocrisy and dissimulation in late-sixteenth- and early-seventeenth-century England and to endeavour to place them in their cultural and intellectual, educational, and civic contexts. A prevailing orthodoxy bids us to see these themes as an overarching cultural and social *mentalité* of the period. I want to suggest that such a sweeping claim is not particularly helpful if we want to gain an understanding of what the early modern authors were doing in their accounts of hypocrisy and dissimulation. I shall argue instead that the characteristics of hypocrisy and dissimulation had a specific role in attempts to grapple with the intricacies of social and civic life in the early modern period.

The sixteenth and seventeenth centuries in general, and the period between 1550 and 1650 in particular, have often been called the age of dissimulation or the age of hypocrisy (Bouwsma 2000, 117–18; Herdt 2008, 5; Snyder 2009, 1; Villari 1987, 25). Of course, neither dissimulation nor hypocrisy was novel in itself in the early modern period, but historians have insisted that the intensity in which they were discussed and practised was unprecedented. The values and practices of hypocrisy and dissimulation are said to have been central to key social and religious, political, and cultural processes of the early modern period. As one recent scholar has put it, dissimulation was "a mode of resistance to oppressive social, cultural, and religious norms" (Snyder 2009, 47). Insofar as religion is concerned, the Reformation and Counter-Reformation unleashed developments and processes which, for many historians, necessitated dissimulation, lying, and hypocrisy – the development of "the prudential self" (Martin 2004, 32–5). These characteristics, in their turn, prompted, at least according to some scholars, the process of secularisation in early modern Europe (Cavaillé 2002). In social and communal life, mendacity and dissimulation, secrecy and hypocrisy are said to have been the result of growing urbanisation and the erosion of traditional social hierarchies. "Rising social mobility" led to "the consciousness that it is possible to become socially what one is not yet, but that this will require, among other things, that one successfully act the

16   *Markku Peltonen*

part" (Herdt 2008, 5), but also to attempts to maintain those hierarchies (Snyder 2009, 45, 32–3).

In the field of politics, the ubiquity of dissimulation and hypocrisy in early modern Europe has been associated with absolutism and state formation. From the individual's point of view, whether as a mere subject or a courtier, the repressive institutions of absolutism and state formation often demanded secrecy, dissembling and hypocritical behaviour. Such behaviour offered psychological freedom under oppressive absolutism (Martin 2004, 34; Snyder 2009, 47–9). From the ruler's point of view, secrecy, dissimulation, and hypocrisy, especially in the form of reason of state, provided efficient and potent tools for governing subjects and large empires. These values were indispensable for absolutist rulers who wanted to maintain and enhance their state through a monopoly of legitimate violence and increasing tax revenue, through the "social disciplining of an often-tumultuous populace" and "the disciplining of the body politic" (Snyder 2009, 106–8).

These assessments have led recent historians to argue that the ubiquity of hypocrisy and dissimulation in early modern Europe was ultimately embedded in contemporary culture. William J. Bouwsma, for instance, acknowledges that the cultural "discontents" of the period were not "unrelated to the material discomforts of the age: to warfare, civil and foreign, now aggravated by religious hatreds and gunpowder, and to the social disruptions caused by the great price rise of the later sixteenth century" (Bouwsma 2000, 129). But he insists even more strongly that the major "shift in the cultural atmosphere" which took place by the late sixteenth century and which made "many cultivated Europeans... increasingly anxious and unhappy" could be explained by "the culture itself" (Bouwsma 2000, 112). This culture – "the Renaissance culture of liberation" – consisted of liberating, not only of knowing, time, space, politics, and religion, but also of "the self" from "the traditional model of hierarchy of discrete faculties governed by reason" (Bouwsma 2000, 165). "The self", Bouwsma writes, "*had* become fluid and problematic" and "troubling doubts about the shape of the 'true' self, even doubts of its existence" had arisen (Bouwsma 2000, 135). The consequence of all this was both that "the general culture of Europe in this period was probably the most theatrical in its history" and that hypocrisy was thought to be the most prevalent vice of the same (Bouwsma 2000, 132–3, 141–2, 117–8). Dissembling, lying, and hypocrisy are thus said to be at the heart of early modern European religion and society, politics, and culture.

Seeing the early modern period exclusively through the lens of dissimulation and hypocrisy runs the obvious risks of an all-embracing *mentalité* or *Zeitgeist*. At the same time, it leads scholars to make specious claims about other periods of history, periods that they are not actually studying. In order to distinguish the sixteenth and seventeenth centuries as a period of dissimulation and hypocrisy, scholars have concluded, for

Hypocrisy, Dissimulation, and Education for Civic Life 17

instance, that the "discussions of dissimulation were anathema... for the Enlightenment" (Snyder 2009, 176). But such a conclusion can be difficult to endorse by those who actually study dissimulation, hypocrisy, and mendacity in the eighteenth century. One such scholar writing about hypocrisy in eighteenth-century political thought has recently concluded that "the question of when, why, and how it might be acceptable to conceal one's true political principles and hide behind a mask of piety and virtue had become one of the major themes of eighteenth-century political argument" (Runciman 2008, 77–8). Seeing certain periods or centuries as that of dissimulation, hypocrisy, or indeed something else is therefore not particularly helpful.

Instead of studying dissimulation and hypocrisy as the *mentalité* of the early modern period, we might do better to study their various expressions and usages in their specific historical contexts, what their advocates were doing in these expressions and usages, and how and why these expressions and usages were similar or different from those which went beforehand or came thereafter. For instance, we can examine, as Perez Zagorin and others have done, the ways in which different religious groups and minorities explored and employed various ways of lying in early modern Europe (Zagorin 1990). Similarly, in the political and social arena, rather than making any overall assumptions about their hypocritical and dissembling character, we can explore how these values were advocated, objected to, or perhaps ignored in different situations and what these people were doing in advocating, objecting to, or ignoring hypocrisy and dissimulation.

The present essay attempts to do precisely this. It makes no assumptions about the overall hypocritical or dissembling nature of the sixteenth and seventeenth centuries. The aim is instead to offer a fresh perspective on how dissimulation and hypocrisy had a distinctive place in early modern education. I will first examine hypocrisy and dissimulation in the Renaissance tradition of civility and civil conversation by focussing on the best-known work of this tradition – Stefano Guazzo's *The Civile Conversation*. I will then move to explore how dissimulation and similar values were discussed and advocated in the *ars rhetorica* taught in the grammar school (Dini 2000, 118). In both cases, I seek to demonstrate the importance of hypocrisy and dissimulation. In his account of civil conversation, Guazzo maintained that hypocrisy, dissimulation, and flattery were its necessary parts. In rhetoric manuals, published for the grammar school, dissimulation was also thought to be important for a good orator. In the final section, I turn to discuss the relationship between civil conversation and rhetoric. Although they were in many ways contrasting traditions, I seek to demonstrate that in the context of Renaissance England they were relatively close to each other. In the contexts where I examine them, neither dissimulation nor hypocrisy was advocated as a means to avoid religious persecution or to find a sanctuary

18   *Markku Peltonen*

against repressive absolutism in inner self, to carve out a brilliant career in the royal court, or to maintain sovereignty and enhance tax revenue. They were rather seen as a significant part of social and civic life. Dissimulation and hypocrisy were important characteristics of not just courtiers and nobles but anyone who was intent upon leading a successful public life. They, I argue, empowered the pre-revolutionary citizen.

II

What were hypocrisy and dissimulation? Traditionally, there was a clear distinction between them. For Thomas Aquinas and others, whereas *"dissimulation* is any form of deceptive self-presentation through one's actions, *hypocrisy* specifically denotes the simulation of virtue" (Herdt 2008, 80). This emphasis on the appearance of virtue in hypocrisy can be detected in sixteenth-century England as well. Thus Nicholas Bodrugan, discussing the Scottish clergy in 1548, noted that "by hypocrisy they alway had this gifte to shewe their vertue to the uttermost and hide their faultes to the secretest, so that their virtue appeareth more then it is, & their vice lesse" ([Bodrugan] 1548, h.iir). By and large, however, early modern English writers did not distinguish between hypocrisy and dissimulation. These concepts might have covered slightly different semantic fields, but they were often used to describe each other. Thomas Elyot, in his dictionary, defined "hypocrisis" as "false dissimulation" (Elyot 1538, s.v. 'Hypocrisis'). Others paired them, one author maintaining that "all their outward shew of holinesse was nothing but dissimulation, hypocrisie, and lustfull sacriledge" (Charron [1608?], 445; [Hall] 1604, G7v; Robinson 1623, 26). Yet others described a 'hypocrite' as someone who was "cunningly dissembling", or simply equated "the hypocrites and dissemblers" (G[ainsford] 1616, 66; Prynne 1633, 449, 141, 547; Robinson 1625, 232). Both terms often appeared together in a list of similar vices. Richard Robinson described "simplicite" as "a singular virtue, which properly and plainly speaketh and doth those things which are unfeined, uncorrupt, without simulation, adulation, collusion, hypocrisie, doublenesse of hear[t]e, or sinister externall dealing in doctrine and doings of life & manners" (R[obinson] [1579], H3r).

Both dissimulation and hypocrisy denoted the characteristic of appearing to be something else than one really is and they were often described as mask-wearing. Although "frendeshype", Thomas Elyot insisted, must be based on "equall benevolence", it was also important that there was "equall demonstracion" because "thinges are most judged by outward tokens". But since "hypocrisy" had "so great a preemynence", such outward tokens of friendship could easily be used to deceive (Elyot 1539, A.iiv). Robert Pricket assured that the Earl of Essex had not been "hollow, like the Vaults of hell" and had fled "from base hypocrisy" (Pricket 1604, C4r). Similarly, Joseph Hall exhorted everyone "to carry

Hypocrisy, Dissimulation, and Education for Civic Life 19

our selves in an honest and simple truth, free from a curious hypocrisy, & affectation of seeming other than we are" (Hall 1606, 16–17). The origins of the term hypocrisy were, of course, in ancient Greek drama and the Greek term *hypokrisis* meant the playing of a part. As the separatist theologian, John Robinson, explained, "hypocrites have their names from stage-players, as rayther [sic] playing than working that which is good and virtuous; and the same onely upon the stage, and to please lookers on" (Robinson 1625, 260). This etymological link between hypocrisy and theatre was used with great vehemence by those who opposed theatre in the early seventeenth century. "If we", wrote William Prynne in his tirade against theatre, "seriously consider the very forme of acting Playes, we must needs acknowledge it to be nought else but grosse hypocrisie" (Prynne 1633, 156).

Hypocrisy had strong religious overtones. Both Elyot and John Rider defined it in their dictionaries as "fayned holynesse" (Elyot 1538, s.v. 'Hypocrisis'; Rider 1589, s.v. 'hypocrisis'). The Edwardian *Booke of the Common Prayer* included it in a list of vices, "blindnes of heart... pryde, vainglory, & Hypocrisy,... envy, hatred and malice, and all uncharitableness" (*The Booke* 1549, cxxr). It was, as one author maintained, "the poison of true religion" (G[ainsford] 1616, 67). Papists in general and "their Priests, their Monkes, and Friers" in particular were often depicted as hypocrites (Prynne 1633, 446; Tyndale 1548, Dr). Francis Bacon wrote about "the hipocrisie of fryars" (Bacon 2012, 170). Yet, it was also often used in a secular context. John Robinson distinguished between "*Religious Hypocrites*" and "civill Hypocrites". The former were those who had "a certain zeal... for and in the duties of the first Table" and who "repute themselves highly in Gods favour" though they lacked in goodness and love towards other men. "Civill Hypocrites", on the other hand, behaved with civility, conversing "honestly, and kindly with men", and thus presumed "great acceptance from God", although "they have little care to know his will in his Word" and even less "to observe his Precepts, and Ordinances" (Robinson 1625, 41–2). So, whereas a religious hypocrite wore a religious mask without benevolence to others, a civil hypocrite wore a polite mask without Christian interior.

Robinson's account points to an important fact about early modern discussions of hypocrisy and dissimulation. They were often closely associated with civility. Of course, those who fulminated against court and courtly life saw it as a place of dissimulation and hypocrisy. Courtiers, according to Antonio de Guevara's dispraise of them, did not only "flatter, & begge" for obtaining "a little favour"; they also had a "dissemblyng heart that under a pretence to be clere and loyall, make men to judge that hypocrisy is devocion" (Guevara 1548, d.iv–d.iir). According to Pierre Charron, "hypocrisie and dissimulation" were "a notable quality of Courtiers, and in as great credit amongst them as vertue" (Charron [1608?], 445). But civility was also associated with hypocrisy

20 *Markku Peltonen*

outside such anti-court discourse. Grey Brydges, in *A Discourse against Flatterie*, described flattery as "nothing else but false friendship, fawning hypocrisy, dishonest civility, base merchandise of words, a plausible discord of the heart and lips" ([Brydges] 1611, 4; Charron [1608?], 441, 442, Howard 1557, 97r).

Brydges's phrase, "base merchandise of words", provides us with an obvious pointer to the other area where dissimulation and hypocrisy were often discussed – rhetoric. Of course, words had a central place, together with deeds, in early modern civility. When, for instance, Thomas Gainsford pointed out that hypocrisy was about such outward things as "the attire, gesture, countenance, words, and actions" (G[ainsford] 1616, 66–7), there is little doubt that he had civility in mind. But when Thomas Lever preached at St. Paul's in 1550 that "the people of the country use to saye, that their gentlemen and officers were never so full of fayre words and evill deeds (which is hypocrisy) as they nowe be" (Lever 1550, C.iir), it seems clear that he had eloquence in mind, where words were hardly less central. Guevara argued that a "dissembling heart" caused men to take "hypocrisy as devocion" but also "muche bablyng" as "eloquence" (Guevara 1548, d.iir). In the translation of Heinrich Bullinger's antidote against Anabaptists, published in 1548, hypocrisy, flattery, and eloquence were even more closely linked to one another. "Al mortal men", the tract maintained, were "exceadyng studiouse, of new thynges", so much so that they were often deceived by "hypocrisy, and vaine blandiloquence or flatteryng" (Bullinger 1548, Biiir–v).

III

So far, I have explored the negative depictions of hypocrisy and dissimulation. I have done this not only to show the closeness of hypocrisy and dissimulation to each other but also to indicate their proximity to civility and rhetoric in early modern England. I now turn to the first of these topics – the Renaissance tradition of civility and civil conversation. I focus on a well-known treatise which was explicitly a conversational treatise and guide, and whose title created the term for this whole genre – Stefano Guazzo's *The Civile Conversation* (1574). The first three books, translated from French, were published in 1581 and five years later in 1586 the fourth book, translated from Italian, completed the treatise (Guazzo 1586). It is a dialogue between William Guazzo, the author's brother, and the physician Annibal. My aim is to show that, according to Guazzo, hypocrisy, dissimulation, and mendacity more generally, were central to social and civic life.

Guazzo and Annibal's conversation began as a debate about solitary life, which Guazzo is defending. He argues that "the companie of many is greeuous unto me, and that contrariwise, solitarinesse is a great comfort and easie of my travels" (Guazzo 1586, 3r). He of course acknowledges

Hypocrisy, Dissimulation, and Education for Civic Life   21

that "for the service of my Prince, I must of force be conversant not onelie with other Gentlemen his servants, but also in the court to discourse & deale with diverse persons of diverse countries & nations" but hastens to add that he does that "against the heart" (Guazzo 1586, 3r). It demands considerable effort "to understand other mens talke, to frame fit answeres thereto, and to observe such circumstances, as the qualitie of the persons, and mine owne honour require: which is nothing else but paine & subiection" (Guazzo 1586, 3r). Annibal counters this by insisting that "a man, being a compagnable creature, loveth naturallie the conversation of other men" (Guazzo 1586, 4v) and goes on to argue that conversation is necessary in practically all pursuits of human life. Consequently, a solitary man is nothing but "a beast" (Guazzo 1586, 9v). Guazzo then defends solitary life partly as "the perfection of man" (Guazzo 1586, 13r) and partly as a way of avoiding injuries. There is so much malice in the world, he declares, "that if you addict your selfe to devotion, and the exercise of charitie, you are taken for an hypocrite", and "if you be affable and courteous, you shall be called a flatterer" (Guazzo 1586, 13v).

Annibal, although he insists that the corruption of the world must not prompt one to renounce one's goodness, grants Guazzo's general point about civil conversation and hypocrisy. This emerges in his account of civil conversation. He begins by emphasising that his "meaning is not to discourse formally of their [ie. conversants'] dutie, neither to lay before you all those moral vertues which pertaine to the perfection & happie state of lyfe" (Guazzo 1586, 21v). Moral duties and virtues did not pertain to civil conversation. On the contrary, civil conversation is related, Annibal explains to his interlocutor, "to the manners and conditions which make it civile" (Guazzo 1586, 22r). It follows that, instead of internal virtues, attention should be paid to outward manners. "We ought to consider", Annibal points out, "that our name dependeth of the general opinions" (Guazzo 1586, 24v). But what about hypocrites? As Guazzo phrases it: "howe shall I behave my selfe with some, whom I knowe farre more wicked than those whome you have spoken of, albeit by their dissembling hypocrisie, they are accounted of everie man for honest men?" (Guazzo 1586, 25r). This might "trouble your conscience" Annibal admits, but insists that, as long as "they are not reputed evill", men must be regarded good (Guazzo 1586, 25r). When Guazzo challenges this, Annibal retorts that if a gentleman did not observe accepted customs, "hee shall be mocked" (Guazzo 1586, 25v). Social life, in other words, necessitated dissimulation and hypocrisy.

The same conclusion is reiterated in Annibal and Guazzo's subsequent discussions of "evill tongued" people and "flatterers". There are, Annibal explains, two different kinds of "evill tongued" people: "the one ill, which you ought to flie: the other farre worse, whose companie you ought not to avoide" (Guazzo 1586, 27v). The first group consisted

22   Markku Peltonen

in those who disparage and muckrake other people openly and often in front of these very people. Such "evill tongued" people, although they were annoying, could be ignored; "their words are not much credited", "they doe nothing but raise a dust" and they could be excluded from civil conversation (Guazzo 1586, 27v–28r).

Annibal listed no less than ten different characters in the second group, the three most important being "Rhetoritians", "Poets" and "Hypocrites". Rhetoritians were those who used "a certaine figure, called by the Maisters of Eloquence *Occupatio*". This figure, often also called *occultatio*, *praeteritio*, or *paralepsis*, was used, as Henry Peacham pointed out, "when the Orator faineth and maketh as though he would say nothing in some matter, when notwithstanding he speaketh most of all" (Peacham 1593, 130). Poets were no less students of eloquence than rhetoricians. They often employed, Annibal says, the figure *antiphrasis*, which Peacham defined as "a forme of speech which by a word exprest doth signifie the contrary" (Peacham 1593, 24). Poets, "speaking by contraries, wil give in mockage the name of faire to a woman that is foule" (Guazzo 1586, 28v). The third character consisted in "ill tongued hypocrites, who under the colour of griefe and compassion, to be better beeleved, lamentablie rehearse the ill haps of others" (Guazzo 1586, 28v). Although these and several other characters included in this group were clearly annoying, and were, in fact, "farre worse than the other", they must, Annibal was convinced, be tolerated, and "be admitted into Conversation" (Guazzo 1586, 28r).

Why? Simply because the rules of civil conversation demanded it. As long as men had a good outward reputation, they could not be excluded from civil conversation. Thus those in the former group of evil tongued were generally known to be such, they had "a marke on their forehead, and are knowne for infamous persons". Hence, they could be overlooked. The second group, while more insidious, were "not marked on the forehead", which meant, as Annibal patiently explains, that "they are not excluded from the companie of others" and that "we cannot refuse their companie" (Guazzo 1586, 31r). Annibal provided Guazzo with some antidotes against "the venim of their serpentine tongues" (Guazzo 1586, 31r).

The case of flattery, which Guazzo and Annibal proceeded to discuss after evil-tongued people, was very similar. Whereas Annibal deemed flatterers to be "tolerable", Guazzo maintained that they should in fact be "desirable" (Guazzo 1586, 32v) and launched into a long defence of flattery. Of course, everyone reproved flattery "in word, yet everie one commendeth it in heart". Flattery, he went on, was "the waie to make friends and winne preferment" (Guazzo 1586, 32v–33r). More generally, if one wanted "to bee acceptable in companie", it was incumbent "to avoide contention" and to have resort to flattery and "to consent to other mennes sayings" (Guazzo 1586, 34r). Guazzo singled out two

Hypocrisy, Dissimulation, and Education for Civic Life 23

kinds of people who constantly used flattery. First, "schoolmaisters" extolled their pupils" mediocre performances "to incourage them to goe forward from good to better" (Guazzo 1586, 33v). Similarly, "fine Oratours ... teach men to insinuate, & by coloured words to creepe into mens bosomes" (Guazzo 1586, 33v). Guazzo concluded his account of flattery by declaring "that to winne favour, and happily to atchieve our purposes, we must always have praising and pleasing wordes in our mouth" (Guazzo 1586, 34v). Annibal did not accept Guazzo's point of view, and in the end they agreed that flattery was not desirable but at least tolerable.

One of Guazzo's central conclusions in his treatise was that hypocrisy and flattery, dissimulation, and mendacity were necessary in social and civic life. They were more important than moral virtues. Another important conclusion he drew was that there was a close relationship between hypocrisy and dissimulation on the one hand and rhetoric on the other.

IV

Rhetoric had a central place in early modern grammar school curriculum. Whereas the lower forms focussed on grammar – so that they were able to read, write, and speak Latin – by the fourth or fifth form (in the early seventeenth century even as early as the third form) the schoolboys started to study rhetoric – first with letter-writing (Mack 2002; Skinner 1996). In what follows, I shall focus on the moral ambiguity of Renaissance rhetoric in general and on dissimulation's role in it in particular. The attack on the moral standing of the teaching of the *ars rhetorica* from Plato onwards has been a scholarly commonplace for a long time, and rhetoric, despite its pedagocical importance, was often censured in Renaissance England (Peltonen 2013, 218–42). Recent scholars have examined and highlighted important aspects of Renaissance rhetoric, which contributed to its moral ambiguity and thus underlay those censures. Quentin Skinner, in particular, has examined two central aspects of Renaissance rhetoric which aroused the most vehement moral critique. First, the ability to speak *in utramque partem*, on both sides of any question (Hankins 1996, 120–3; Skinner 1996, 138–80; 2002a, 2002b, 2007). The "governing assumption" of the *ars rhetorica* was, as Skinner has put it, "that in any discussion about moral and civil affairs it will always be possible to mount a plausible argument on either side of the case" (Skinner 2002a, 267). The moral ambiguity of this skill becomes readily obvious in Erasmus's comment, made in *De conscribendis epistolis*, which was widely used in English grammar schools and elsewhere for teaching letter-writing, that "nothing is so inherently good that it cannot be made to seem bad by a gifted speaker" (Erasmus 1985, 145–6). The other and even more important aspect of rhetoric, which

24 *Markku Peltonen*

Skinner has emphasised and which contributed to its morally ambiguous character, was the figure of *paradiastole*. This figure enabled the orator "to redescribe a given action or situation in such a way as to augment or extenuate its moral significance" (Skinner 2002a, 271).

There is a further aspect of moral ambiguity in the Renaissance *ars rhetorica*. This is the fact that it instructed its practitioners to view the virtues, the core of classical moral philosophy, not so much as moral values than as weapons to be used in rhetorical warfare (Peltonen 2012). Underlying this was what can be called the instrumentalist view of speech-making. Since the ultimate aim was to persuade the audience and thus "always to have the victorie", as Thomas Wilson put it in *The Arte of Rhetorique* of 1553 (Wilson 1553, 5r–v), the governing assumption was to invent arguments which would move the audience and thus to bring victory to the orator (Peltonen 2013, 74–9).

The instrumentalist notion of speech-making had a number of important consequences, which further emphasise the moral ambiguity of Renaissance rhetoric. In order to persuade his audience, the orator needed to think hard about his arguments and to ensure that they fitted the bill. He had, for instance, carefully to appraise every part of the speech and every possible argument from his own but also from his adversary's point of view. An important part of this was to win the audience's benevolence. This, as the early-seventeenth-century schoolmaster of Winchester College, Hugh Robinson, explained to his pupils, could be done if they, in the *exordium* of their speeches, properly established their ethos and thus "aptly and modestly praise themselves and their cause" ([Robinson] 1616, 32).[1] But it could also be advantageous for the victory to deprecate and even ridicule the adversary. This was so, the most popular school textbook of the early modern period pointed out, because "in a Free Republic slanderers often bring great commodity" (Aphthonius 1575, 164r).[2] Another school manual told schoolboys that they could make "the person of our adversary an object of hatred if we accuse him of pride, cruelty, treachery and malice"; they could produce envy by revealing the adversary's excessive "power, riches, friends, fame and faction" and they could bring him into "contempt" by disclosing his "laziness, negligence, luxury and cowardice" (Valerius 1580, 14–15).[3]

School manuals stopped short of drawing any outright hypocritical conclusion from their discussions of ethos. However, at least one Anglophone manual did point out that insofar as ethos was concerned what mattered most was what things looked like, not how they actually were. "The onelie meanes" for orators, he wrote, "to winde themselves into the hearts of the people" was "to seem religious and virtuous" or "to shaddowe foorth in some apparent manner, a desire in them to further the publique good of the State and Commonweale" ([Turval] 1608, 22r–v). Hypocrisy, we should remember, denoted the simulation of virtue.

Hypocrisy, Dissimulation, and Education for Civic Life   25

Similar considerations were of utmost importance for the orator in the invention of the actual arguments of his speech. The effectiveness of the arguments rather than their intrinsic moral value must be the orator's top priority. In deliberative rhetoric, for instance, where *honestas* and *utilitas* were the two values on which one's arguments should be based, the choice between them entirely depended on their efficacy. William Pemble, in his school manual, *Enchiridion Oratorium*, of 1633, listed efficient maxims for schoolboys to be used in deliberative rhetoric. If the boy wanted to prefer *utilitas* and therefore to emphasise profit and safety, he could declare in his speech that "without safety, no-one can use virtues" and "it must not be at all necessary to value honesty, which does not bring welfare" (Pemble 1633, 25).[4] But if he prioritised *honestas*, he could maintain contrary values, declaring, for instance, that "he lives in safety, who lives honestly, not he who lives in present safety", or that "he who lives disgracefully cannot possess safety forever" (Pemble 1633, 26).[5]

The truth of one's arguments was likewise considered from an instrumental point of view. Of course, true arguments strengthened the orator's case, but it was sufficient that they appeared to be so. As an epistolary manual explained, whether our arguments "are true or false does not always matter" (Brandolini 1573, B2v).[6] Another school handbook noted that "a fact, whose truth is not credible, is not so useful [in an oration] as that which is false yet probable" (Butler 1629, E4r).[7]

Yet another important element of the *ars rhetorica*, which could bring an accusation of moral ambiguity against it, was the centrality of emotional appeals. Persuasion was achieved sometimes by "reasons", sometimes by "mooving mens affections" (P[histon] 1584, A4r). "It is more useful", Pemble maintained, "to govern the auditors by the vehemence and passion of the mind rather than by judgment or deliberation" because "most people judge by the agitation of the mind rather than by the dictated truth and the norms of justice or by laws" (Pemble 1633, 54).[8] The orator should ignore truth and justice and instead feign certain passions and emotions. As Quintilian endeavoured to defend rhetoric, "they allege also that rhetoric makes use of vices... in speaking falsehoods and exciting emotions" (Quintilian 2001, 2.17.26–7). Amplification was the main means of exciting the listeners' emotions, and again it was suggested that this entailed the use of mendacity. Quintilian suggested that for the sake of amplification the orator could tell false tales (Quintilian 2001, 8.3.70).

V

So far in my brief account of the *ars rhetorica* I have highlighted some of its teachings, which suggested moral ambiguity and a certain kind of mendacity. I shall now turn to those teachings of the *ars rhetorica* where the orator was specifically advised to use dissimulation. Most of my

26 Markku Peltonen

examples come from pre-revolutionary school manuals, which means that boys were supposed to learn about dissimulation in the grammar school. There were two important places in the *ars rhetorica* where dissimulation was needed. The first occurred in the construction of *exordium*. This was the part of the speech, as we have seen, where the orator had to win the favour of his audience. To accomplish this, the orator needed to pay tribute to his audience, disparage his adversary, and modestly praise himself and his cause.

Nevertheless, rhetoric manuals further advised what the orator should do if he found himself on the back foot at the beginning of his speech. This could happen if his listeners were weary or his adversary had won their goodwill or he defended a shameful cause. In the last case, the orator must explain how his cause was not in fact disreputable. The most potent way of doing this, both classical and early modern rhetoricians agreed, was to use dissimulation. The *Ad Herennium* and Cicero's *De inventione* both of which were commonly used in early modern grammar schools, advised to use "dissimulation", that is to say, to mislead the audience by appearing to defend something else than one was in fact defending ([Anon] 1954, 1.7.11; Cicero 1949, 1.17.24).[9] Numerous early modern Anglophone manuals followed suit, but so did many early modern school textbooks. Epistolary manuals recommended to creeping into the listener's mind "secretly by dissimulation", as Georgius Macropedius put it in *Methodus de conscribendis epistolis* – a popular school manual, which was printed more than ten times in England between 1573 and 1640 (Brandolini 1573, B6r; Macropedius 1580, Aviiv). The Dutch humanist Cornelius Valerius's *In universam bene dicendi rationem tabula*, published in London in 1580, advised that we need to "excuse" the "disgracefulness of our cause" and that this should be accomplished "by cunning and secret" (Valerius 1580, 13).[10] The schoolmaster of Winchester College, Hugh Robinson, echoed the words of the *Ad Herennium* when he told his pupils that they could "secretly prepare and stroke the listener's mind by dissimulation" ([Robinson] 1616, 30).[11] One manual from the 1620s suggested the use of "deceit" and "flattery" for "creeping into the listener's mind", whereas another openly suggested resorting to "dissimulation" (Butler 1629, D3v; Vicars 1628, 7).[12] The most popular early-Stuart textbook did not mention dissimulation but explained that, when the orator defended a "disgraceful, dubious, base or obscure" cause, he should redescribe it and declare that he speaks about "great, necessary, novel, useful [and] pleasant matters" (Farnaby 1629, 7).[13] William Pemble opened his account of *insinuatio* by maintaining that the orator must win the audience "by dissimulation and secret circumlocution" (Pemble 1633, 61).[14] In case of a disgraceful cause, it was best, he continued, to follow Cicero's "admirable" instructions. According to one of them, the orator "should

Hypocrisy, Dissimulation, and Education for Civic Life 27

dissimulate that he is defending what is supposed to be defended" (Pemble 1633, 61).[15]

Another and more important place in their rhetoric classes where schoolboys were exhorted to use dissimulation was in inventing arguments for deliberative orations. In such orations, the orator, as we have seen, should call forth the characteristics of honesty and utility. It was in their analyses of utility that many rhetoricians and schoolmasters examined the use of dissimulation. Whereas Cicero, in the *De partitione oratoria*, observed that *utilitas* often competed with *honestas* or moral value (Cicero 1942, 25.89),[16] the *Ad Herennium* mentioned dissimulation. It divided utility in political speeches initially into "security and honesty" and further divided "security" into "strength" and "fraud". When the orator appealed to "fraud", he was to speak about "money, promise, dissimulation, promptness, deception" ([Anon] 1954, 3.2.3).[17] Again, English textbooks followed these accounts very closely. Above all, William Pemble examined the use of dissimulation. Public utility, he wrote, consisted of "welfare and liberty" on the one hand and "greatness and power" on the other. In the case of "welfare and liberty", the orator could enlarge on numerous topics, including

> making of laws, manner of providing money, peace and war, and instruments of both. Armies, arms, engines of war, sailors, the allied and auxiliary troops, harbours, guarding of borders, transportation, provision of necessary victuals, the means of agriculture, commerce and similar things which make the commonwealth safe and secure with power.
>
> (Pemble 1633, 23)[18]

In addition to this list, which was based on Aristotle's *Rhetoric*, Pemble followed the *Ad Herennium* and explained to schoolboys that the orator could discuss "fraud and counsel". This could be done by "corrupting the enemies with large sums of money, by timely promises and dissimulations and by quick simulations and by lies". It was common, Pemble also explained to schoolboys, "to deliberate whether it is useful (when we are unable to do it by force) to safeguard the republic by fraud" (Pemble 1633, 23).[19]

Anyone who received training in early modern grammar schools was thus taught that fraud, dissimulation, and mendacity were integral parts of speech-making. Schoolboys were told that they could use dissimulation if they were defending a morally questionable or disgraceful cause. They also learned that in their political speeches they could resort to fraud and dissimulation. It should be emphasised that these were no clandestine methods to be employed, if at all, as secretly as possible. On the contrary, they were arguments to be used in highly public speeches.

VI

Did Guazzo's depiction of civil conversation and the *ars rhetorica* expounded in school manuals have something in common? Words and speech assumed a paramount place in both, but these two accounts were in many ways contrasting contexts. Civility and courtesy manuals appeared to be primarily intended for courtiers, nobles, and gentlemen, to advise them how to conduct themselves politely in different situations. The *ars rhetorica*, by contrast, was taught at grammar schools and universities and its aim was to instruct how to speak or write persuasively – how the orator can win his audience to his side. Moreover, the primary reason for acquiring a mastery of the *ars rhetorica* was civic and political. Profound knowledge of its rules and definitions was said to be indispensable for civic and political participation (Peltonen 2013, 11–97; Skinner 1996, 66–110). There seemed, then, to have been a profound difference between an oration and a civil conversation. Cicero had already distinguished between "vehement speake" and "comon talk", as they were translated by Nicholas Grimalde in 1556. Whereas vehemence and victory were the defining character of an oration, gentleness and pleasure were those of a conversation (Peltonen 2003, 24; 2013, 63–5).

Nevertheless, in the context of late-sixteenth- and early-seventeenth-century England these two traditions, as Jennifer Richards has powerfully argued, seemed to have been closer than might appear (Richards 2003). First, to a large extent they both derived from the classical republican tradition of Cicero. Many of the courtesy books were written in the dialogue form, which has obvious links to the classical culture of the *ars rhetorica*. Second and more importantly, in sixteenth-century England, the Italianate courtesy books were located in the context not so much of courtiers and nobles than of humanist scholars, who also promoted rhetoric. It follows that the courtesy books should be seen at least in part in the context of the humanists' emphasis on *negotium* and active life rather than "the individualistic and competitive paradigm" of court culture (Richards 2003, 14). By the same token, they did not necessarily, as has often been assumed, "defend the privileges of an established elite" (Richards 2003, 15); they had, after all, numerous readers from humble backgrounds. Early modern courtesy books in general and Guazzo's *Civile Conversation* in particular should be read, in other words, in the same context of expanding civic and political participation than the grammar school manuals of the *ars rhetorica* (Peltonen 2013, ch. 2). From an early modern English point of view, Guazzo, as well as rhetoric manuals, taught their readers how to participate in the civic and public life of their local and national community.

This contextual proximity emerges clearly in Guazzo's treatise. As we have seen, Guazzo saw civil conversation and rhetoric close to each

Hypocrisy, Dissimulation, and Education for Civic Life   29

other. Furthermore, when Guazzo asks Annibal to talk about philosophy he retorts that he is not "a Philosopher" but "a mere Citizen" (49v). Therefore, he is not ready to talk about philosophy but only about "Civile Conversation", which he divided into "private" and "publike". Whereas the former treated conversation which took place "at home" and "in the house", the latter dealt with "publike Conversation" (51v). Rhetoric and public conversation overlapped. Annibal and Guazzo agreed that in a public conversation "we should move affections, and perswade mens minds with the tongue". Effectively, this was a definition of rhetoric as much as of public conversation. It comes as no surprise, therefore, that Guazzo told his interlocutor: "you cannot choose but you must have recourse to the precepts of Rhetorike" (57r). In so much as civil conversation aimed at persuading the audience at a public arena, it shared common ground with rhetoric. They enabled both the conversant and the orator to participate and exercise power in the civic life of their community.

VII

I have argued in this essay that dissimulation and hypocrisy had a distinctive position in early modern education. This does not appear to be so because of the oppressive social, cultural, and religious norms of the period. Schoolboys were taught in their rhetoric classes how to use dissimulation and to simulate virtue in written and oral speeches; and conversational manuals, likewise, emphasised the necessity of dissimulation and hypocrisy. In both cases it was neither religious or political repression, nor the erosion or maintenance of social hierarchies, nor even state formation or "the Renaissance culture of liberation" which caused this. On the contrary, the importance of dissimulation and hypocrisy was predicated on the importance of rhetoric and civil conversation in early modern political participation. Rhetoricians and the theorists of civil conversation were convinced that hypocrisy and dissimulation were necessary for persuading one's audience and thus in exercising political power.

Notes

1 "Si Nos nostramq; causam apte ac modeste laudemus".
2 In Repub. "Libera magnam saepenumero commoditatem afferunt conviciatores".
3 "*A persona adversarij nostri*, si eum vel in odium adducamus, ut si superbiam, crudelitatem, perfidiam, malitiam accusemus: vel in invidiam; ut si nimiam potentiam, opes, & copias amicorum, nobilitatem & factionem proferamus: velin contemptionem; si inertiam, negligentiam, luxuriam, & ignaviam aperiamus".
4 "Sine ea [ie. incolumitas] virtutibus neminem posse ... Honestum nihin oportere existimari quod salutem non pariat".

30 *Markku Peltonen*

5 "Eum tute vivere qui honeste vivat non qui sit in present incolumis. Qui turpiter vivat incolumen in perpetuum esse non posse."
6 "Verae, an falsae sint, non semper refert".
7 "Verum, cuius veritas non est credibilis, non tam Causae prodest, quam falsum verisimile".
8 "Utilissimum enim hoc est & impetu quodam animi & perturbatione magis quam judicio aut consilio auditor regantur. Plura enim multa homines iudicant aliqua permotione mentis quam veritate praescriptio & juris norma aliqua aut legibus itaque".
9 "Insinuatio eiusmodi debet esse ut occulte, per dissimulationem, eadem illa omnia conficiamus". "Et dissimulare te id defensurum quod existimeris".
10 "Callide & latenter".
11 "Cum occulte per dissimulationem Auditoris animum preparamus & demulcemus".
12 "Fallacia blandimentia, auditors animo paulatim surreptit".
13 "In causa Turpi, Dubia, Humili, Obscura ... nos dicturos de rebus magnis, necessaris, nouis, vtilibus, iucundis".
14 "Dissimulatione & circuitione occulte".
15 "Dissimulabit se id defensurum, quod existimatur defensurus".
16 "Persaepe evenit ut utilitas cum honestate certet".
17 "Dolus consumitur in pecunia, pollicitatione, dissimulatione, maturatione, mentitione".
18 "Salus & libertas, ut Leges fereandae, pecuniarum parandarum ratio, bellum et pax, instrumenta utriusque. Classes, arma, tormenta, nautae, milites socij et auxilia, portus custodia regionis, commeatus et res ad victum. Agrorum colendorum ratio, commercium et similia quae civitatem tutam et incolumen quasi per vim praestant."
19 "In pecuniis ad corrumpendos hostes elargiendis, in pollicitationibus dissimulationibus maturationibus et simulates festinationibus, mendaciis aliisq; artificiis de quibus saepe deliberator, and utile sit (eum per vim nequeamus) fraude rempublicam tueri".

Works Cited

[Anon.] 1954. *Ad C. Herennium*. Translated by Harry Caplan. London: Loeb.

Aphthonius. 1575. *Aphthonii sophistae progymnasmata, partim a Rodolpho Agricola, partim a Ioanne Maria Cataneo Latinitate donata: cum luculentis & vtilibus in eadem sholijs Reinhardi Lorichij Hadamatij*. London.

Bacon, Francis. 2012. *The Oxford Francis Bacon I: Early Writings 1584–1596*. Alan Stewart and Harriet Knight eds. Oxford: Clarendon Press.

[Bodrugan, Nicholas]. 1548. *An Epitome of the Title the Kynges Maiestie of Englande, Hath to the Souereigntie of Scotlande*. London.

The Booke of the Common Prayer. 1549. London.

Bouwsma, William. 2000. *The Waning of the Renaissance 1550–1640*. New Haven, CT: Yale University Press.

Brandolini, Aurelio. 1573. *De ratione scribendi, libri tres*. London.

[Brydges, Grey]. 1611. *A Discourse against Flatterie*. London.

Bullinger, Heinrich. [1548]. *An Holsome Antidotus or Counter-poysen, agaynst the Pestylent Heresye and Secte of the Anabaptistes*. Translated by John Véron. [London].

Butler, Charles. 1629. *Oratoriae libri duo*. Oxford.

Hypocrisy, Dissimulation, and Education for Civic Life 31

Cavaillé, Jean-Pierre. 2002. *Dis/simulations. Jules-César Vanini, François La Mothe Le Vayer, Gabriel Naudé, Louis Machon et Torquato Accetto: Religion, morale et politique au XVIIe siècle*. Paris: Honoré Champion.

Charron, Pierre. [1608?] *Of Wisdome Three Books*. Translated by Samson Lennard. London.

Cicero, Marcus Tullius. 1942. *De partitione oratoria*, in Cicero, *De oratore III, De fato, Paradoxa Stoicorum, De partitione oratoria*. Translated by H. Rackham. London: Loeb.

———. 1949. *De inventione*, in Cicero, *De inventione, De optimo genere oratorum, Topica*. Translated by H. M. Hubbell. London: Loeb.

Dini, Vittorio. 2000. *Il governo della prudenza: Virtù dei privati e disciplina dei custodi*. Milano: FrancoAngeli.

Elyot, Thomas. 1538. *The Dictionary*. London.

———. 1539. *The Castel of Helthe*. London.

Erasmus. 1985. *On the Writing of Letters*. Translated by Charles Fantazzi. In *Literary and Educational Writings*, vol. 25 of the *Collected Works of Erasmus*. Edited by J. K. Sowards. Toronto: University of Toronto Press.

Farnaby, Thomas. 1629. *Index rhetoricus, scholis & institutioni tenerioris aetatis accommodatus*. London.

G[ainsford], T[homas]. 1616. *The Rich Cabinet Furnished with Varietie of Excellent Discriptions, Exquisite Charracters, Witty Discourses, and Delightfull Histories, Deuine and Morrall*. London.

Guazzo, Stefano. 1586. *The Civile Conversation*. Translated by George Pettie and Barth Young. London.

Guevara, Antonio de. 1548. *A Dispraise of the Life of a Courtier, and a Commendacion of the Life of the Labouryng Man*. [Translated from French by Francis Bryan]. London.

[Hall, Joseph]. 1604. *Two Guides to a Good Life*. London.

Hall, Joseph. 1606. *Heauen upon Earth, or of True Peace, and Tranquillitie of Minde*. London.

Hankins, James. 1996. "Humanism and the Origins of Modern Political Thought". In *The Cambridge Companion to Renaissance Humanism*, edited by Jill Kraye, 118–41. Cambridge: Cambridge University Press.

Herdt, Jennifer A. 2008. *Putting On Virtue. The Legacy of the Splendid Vices*. Chicago, IL: University of Chicago Press.

Howard, Henry. 1557. *Songes and Sonettes*. [London].

Lever, Thomas. 1550. *A Fruitfull Sermon Made in Poules Churche at London*. London.

Mack, Peter. 2002. *Elizabethan Rhetoric. Theory and Practice*. Cambridge: Cambridge University Press.

Macropedius, Georgius. 1580. *Methodus de conscribendis epistolis*. London.

Martin, John Jeffries. 2004. *Myths of Renaissance Individualism*. London: Palgrave.

Peacham, Henry. 1593. *The Garden Of Eloquence*. London.

Peltonen, Markku. 2003. *The Duel in Early Modern England. Civlity, Politeness and Honour*. Cambridge: Cambridge University Press.

———. 2012. "Virtues in Elizabethan and Early Stuart Grammar Schools". *The Journal of Medieval and Early Modern Studies* 42(1): 157–79.

32 Markku Peltonen

———. 2013. *Rhetoric, Politics and Popularity in Pre-revolutionary England.* Cambridge: Cambridge University Press.

Pemble, William. 1633. *Enchiridion oratorium.* Oxford.

P[histon], W[illiam]. 1584. *The Welspring of Wittie Conceits.* London.

Pricket, Robert. 1604. *Honors Fame in Triumph Riding.* London.

Prynne, William. 1633. *Histrio-mastix. The Players Scvrge, or, Actors Tragaedie, Divided into Two Parts.* London.

Quintilian. 2001. *Institutio oratoria.* Edited and translated by Donald A. Russell, 5 vols. London: Loeb.

Richards, Jennifer. 2003. *Rhetoric and Courtliness in Early Modern Literature.* Cambridge: Cambridge University Press.

Rider, John. 1589. *Bibliotheca scholastica. A Double Dictionarie.* Oxford.

[Robinson, Hugh]. 1616. *i. Preces, ii. Grammaticalia quaedam, iii. Rhetorica brevis.* Oxford.

Robinson, John. 1625. *Obseruations Diuine and Morall. For the Furthering of Knowledg, and Virtue.* [Amsterdam].

R[obinson], R[ichard]. 1579. *The Vineyarde of Vertue Collected, Composed, and Digested into a Tripartite Order.* [London].

Robinson, Thomas. 1623. *The Anatomie of the English Nunnery at Lisbon in Portugall.* [London].

Runciman, David. 2008. *Political Hypocrisy. The Mask of Power, from Hobbes to Orwell and beyond.* Princeton, NJ: Princeton University Press.

Skinner, Quentin. 1996. *Reason and Rhetoric in the Philosophy of Hobbes.* Cambridge: Cambridge University Press.

———. 2002a. "Moral Ambiguity and the Renaissance Art of Eloquence". In *Visions of Politics,* edited by Quentin Skinner, vol. 2, 264–85. Cambridge: Cambridge University Press.

———. 2002b. "Hobbes on Rhetoric and the Construction of Morality". In *Visions of Politics,* edited by Quentin Skinner, vol. 3, 87–141. Cambridge: Cambridge University Press.

———. 2007. "*Paradiastole.* Redescribing the Vices as Virtues". In *Renaissance Figures of Speech,* edited by Sylvia Adamson, Gavin Alexander, and Katrin Ettenhuber, 149–63. Cambridge: Cambridge University Press.

Snyder, Jon R. 2009. *Dissimulation and the Culture of Secrecy in Early Modern Europe*: Berkeley: University of California Press.

[Turval, Jean l'Oiseau de]. 1608. *Essaies Politicke, And Morall.* London.

Tyndale, William. 1548. *The Practyse of Prelates.* London.

Valerius, Cornelius. 1580. *In universam bene dicendi rationem tabula.* London.

Vicars, Thomas. 1628. *Cheiragogia. Manuductio ad artem rhetorica,* 3rd ed. London.

Villari, R. 1987. *Elogio della dissimulazione. La lotta politica nel seicento.* Roma: Laterza.

Wilson, Thomas. 1553. *The Arte of Rhetorique.* London.

Zagorin, Perez. 1990. *Ways of Lying. Dissimulation, Persecution, and Conformity in Early Modern Europe.* Cambridge MA: Harvard University Press.

2 Trading in Gratitude
John Donne's Verse Epistles to His Patronesses

Silvia Bigliazzi

Gratitude as Transaction

The sixteenth- and seventeenth-century flourishing of courtesy books and letter manuals in England testifies to a widespread preoccupation with how to style oneself in society. Different kinds of transactions took place under the guise of friendly courtly relations in which both patron and client had their share. As Curtis Perry put it,

> Recipients of royal favour were much courted..., for they were influential and had the opportunity to broker suits for others. The ability to reap benefits for clients was one way of demonstrating and maintaining prestige, and therefore much of the wealth doled out through the court was distributed to various associates of successful courtiers. As a result, the social and political world of the upper classes organised itself into shifting and overlapping networks of patronage that served, among other functions, as conduits to distribute royal bounty in the forms of grants, patents, and offices. A great courtier would tend to have a sizeable number of dependants and clients, whose reciprocated services helped to cement the social and political importance of their patron.
>
> (2010, 304–5)

This mutual interest was encoded in a practice of exchange of literary works and epistles as part of a process that thrived upon a tacit accord between patron and client to consolidate or develop new bonds and, at the same time, channel requests for preferment or financial support. To this end, showing gratitude was a crucial matter. It entailed subtle and often artful strategies which came to be codified in precise discursive patterns and styles.

Indeed, ungratefulness, but also feigned gratitude, were topics frequently discussed and criticised by moralists as conducive to the degeneration of ethics. Writers and thinkers such as Elyot, La Primaudaye, and Montaigne expended much ink on this issue. In his 1531 *The Boke Named the Governour*, Sir Thomas Elyot qualified ingratitude as the "most damnable vice" along with hypocrisy and failure to dispense

34 *Silvia Bigliazzi*

rewards ("He is unkynde that dissimuleth, he is unkynde that recompenseth not. But he is most unkynde that forgeteth"; 1531, 2.13 "The division of Ingratitude and the dispraise thereof", 136). In 1586, Pierre La Primaudaye offered a lengthy discussion of the same pernicious vice, deeming it the cradle of troubles of the mind of all kinds: "Ingratitude stirs unquiet thoughts, and uncertain desires, which is an argument of the imperfection of their [the unthankful men's] reason, and of their ignorance of what which is good" (1586, ch. 40 "Of Ingratitude", 426). He criticised the example of the "vassaile", who, "for the least denial or hard countenance which he receiveth of his lord, forgetteth all the good turnes, furterhances and favours, which before that time he had done unto him", and likewise found it despicable that the son might complain of his father, "the brother of the brother" and "the servant of the master" (ibid., 428). When it was the prince or master who showed ungratefulness, the welfare itself, together with the arts and sciences, as well as all progress, he claimed, "languish[ed]" and were "extinguished little and little through the ingratitude and covetousnes of those that rule" (ibid.). On the vice of ingratitude in family and social bonds, both Elyot and La Primaudaye wrote extensively, exploring the subtle psychological reasons for the envious time-server's betrayal of friendship in exchange for chances of preferment. La Primaudaye's conclusion was that "if there be hope of recompence, the benefactor deserveth not all the name of a liberall man, but of one that giveth out to usurie" (ibid., 433). Moral integrity and freedom are clearly the issues at stake here.

Yet, trading in gratitude was precisely what courtiers often did. Montaigne was ready to criticise bonds of patronage which deprived man of his liberty, and stigmatised them as downright commercial dealings. In chapter 25, book 1, of his *Essays* ("Of the Institution and education of children; to the Lady Diana Foix, Countess of Gurson") he recommended that the young man "shall not be preferred to any place of eminencie above others for repeating of a prescript part"; nor will he "defend any cause, further than he may approve it"; nor "shall he bee of that trade where the libertie for a man to repent and re-advise himselfe is sold for readie money". In fact, when "the judgment of a man... is waged and bought, either it is less free and honest, or else it is blemished with oversight and ingratitude" (Montaigne 1603, 73). If Montaigne was so trenchant it was because he bitterly knew that man does not care much about selling off his own liberty in certain circumstances. Examples of the duplicitous courtier proved him right. Of course this also entailed a concern over threats of social and political subversion, because if inward disposition could be camouflaged, a criminal mind also could (see e.g. Maus 1995). But in the case of court advancement, this was not an issue. The transactional system, in fact, developed specific codes of conduct and communication, which were to be known to and shared by the participants if they were to succeed in encrypting covert messages. Such coded discourse evidently prospered upon an awareness of the instabilities of meaning inherent in language, which allowed for an exploitation of polysemy through agreed strategies. Compliment was one of these. It relied upon the possibility to don different masks depending on circumstances, which, as the reverse of the coin, unveiled the courtier's substantial weakness and fluctuability in the social scale, disclosing that position had no guarantee other than the promises securable through the suitor's own discursive ability. Epistolary exchanges, in particular, offered the poet-client the chance to present himself as a grateful and obedient servant, which required of him a good amount of double discourse.

The examples I will provide in the following pages come from a selection of prose and verse letters that John Donne sent to some of his patronesses during the so-called Mitcham years (1607–10), when he was trying to make up for his career failures by entering this transactional system of patronage. His principal correspondent was Lucy Harrington, Countess of Bedford, with whom he became closely acquainted around 1607. He exchanged with her regular letters, "established upon visits to her houses", especially in "1608 and the first half of 1609", before interrupting contacts in 1614, after a last, embarrassing plea for financial help – he sent her an obsequy for the death of her brother John in 1613–14 with request for money.[1]

Donne's rhetorical and argumentative strategies, as exemplified especially in one of his verse epistles belonging to the time when he was closest to the Countess (1609–10), offer a sample of the complex discursive practices that shaped their relationship. His inventiveness in fabricating a double discourse of praises and requests discloses the nature of the social negotiation at work while secretly hinting at his own intolerance of it. As Marotti suggested, "the playfully adversarial relationship he liked to establish with his readers resurfaces in the complimentary poems as an expression… of the strong resentment he harboured about the role as a deferential suitor he assumed in such verse" (Marotti 1986, 206–7). We shall see how his expression of gratitude might be read as double-edged, and will explore his rhetorical ingenuity in weaving his own restiveness into conventional pieces of compliment.

Hypocrisy, Letter-Writing, and the Power of Allegory

Commonly used, since its entrance in the English language, to denote duplicity and falsity,[2] in Ancient Greek the word hypocrisy (*hypokrisis*) originally bore a distinctively different meaning. In the Ionic dialect it signified reply, answer (Herodotus, *Histories* 1.116), while in its Attic usage it was a technical term for the playing of a part on stage[3] as well as the delivery of an oration (Aristotle, *Rhetoric* 3 1403b18–22). A metaphorical meaning more clearly endowed with moral condemnation,

36 *Silvia Bigliazzi*

stressing the falsity of outward show and acting,[4] developed only at a later time within a religious context, as testified to in both the Septuagint (2 Macc. 6.25) and the New Testament (Matthew 23, 28–29). It is not by chance that Tertullian (*De Spectaculis* 23) took up precisely this figurative acceptation derived from the neutral Aristotelian definition of stage playing in order to level a ponderous attack against spectacles. The anti-theatre polemics of the sixteenth and seventeenth century in England was fuelled precisely by such violent statements.[5] But the indictment of hypocrisy was most violent in the theological polemics. Protestants and Catholics were involved in an exchange of accusations which, at least at its inception, saw the former charge the latter with duplicity and the latter retaliate with blames of heresy. As has been contended, the two questions in fact were close, in that both were concerned with the same urge to probe 'inner intentions' (see e.g. Weightman 1992, 7–8). Indeed, the Reformation awakened a painful awareness of the possibilities of lying (Zagorin 1990), and suspicion towards all forms of potential or actual masking of one's identity and aims became a hallmark in debates on religious conformity as well as communal welfare.

Already in 1562, and again in 1574, a series of laws called Statutes of Apparel reviving earlier sumptuary laws were issued in order to cut on expenditures but also maintain through rules for attire a class system that certified one's social identity via clothing. Although widely ignored and therefore ineffective, their existence, as Vincent suggested, was important symbolically, as they "articulated a statement of desired intent, expression therein a governmental and cultural preference for a particular ordering of society". After all, Vincent argued, "[d]ress, as the apparel laws attest, could be used to make false claims about status and wealth, and these false claims were felt to be a threat to the status quo" (2003, 143). A few years later, in 1587, yet another edict condemned the "inordinate excesse in apparel, contrary to both the good lawes of the Realme, and to her Maiesties former admonitions by her Proclamations". It especially underlined their 'symbolic' contrariness "to the confusion of degrees of all estates, among whome diversities of apparell hath been always a special and laudable marke". Wild moralists ceaselessly ranted against that confusion, labelling it monstrosity,[6] an idea which shared in the early modern diffused awareness that "'seeming' might not be the same as 'being'" (Vincent 2003, 10). It is not by chance that, as Peter Burke suggested, the term 'sincerity' came into regular use by the end of the sixteenth century and reached a peak in the following one,[7] in a period when discussions of the effects of dissembling flourished in various contexts.

Amongst the "chiefe conditions and qualities in a Courtier" listed by Castiglione at the end of *The Courtesan*, not being a "lyer" nor a "fonde flatterer" occupied a prominent place. Manners should not display affectation (*affettazione*), and artifice ought to be concealed through "recklessness", as Hoby anglicised the Italian *sprezzatura*; in short, a good courtier was expected

> To shon Affectation or curiosity above al thing in al things… [to]… use a Reckelesness to cover art, without minding greatly what he hath in hand, to a mans seeminge…. To reason of pleasaunt and meerie matters… without dissimulation or flatterie… to be francke and free with him [with the Prince or Lord…], always putting him in minde to folow vertue and to flee vice… and to shut his eares against flatterers, whiche are the first beeginninge of self leekinge and all ignorance.
> (Castiglione 1561, "A breef rehersall of the chiefe conditions and qualities in a Courtier", Vv.iiii.r, Zz.ii.r, Zz.ii.v)

A few decades only after the circulation of Hoby's translation, Francis Bacon entitled one of his essays "Of Simulation and Dissimulation". He distinguished three degrees of what he called a "hiding and veiling of a man's self" (2002, 350):

> For the first of these, Secrecy; it is indeed the virtue of a confessor… an habit of secrecy is both politic and moral. And in this part, it is good that a man's face give his tongue leave to speak. For the discovery of a man's self by the tracts of his countenance is a great weakness and betraying; by how much it is many times more marked and believed than a man's words.
> For the second, which is Dissimulation; it followeth many times upon secrecy by a necessity; so that he that will be secret must be a dissembler in some degree…. So that no man can be secret, except he give himself a little scope of dissimulation; which is, as it were, but the skirts or train of secrecy.
> But for the third degree, which is Simulation and false profession; that I hold more culpable, and less politic; except it be in great and rare matters. And therefore a general custom of simulation (which is this last degree) is a vice, rising either of a natural falseness or fearfulness, or of a mind that hath some main faults, which because a man must needs disguise, it maketh him practise simulation in other things, lest his hand should be out of ure.
> (Bacon 2002, 350–1)

Bacon's position was not isolated.[8] It was consonant with theories of duplicity as a falsifying potential inscribed in language that at the time circulated in books of rhetoric and oratory.[9] In his *Arte of English Poesy* (1589), George Puttenham famously wrote that:

> As figures be the instruments of ornament in every language, so be they also in sorte *abuses or rather trespasses in speech*, because they

38 *Silvia Bigliazzi*

passe the ordinary limits of common utterance, and be occupied of purpose to *deceive the ear and also the mind*, drawing it from plainness and simplicity to a certain *doublenesse*, where by our talk is the more *guileful and abusing*. For what else is your Metaphor but an *inversion* of sense by transport, or your allegory by a *duplicitie of meaning or dissimulation under covert intendments*; one while *speaking obscurely* and in *riddle* called Aenigma; another by common proverb or Adage called Paremia; then by merry skiff called Ironie; then by bitter taunt called Sarcasmos…

> (1589, 3.7 "Of figures and figurative speaches", 128, my emphasis)

Puttenham's censorious attitude towards the abusing potential of ornamentation, and his recommendation wisely to use discretion and "decency",[10] focused especially on the figure of allegory, or "false samblant". His critique was rooted in its power to deflect meaning from its natural signification, a prerogative which was also of other figures, such as irony, riddle, and hyperbole; through their use, in fact,

we may dissemble, I meane speake otherwise then we thinke, in earnest as well as in sport, vnder couert and darke termes, and in learned and apparant speaches, in short sentences, and by long ambage and circumstance of wordes, and finally as well when we lye as when we tell truth. To be short euery speach wrested from his owne naturall signification to another not altogether so naturall is a kinde of dissimulation, because the wordes beare contrary countenaunce to th'intent.

> (Ibid., 155)

And yet,

[t]he use of this figure [allegory] is so large, and his vertue of so great efficacie as it is supposed no man can pleasantly utter and persuade without it, but in effect is sure never or very seldome to thrive and prosper in the world, that cannot skilfully put in use.

> (Ibid.)

This is why

not onely every common Courtier, but also the gravest Counsellour, yea and the most noble and wisest Prince of them all are many times enforced to use it, by example (say they) of the great Emperour who had it usually in his mouth to say, *Qui nescit dissimulare nescit regnare*.

> (Ibid.)

Even more explicitly Puttenham stated that he had "not impertinently" called that figure of Allegory as "the Courtier or figure of faire semblant", because it is not "perchance more requisite our courtly Poet do dissemble not onely his countenances & conceits, but also all his ordinary actions of behaviour" (ibid, 251; Mucci 2010, 217). Indeed, poetry of compliment was the best example of this allegorical dissemblance and, exactly like politics, availed itself of Bacon's three degrees of self-hiding, from secrecy to simulation.

Although since Cicero dissimulation was reputed pernicious in public intercourse ("ex omni vita simulatio dissimulatioque tollenda est", *De Officiis*, 3.15), in fact the Renaissance acknowledged its usefulness. It was common opinion that the art of politics required both simulation and dissimulation, as Machiavelli famously contended in chapter 18 of *The Prince*: "... quello che ha Saputo meglio usare la volpe, è meglio capitato. Ma è necessario questa natura saperla bene colorire, ed essere gran simulatore e dissimulatore" ("Those best at playing the fox have done better than the others. But you have to know how to disguise your slyness, how to pretend one thing and cover up another": Machiavelli 2009, 70). The courtier too was no less aware of the 'virtues' of hypocrisy in order to gain quick access to power, as well as of the innocent use of dissimulation in pleasant intercourse, as in jesting, "whan a man speaketh one thinge and privilie meaneth another" (Castiglione 1561, "Dissimulacion", book 2, X.i.v). In all such cases, disguising one's inner disposition through outer appearances was akin to dissembling linguistically one's inner thought (Mucci 2010). As Puttenham put it, allegory was indeed an intrinsically political figure.

In some respects epideictic letter-writing participated in the shaping of this culture rooted in allegorical practices. Based on a reappraisal of the medieval *artes dictaminis* through the mediation of Ciceronian oratory, letter-writing met with renovated enthusiasm precisely in the Renaissance thanks to Erasmus's *De Conscribendis* (1522). This treatise offered a detailed classification of letters – "descriptory", "laudatory", "deliberative", "amatorie", "iudiciall", "expostulatorie", "comminatorie", "familiar" etc. – and an accurate discussion of appropriate styles, which was conducive to a renewed attention to how to style oneself in writing. This implied knowledge of rules as well as skill in handling them (Bound 2002; Burke 1997; Burke and Porter 1991; Daybell 2011; Foucault 1988; Porter 1997; Sawday 1997; Smith 1997). The subsequent swell of editions of manuals for the instruction of the mercantile class and of those interested in vernacular epistolography, from William Fulwood's *The Enemie of Idleness* (1568) to Angel Day's *The English Secretary* (1586, revised and extended in 1602), established letter-writing as a rapidly growing genre that crossed "the thin line... to epistolary fiction" (Newbold 2007, 137), especially when topics such as love were in focus (as in Nicolas Breton's *A Post with a Mad Packet*

40 *Silvia Bigliazzi*

of Letters, 1602). Samples were provided according to a typology of recipients, who played a prominent role in the communicative exchange. Fulwood, for instance, recommended that:

> If we speake or write of or to our superiours, we must doe it with all honour, humility and reverence, using to their personages superlative and comparative terms, as, Most high, most mighty, right honourable, most redoubted, most loyall, most worthy, most renownd: and so of the rest according to the quality of their personages: and it is to be noted, that of Superlatives, Comparative, Positive, or Diminutive terms, we must use but three at once at the most.
>
> (1568, 2)

Skill in using style appropriately allowed to "purchace" somebody's benevolence, as Fulwood revealingly put it, and this could be achieved by following set rules: firstly by decently praising him "for his liberality, his bountifulnesse, his iustice, his virtue, &c."; secondly by saying that "he is modest, gentle to every one, and a man not voide of knowledge"; thirdly by avoiding to demand things too great or irrespective of the appropriate time, place and cause; and finally by promising "him service, and continuall obedience" (ibid., 16–18).

These conventions allowed for more than one level of signification. Underneath the praise, verse epistles were pleads for favours, and this dual layer was intended not to be misunderstood, while not appearing too blatant. Depending on the client's ability, these levels could proliferate. Some of John Donne's letters provide precisely such an example. Their extremely elaborate style and ingenious use of allegorical strategies, verging towards downright obscurity, in fact activate unexpected signifying processes. What seems to sneak in between the lines are secret allusions to impatience of the pressures of patronage and its fundamentally hypocritical structure. It is not coincidental that, as will be seen, he wrote revealing lines upon (in)gratitude, at the same time embedding within his own discursive practices of compliment their very critique.

Encoding Duplicity in Donne's Show of (In)Gratitude

In his laudatory letters to his patronesses, Donne's arguments show a deep awareness of the mechanics involved in writing to a superior. He appropriately followed common precepts of humility, devotion, self-abnegation, and circumstantial opportunity, and participated in a transactional exchange showing

> [l]ittle that can be regarded as the direct expression of personal experience, or, indeed, of more than a part, a small part, of the

poet's self; little that is more than half-serious; little that is what a modern reader is accustomed... to call 'sincere'.

(Leishman 1969, 143)

Rather, he constructed versions of his own self that deployed the "complex image of the relations between poet, patroness, society and ethical idealism" (Aers and Kress 1978, 140).

As Cedric Brown (2008) has argued, within a culture of epistolarity, which provided the "material medium... of social exchange" (Schneider 2005, 13), references to memory and gift practices could regulate the mobile relationship between poet and patron. Anxious about how his writings might be received and "constantly referring to his own memory of earlier transactions" (Brown 2008, 65), Donne often talked about his own exchanges with his patronesses, their virtues, and his own thankfulness, drawing the boundaries of their reciprocal interest in trading in mutual gratitude. In this sense his epistles should be looked at as "'performances' to mark specific 'occasions,' whether or not those specific occasions can now be determined with exactitude" (Pebworth 1989, 64). The choice of the topic was not neutral. In one of his letters to the Countess of Bedford, in particular, probably written in late 1609 or 1610, Donne seemed to struggle with courtly language, apparently intolerant of those discursive fetters which Montaigne held up as reflecting the minion's lack of freedom.[11] In that epistle he tackled the issue of writing in response to the Countess, disclosing how deeply it was involved with another, more important, question: his own promotion. This was an issue that he often tackled in his letters to his patronesses through ingenious innuendos embedded in a very compressed style. In a previous epistle of 1607–8 *To Mrs M. H.* (i.e. Magdalen Herbert), shaped according to the medieval model of the *envoi*, he indirectly referred to the Gentlewoman by addressing the letter itself, and elaborately adumbrated his own social advancement through images of 'possession' and 'creation' at the hands of the patroness:

> Yet when her warm redeeming hand, which is
>   A miracle; and made such to work more,
> Doth touch thee, sapless leaf, thou grow'st by this
>   Her creature; glorified more than before.

(ll. 17–20)

Being a "creature" miraculously grown ex nihilo thanks to Lady Magdalen's generative (but also destructive) power clearly stands, as in other similar cases, for his "admission to the desired social group" (Aers and Kress 1978, 145).[12] Donne is well aware of the function of indirectness and of a sophisticated use of metonymy and metaphor (the letter as a "sapless leaf" and an emanation of himself; non-existence at Court as non-existence tout court; the patroness as a Goddess). At the same time, he showcases the potential of his own art and prospective utility at Court, offering a tangible sample of how he could be of use: his verse deflecting praise from the patroness herself ("not her") to her qualities ("her servants") thematises the efficacy of indirectness and his own talent in handling it:

> Yet may'st thou praise her servants, though not her;
>   And wit, and virtue, and honour attend;
> And since they're but clothes, thou shalt not err,
>   If thou her shape, and beauty, and grace commend.
>
> (ll. 29–32)

As Aers and Kress clearly demonstrated, in such letters Donne

> constructed a complicated metaphysics in which a platonic model of eternal value was set off against a market model of use. Donne's critical attitude to the world which excluded him, and his self-estimation were bound up with the former model; yet he clearly wanted a place in the market and so had to assert his use as a secular servant as usher/ideologue.
>
> (1978, 149–50)

In "Madam You have Refin'd me", a letter addressed to the Countess of Bedford possibly around 1608, Donne was even more elaborate. He imaged her patroness's own virtue as a dark text that "need[s] notes", and himself as the interpreter she may want if she wishes to establish a firmer place at Court:

> Therefore at Court, which is not vertues clime,
> Where a transcendent height, (as, lownesse mee)
> Makes her not be, or not show: all my rime
> Your vertues challenge, which there rarest bee;
> For, as darke texts need notes: there some must bee
>   To usher vertue, and say, This is shee.
>
> (ll. 6–10)

Donne here displays his merchandise by marketing his own abilities and readiness to sacrifice his own liberty in return for a post, aware that if he wishes to become 'somebody' he needs to prove profitable. Aers and Kress are conclusive on this:

> This employment not only brings him into existence, creates him indeed (as lines 21–2 make explicit ["Since a new world doth rise here from your light, / We your new creatures, by new recknings goe"]),

but also brings the countess' virtue into the social world, thus indirectly giving her existence and... value. This is an astonishingly delicate combination of begging and self-assertion, and the relations hinted at are very complex. Donne is the created creature, she the creator; he low, she high; he patronized, she patron; he exegete, she dark text; he usher, she virtue; he excluded, she included. Yet she too is excluded until he realises her social potential and value for her. Structurally Lucy and Donne are opposed and yet equated, transforms of each other creating each other from shared invisibility into apparent existence and social value.

(1978, 143)

This mutual interest lying behind the patron-client bond is the premise of also another, subsequent, letter to the Countess of Bedford, where he plays upon the apparent paradox of God's own need of his own creatures in order to receive from them the honour He deserves:

Honour is so sublime perfection,
And so refined; that when God was alone
    And creaturelesse at first, himselfe had none;
...

So from low persons doth all honour flow;
Kings, whom they would have honoured, to us show,
    And but *direct* our honour, not *bestow*.

(ll. 1–3; 7–9, my emphasis)

Once the godly patron is shown the extent to which the courtier is crucial in supporting his/her own social position, the transaction may begin through an exchange of favours and benefits aimed at securing their reciprocal standing 'circumstantially' (see Maurer 1980). To return to the above-quoted "You have refin'd me", the opening lines state very clearly that nothing is endowed with intrinsic value (neither virtue, nor art, nor beauty), and that only circumstances grant it. The formulation is radical: "as they [these things] are circumstanc'd, they bee" (l. 4.). Against a platonic ontology of value equated with ineffable perfection, everyone is measured phenomenally, which opens to strategies of negotiation based on one's marketability.

Depressed at failing to become a civil servant, in the Mitcham years Donne often represented himself as a "nothing" in his prose letters too (Marotti 2006, 41–2); "to be no part of any body", he once wrote to his friend Henry Goodyer, "is to be nothing"; non-belonging to any recognisable social group meant having neither utility nor value:

At most, the greatest persons, are but great wens, and excrescences; men of wit and delightful conversation, but as moales for ornament,

44 *Silvia Bigliazzi*

except they be so incorporated into the body of the world, that they contribute something to the sustentation of the whole. This is made account that I begun early, when I understood the study of our laws: but was diverted by the worst voluptuousness, which is an Hydroptique immoderate desire of human learning and languages: beautifull ornaments to great fortunes; but mine needed an occupation, and a course which I thought I entred well into…. And there I stumbled too, yet I would try again: for to this hour I am nothing, or so little, that I am scarce subject and argument good enough for one of mine own letters: yet I fear, that doth not ever proceed from a good root, that I am so well content to be lesse, that is dead.

(Donne 1651, 51)

In another letter to Goodyer of 15 August 1607, he insisted on his own sincerity in avowing his awareness of being 'useless' and, at the same time, in desperate need to be 'used':

And as wheresoever these leaves [my letters] fall, the root is in my heart, so shall they, as that sucks good affections towards you there, have ever true impressions thereof. Thus much information is in very leaves, that they can tell what the tree is, and these can tell you I am a friend, and an honest man. Of what generall use, the fruit should speake, and I have none: and of what particular profit to you, your application and experimenting should tell you, and you can make none of such a nothing; yet even of barren Sycamores, such as I, there were use, if either any light flashings, or scorching vehemencies, or sudden showres made you need so shadowy an example or remembrancer. But (Sir) your fortune and minde do you this happy injury, that they make all kinde of fruits uselesse unto you; Therefore I have placed my love wisely where I need communicate nothing.

(Ibid., 115)

As in *To Mrs M. H.*, the orchard imagery stands for both his letter and himself, a "barren tree", socially sterile, but "a friend, and an honest man". The passage is very intricate and the sequence of negations contain more than a progress towards self-nihilism. "[N]othing" shifts reference from the poet's own lack of value to Goodyer's liberality, thus certifying that their friendship is sincere and outside of the fetters of patronage, as Montaigne would have it. Yet, if he could assert this with reference to Goodyer, who often helped him to find prospective patrons by making "the crucial introduction" (Stubbs 2008, 214), he could not say the same with regard to those who really might have included him in the desired social group. In his final statement ("I have placed my love wisely where I need communicate nothing") Donne seems to reveal his relief in speaking openly with his friend, which discloses by contrast

Trading in Gratitude   45

his awareness that he should use a different language with the others if he hoped to leave his present state of alienation. He was also aware that offering a service none needed was fruitless, a lesson which he had recently and disappointingly learned. As Stubbs recalls, in yet another letter to Goodyer of 13 June 1607, Donne had asked him to remind the royal secretary, William Fowler, that they had met once, in 1603, in the hope that this memory could help him get the position on the Queen's staff which had become vacant. In that letter Donne "presented himself as "a 'gift' for Fowler to do with as he pleased, though the official might have forgotten the 'right and power' he still held over his human property"; but although "Donne might describe himself as the secretary's 'possession'... nobody was interested in a free gift" (ibid.).

Memory of gifts and letters as reminders of himself to his patrons was a main preoccupation with Donne, whose epistles frequently voiced "the anxieties caused by slowness or lack of response" (Brown 2008, 65). "T'have written then" focuses precisely on the topic of writing back as a gift practice loaded with controversial connotations. As has been pointed out (Grierson 1951, 160; Milgate 1967, 262), in his 1623 sermon "Preached upon the Penitentiall Psalmes" Donne was to ground his critique of ingratitude in a long tradition of moral attacks, which he recalled by mentioning that

> in all Solomons bookes you shall not finde halfe so much of the duty of thankfulnesse as you shall in Seneca and in Plutarch. No book of Ethicks, of morall doctrine is come to us, wherein there is not almost in every leafe some detestation, some anathema against ingratitude.

As Seneca famously wrote, "Non referre beneficiis gratiam et est turpe et apud omnes habetur" (*De Beneficiis*, 3.1.1.). Yet in 1609–10, when Donne composed that letter to the Countess of Bedford, the issue of gratitude appeared to him more complicated than would later seem. At that time he was still trying to bargain his career at Court, and the culture of patronage he had to cope with involved a whole range of morally debatable issues he could not openly question, including having to show gratefulness. We know that he exchanged with the Countess both prose and verse letters, although none of hers is extant; yet reference to them is contained in one of Donne's epistles in which he asks to be given the verses she had written for him and he had seen in Twickenham:

> Happiest and worthiest Lady, I do not remember that ever I have seen a petition in verse, I would not therefore be singular, nor adde these to your other papers. I have yet adventured so near as to make a petition for verse, it is for those your Ladiship did me the honour to see in Twicknam garden, except you repent your making; and having mended your judgement by thinking worse, that is, better,

46 *Silvia Bigliazzi*

because juster, of their subject. They must needs be an excellent exercise of your wit, which speaks so well of so ill: I humbly beg them of your Ladiship, with two such promises, as to any other of your compositions were threatenings: that I will not shew them, and that I will not believe them; and nothing should be so used that comes from your brain or heart.

(Donne 1651, 67)

From his correspondence with Goodyer, we also know that he acknowledged the Countess as the only one who "hath the power to cast the fetters of verse upon my free meditations" (ibid., 117). Although the word "fetters" here refers to the constraints of metrics, it evokes memories of other bondages enmeshing the poet-client in burdensome social negotiations, and sounds as a metaphor for the way those bonds harnessed his "free meditations". Letter-writing was itself a form of social fetters, binding him to write back at the right time, even if unwilling, but also causing anxiety about possible delays. Thus, when in a prose letter to the Countess he strove to demonstrate that letter-writing transcends time, as letters bear something which "is eternall, and out of the measure of time", he was, contrariwise, voicing concern over time and date, as well as his own belatedness: his epistle had come "not the same day [when her brother had told her that he had written]", nor bore "the same date as his". There followed his justification:

for though in inheritances and worldly possessions we consider the dates of Evidences, yet in Letters, by which we deliver over our affections, and assurances of friendship, and the best faculties of our souls, times and dates cannot have Interest, nor be considerable, because that which passes by them, is eternall, and out of the measure of time. Because therefore it is the office of this Letter, to convey my best wishes, and all the effects of a noble love unto you, (which are the best fruits that so poor a soil, as my poor soul is, can produce) you may be pleased to allow the Letter thus much of the souls privilege, as to exempt it from straitnesse of hours, or any measure of times, and so beleeve it came then.

(Donne 1651, 22–3)

"T'have written then" opens precisely on the same issue. As Marotti has argued (1986, 223–5), this is a troubling and extremely convoluted epistle in which Donne acknowledges his "patroness's courtly maneuverings" under the guise of compliment, and tries to profit from them. Characterised by discontinuities and abrupt changes – mainly after lines 30 and 71, where he first turns the praise into a satire of the world's corruption, and then moves on to the final part of his letter – the poem shows Donne's attempt to assert his own authority as advice dispenser, but also to insinuate his difficulties in having to put up with courtly dealings. His impatience surfaces in the opening lines, where he wonders about the consequences of replying to the Countess – or not doing so – straightaway:

> T'have written then, when you writ, seemed to me
>> Worst of spiritual vices, *simony,*
> And not to have written then, seems little less
>> Than worst of civil vices, *thanklessness.*
>
> (ll. 1–4, my emphasis)

These lines deserve more attention than they have attracted so far, as they encapsulate within a seemingly straightforward reflection upon ingratitude an indirect clue touching on the poet's own attitude towards the Countess and the patronage system. The argument unfolds as follows: replying by return post ("then, when", l. 1) to her epistle might appear as trafficking in sacred things: assuming their friendship as sacred, writing back very quickly would be proof of interested hastiness and therefore of 'trading in gratitude' ("simony"). This last remark exposes the hypocrisy of the exchange, while pretending to dispel all suspicion that the letter might precisely be a 'gift' to cash in advancement. Thus, on the one hand, mention of simony supports the flattering purpose of showing devotion towards the Countess's 'sacred friendship'; on the other, his condemnation of hasty letter-writing as evidence of social interest unveils the truism that stands behind all courtly relationship: writing to a patroness at any time cannot be wrested from interest of preferment, and doing it quickly simply makes it more blatant.

This is the covert statement embedded in the first two lines; the following two discuss the opposite case of not responding at once, and find fault also with this, considering it civil ingratitude. No third option is put forward to overcome the impasse, and in the next six lines Donne further elaborates on those alternatives:

> In this, my *debt* I seemed loth to confess,
>> In that, I seemed to shun *beholdingness.*
> But 'tis not so, *nothings,* as I am, may
>> *Pay all they have,* and yet *have all to pay.*
> Such *borrow in their payments,* and *owe more*
>> By having *leave to write so,* than before.
>
> (ll. 5–10, my emphasis)

At this point Donne has no difficulty in stating that the relation he is talking about is based upon a credit-debit system; his explicit use of a financial metaphor in ll. 7–10, while contradicting his denial of personal interest in l. 2 and implicitly revoking the sacredness of his friendship

48 *Silvia Bigliazzi*

with the Countess (what was condemned as simony is now acknowledged as debt), unveils the logic actually at work in their exchange and the pressures he feels, like all the other "nothings" he compares himself to. While civil and spiritual vices no longer find place here, the focus is upon downright obligation with little manifest moral overtones. In the short space of ten lines, his change of attitude towards untimely letter-writing suggests the presence of some secret counter-discourse concerning letter-writing itself as a fettering bond.

This hypothesis is supported by yet another contradiction, this time involving a shift in perspective, from the client's vice to the patron's own pressures. In lines 5 and 6, the deictic markers "this" and "that" cohesively refer back to the previous lines, the closest and the farthest, respectively (3–4 and 1–2). Accordingly, "[i]n this" introduces an explanation of unthankfulness, while "[i]n that" of simony, so that the sequence is cast as a chiasmus: simony (hasty writing) (A) – thanklessness (belated reply) (B) – resistance to confess his debt (B) – shunning beholdingness (A). This structure qualifies simony as the vice of avoiding obligation of gratitude for financial interest, and thanklessness as that of refusing to acknowledge one's debt of gratitude in time. At this point the two alternatives deriving from contrary choices in respect to when to write are eventually reconciled through transitivity. This poses a logical contradiction, and it is precisely through it that a focalisation upon the idea itself of obligation may be encoded in his argument. If we look at those lines more closely, the series of equivalences show slight semantic shifts: the first series (ll. 1–2, 6) equate (1) 'hasty writing' with (3) 'avoidance of gratitude'; the second (ll. 3–4, 5) correlate (1) 'delayed writing' with (3) 'resistance to confess gratitude'. In either case, a financial metaphor (2) surfaces to deny that what he is talking about is marketing friendship:

1   hasty writing = (2) vice of simony (marketing sacred friendship) = (3) avoidance of the debt of gratitude
2   delayed writing = (2) ingratitude (civil vice) = (3) resistance to confess his debt of gratitude.

By stating that freedom from obligation is the result of both not replying and replying at once, on the one hand he disowns indebtedness ("my debt I seemed loth to confess", l. 5), and on the other he does what he is required to in order to get what he wants and then forgets about it ("I seemed to shun beholdingness", l. 6). In either case he refuses to acknowledge the debt of gratitude, that is obligation, which is precisely what becomes prominent in the following four lines (7–10) in explicitly financial terms. Thus the argument progresses through three steps: (1) compliment and condemnation of the client's own vice (simony or ingratitude) (ll. 1–4); (2) foregrounding of obligation in all cases as a debt (financial constraint) (ll. 5–6); (3) dependency of the client upon the patron.

Trading in Gratitude 49

This tortuous playing with equivalences and oppositions cannot be coincidental and alerts the reader to the presence of a different message from the surface one, something that could not be pronounced aloud: a secret desire to free himself from obligation. Denying this desire only meant affirming it through litotes and the apparent rigour of deductive reasoning, leading to an aporia that stressed exactly that message. Positing an irresolvable choice finally concurred to showing the poet's carefulness in depicting his own deeply embarrassed position.

This is why what follows clears the way from hints of restiveness, possibly passing off those present in these lines as witty playing with compliment. As Marotti has argued,

> [o]nce Donne achieved a degree of social familiarity with Lady Bedford, he operated poetically on the assumption that she was able to appreciate his mischievously witty playing with the conventions of praise: what was, for him, partly a manifestation of his discomfort with suitorship, was probably meant to be enjoyed by her as a compliment to her intelligence and sophistication.
>
> (1986, 209)

At this point compliment had to become prominent once again to counterbalance a potentially subversive discourse. Following the same metaphor of buying and paying back, he thus developed the following four lines (7–10), where he fashioned a version of himself as a "nothing" set against the assumed 'all-ness' of the Countess; his own nothingness, like that of all the other petitioners caught in the meshes of the bond of gratitude, was the apt foil to pay the necessary tribute to the Countess, while bargaining his own freedom. The financial metaphor conveys precisely this idea, because casting all petitioners as insolvent debtors encloses them within a claustrophobic relation of permanent borrowing and paying. Having leave to write (l. 10), in fact, is itself an obliging grant on the part of the creditor, who, by allowing him access to private correspondence, further increases his dues, thus closing in upon the debtor the circle of an interest-based relation. The poet will never be able to balance out, and this makes the bond unsolvable. Again a chiasmus frames all the suitors symbolically, entrapping them within a circle from which there is no way out: "Pay all they have, and yet have all to pay" (l. 8). La Primaudaye's accusation of usury levelled at princes seems to have sneaked into these lines, whose commendatory rhetoric turns this ingenious apology into an implicit accusation.

The next lines resume more plainly the laudatory bend of the servant-poet whose value is measured against his capacity to be of use. Thus premised by issues of gratitude and letter-writing as gift presentation,

50 *Silvia Bigliazzi*

his argument may now play with different masks of the poet's own self in order to demonstrate how useful the 'nothing' that he is may yet be:

> Yet since rich mines in barren grounds are shown,
>> May not I yield (not gold) but coal or stone?
> Temples were not demolished, though profane:
>> Here Peter Joves's, there Paul hath Dian's fane.
> So whether my hymns you admit or choose,
>> In me you have hallowed a pagan Muse,
> And denizened a stranger, who mistaught
>> By blamers of the times they marred, hath sought
> Virtues in corners, which now bravely do
>> Shine in the world's best part, or all it; you.
>
> (ll. 11–20)

He is the mine in a barren ground capable of yielding "coal or stone" (ll. 11–12), a sterile ground that still produces something good; he is also the "profane temple" and "pagan Muse" (l. 16) capable of enshrining in poems the divinity of his patroness; finally, he is the "stranger" who will be denizened at Court (l. 17) if she will only accept his "hymns" (l. 15). The transactional rationale of this relationship is only too apparent.

But once again obscurity soon replaces straightforward allegory, suggesting that things may stand or signify differently from the way they appear. A few lines below, close to the end, he elaborates further on the Countess's virtue, stating that she will not accept two truths (the world's evil and her own virtue), and this accounts for a defective virtue in her (l. 73). The consequence is that her extreme humility (l. 77, "too much one") makes her mistrust her own virtue (l. 78), while her ignorance of evil-doing impedes her compassion for those who commit it:

> But I must end this letter, though it do
>> Stand on two truths, neither is true to you.
> Virtue has some perverseness; for she will
>> Neither believe her good, nor others' ill.
> Even in you, virtue's best paradise,
>> Virtue hath some, but wise degrees of vice.
> Too many virtues, or too much of one
>> Begets in you unjust suspicion,
> And ignorance of vice, makes virtue less,
>> Quenching compassion of our wretchedness.
> But these are riddles...
>
> (ll. 71–81)

In short, perfect virtue requires to be compounded with knowledge of vice, and its ignorance is itself depraved; therefore, the Countess should

Trading in Gratitude 51

not have doubts about herself, nor ignore the evils in the world, but understand them and feel sympathy for human wretchedness. The implication is clear: Donne is asking for both understanding and material help. But the words "perverseness" and "unjust" applied to the Countess reverberate with the implications of latent intolerance of their own relationship emerged before, offering yet another instance of a widespread tactics of indirectness that eventually crystallises in Donne's acknowledgement of his own discursive obscurity and talking in riddles ("But these are riddles", he stops short at line 81).

As in the argumentative short-circuit of the first lines, also here the allegorical code of duplicity is finally exposed the moment it is used, as if the poet wished to frame compliment within a self-referential discourse hinting at its complex allusiveness. In this respect, it is revealing that it is one of Puttenham's figures of "false semblant", the riddle, that eventually exhibits the paradoxical position Donne found himself in, ironically stigmatising his own impatience of compliment and its use in his strenuous attempts to become the poet-servant he was never to be.

Notes

1 Brown (2008, 69); a discussion of the letter accompanying the obsequy with request for money is at 78–81. On the relation between Donne and the Countess within the context of a gradual decline of the patronage system see Thomson (1949).

2 The first attestation recorded in the *Oxford English Dictionary* with the meaning of "The assuming of a false appearance of virtue or goodness, with dissimulation of real character or inclinations, esp. in respect of religious life or beliefs; hence in general sense, dissimulation, pretence, sham" is *Ancrene Riwle*, dating *c*1225, 254: "Of alle cuðe sunnen as of prude ... of yprocrisie" (Proffitt 2016).

3 As for instance in Aristotle's *Nicomachean Ethics* (1118a8), where the term technically identifies the actors' (*hypokritai*) performance as opposed to the chorus's (*tragodoi*).

4 Liddell-Scott-Jones, *Greek-English Lexicon* cites as first entries an epigram ascribed to Polybius and Polybius 35.2.13.

5 In his 1582 *Playes Confuted in Five Actions* Gosson clearly stated that the idea that stage plays are the doctrine and invention of the devil may be gathered from Tertullian. A year later, in 1583, Philip Stubbes again mentioned Tertullian and condemned the players for the same reason in his *Anatomy of Abuses* (ch. 13 "Of Stage-playes, and Enterludes, and their Wickednes") warning them against God's wrath ("and doo these Mockers and Flowters of his Maiefty, these dissembling *Hipocrites*, and flattering *Gnatoes*, think to escape unpunished? beware, therefore, you masking players, you painted sepulchres, you double dealing ambodexters"). He notoriously described theatres as the schools of all vices rooted in hypocritical duplicity; Stubbes (1877–79, 141, 145).

6 Stubbes was famously one of the most extreme:

> There is such a confuse mingle mangle in apparel in Ailgna [i.e. England], and such preposterous excess thereof, as every one is permitted to flaunt it out, in what apparell he lust himselfe, or can get by anie kind of meanes.

52 Silvia Bigliazzi

> So that it is very hard to knowe, who is noble, who is worshipfull, who
> is gentleman, who is not.
>
> (Ibid. 34)

Stubbes also cited Schoolmaster Richard Averell's *Merualous Combat of
Contrarieties* (1588) for his attack on those women who

> from the top to the toe, are so disguised, that though they be in sexe
> Women, yet in attire they appeare to be men, and are like Androgini,
> who counterfayting the shape of either kind, are in deede neither, so
> while they are in condition women, and oulde seeme in apparrell men,
> they are neither men nor women, but plaine Monsters.
>
> (Ibid., 254)

7 More precisely, in the 1600–49 period, according to the *OED* timeline, s.v.
  'sincere'. As Burke noted,

> Shakespeare used the terms "sincerity", "sincere" and "sincerely" thirteen
> times in his printed works (Sidney and Jonson used the terms twice each,
> while Milton, by contrast, used them forty-eight times in his prose works
> alone). The advice Polonius gives Laertes in *Hamlet* "to thine own self be
> true" may have been a commonplace but it was a relatively new common-
> place. What is more, the term 'sincere' was becoming a fashionable one in
> other languages during this period, notably Italian and French (Montaigne
> was one of the first recorded users).
>
> Burke (1997, 19–20)

8 As Vickers points out, his discussion overlapped with that of Francesco
  Guicciardini in his *Ricordi*, a work that circulated widely in various languages
  (Bacon 2002, 723). For a fuller discussion of the essay see Dzelzainis (2010)
  (on Guicciardini see 333–4).
9 Bacon's notorious suspicion towards the heuristic value of words brought
  him to stigmatise language as the idol of the market in *Novum Organum*
  (1620) (1.43). At a later date, in *Leviathan* (1651), Hobbes would famously
  expound on the instability of language: "names of such things as affect us,
  which please, and displease us, because all men be not alike affected with the
  same thing, nor the same man at all times, are in the common discourses of
  men, of inconstant signification"; words

> besides the signification of what we imagine of their nature, have a sig-
> nification also of the nature, disposition, and interest of the speaker; such
> as the names of Vertues, and Vices. For one man calleth Wisdome, what
> another calleth fear; and one cruelty, what another calleth justice; one
> prodigality, what another magnanimity; and one gravity, what another
> stupidity, & c. And therefore such names can never be true grounds for
> any ratiocination. No more can Metaphors, and Tropes of speech: but
> these are less dangerous, because they profess their *inconstancy*; which
> the other do not.
>
> Hobbes (1996, 1.4 "Of Speech", 31)

10 So albeit we before alleaged that all our figures be but transgressions of
   our dayly speach, yet if they fall out decently to the good liking of the
   mynde or eare and to the bewtifying of the matter or language, all is
   well, if indecently, and to the eares and myndes misliking (be the figure
   of it selfe neuer so commendable) all is amisse, the election is the writers,
   the iudgement is the worlds, as theirs to whom the reading apperteineth.
   But since the actions of man with their circumstances be infinite, and the
   world likewise replenished with many iudgements, it may be a question

who shal have the determination of such controversie as may arise whether this or that action or speach be decent or indecent: and verely it seemes to go all by discretion, not perchaunce of every one, but by a learned and experienced discretion, for otherwise seemes the *decorum* to a weake and ignorant iudgement, then it doth to one of better knowledge and experience: which sheweth that it resteth in the discerning part of the minde, so as he who can make the best and most differences of things by reasonable and wittie distinction is to be the fittest iudge or sentencer of [*decencie*].

Puttenham (1589, 220)

11   a mere and precise Courtier *can neither have law nor will to seake or thinke otherwise than favourable of his Master*, who among so many thousands of his subjects hath made choice of him alone, to institute and bring him up with his owne hand. *These favours*, with the commodities that follow minions Courtiers, *corrupt* (not without some colour of reason) *his libertie*, and *dazzle his judgement*. It is therefore commonly seene that *the Courtiers-language differs from other mens*, in the same state, and to be of no great credit in such matters. Let therefore his conscience and virtue shine in his speech, and reason be his chiefe direction.

Montaigne (1603, 1.26, 73, my emphasis)

12 In the previous lines, in fact, the letter is said to 'have died' as soon as arrived in the presence of the patroness's God-like dazzling eye: "But when thou come'st to that perplexing eye / Which equally claims love and reverence, / Thou wilt not long dispute it, thou wilt die; / And, having little now, have then no sense" (ll. 13–16). The implication is that she has absolute power of both life and death over the suitor.

Works Cited

Aers, David and Gunther Kress. 1978. "'Darke Texts Need Notes': Versions of Self in Donne's Verse Epistles". *Literature and History* 8: 138–58.

Aristotle. 1934. *The Nicomachean Ethics*, in Aristotle, 23 volumes, vol. 19. Translated by H. Rackham. Cambridge, MA: Harvard University Press; London: Heinemann.

———. 1975. *The "Art" of Rhetoric*. Translated by John Henry Freese: *Aristotle* vol. 22 (Loeb Classical Library 193). Cambridge, MA: Harvard University Press; London: Heinemann.

Bacon, Francis. 2002. "The Essays or Counsels Civil and Moral (1625). Newly Enlarged". In *The Major Works*, edited by Brian Vickers. Oxford: Oxford University Press.

Bound, Fay. 2002. "Writing the Self? Love and the Letter in England, c. 1660-c. 1760". *Literature and History* 11: 1–19.

Breton, Nicholas. 1602. *A Post with a Mad Packet of Letters*. London: Printed for John Smethicke.

Brown, Cedric C. 2008. "Presence, Obligation and Memory in John Donne's Texts for the Countess of Bedford". *Renaissance Studies* 22(1): 63–86.

Burke, Peter. 1997. "Representations of the Self from Petrarch to Descartes". In *Rewriting the Self. Histories from the Renaissance to the Present*, edited by Roy Porter, 17–28. London and New York: Routledge.

54 *Silvia Bigliazzi*

Burke, Peter and Roy Porter (eds). 1991. *Language, Self, and Society: A Social History*. Cambridge: Polity.

Castiglione, Baldassarre. 1561. *The Courtyer by Count Baldessar Castilio diuided into foure books*. Translated by Thomas Hoby. London: Imprinted by William Seres.

Cicero, M. Tullius. 1913. *De Officiis*. Translated by Walter Miller. Cambridge, MA: Harvard University Press.

Day, Angel. 1602. *The English Secretary or Method of Writing of Epistles and Letters... Now Newly Revised, and in Many Parts Corrected and Amended*. London: Printed by Thomas Snodbam.

Daybell, James. 2011. "Women's Letters, Literature and Conscience in Sixteenth-Century England". In *The Renaissance Conscience*, edited by Harald E. Braun and Edward Vallance, 82–99. Oxford: Wiley-Blackwell.

Donne, John. 1623. "Sermon Preached upon the Penitentiall Psalmes", *John Donne Sermons* 4. BYU Harold B Lee Library Digital Collections. Available online at https://lib.byu.edu/collections/ (accessed 15 May 2016).

Donne, John. 1651. *Letters to Severall Persons of Honour*. London: Printed by J. Flesher for Richard Mariot.

Dzelzainis, Martin. 2010. "Bacon's 'Of Simuation and Dissimulation'". In *A New Companion to English Renaissance Literature and Culture*, edited by Michael Hattaway, vol. 1, chapter 22. 2329–35. Oxford: Wiley-Blackwell.

Elyot, Thomas. 1531. *The Boke Named the Governour*. London.

Erasmus Roterodamus, Desiderius. 1522 [1985]. *De Conscribendis Epistolis*. In *Collected Works of Erasmus. Literary and Educational Writings*, vol. 4, edited by J.K. Sowards. Toronto, ON; Buffalo, NY; London: University of Toronto Press.

Foucault, Michel. 1988. "Technologies of the Self". In *Technologies of the Self: A Seminar with Michel Foucault*, edited by Luther H. Martin, Huck Gutman, and Patrick H. Hutton, 16–49. Amherst: University of Massacussetts Press.

Fulwood, William. 1568. *The Enemie of Idleness*. London: Henry Binneman for Leonard Maylard.

Grierson, Herbert J. C. (ed.). [1912] 1951. *The Poems of John Donne, Edited from the Old Edition and Numerous Manuscripts*. London: Oxford University Press.

Herodotus. 1920. Translated by A.D. Godley. Cambridge, MA: Harvard University Press.

Hobbes, Thomas. 1996. *Leviathan*, edited by Richard Tuck. Cambridge: Cambridge University Press.

La Primaudaye, Pierre. 1586. *The French Academie*. London: Edmund Bollifant.

Leishman, James Blair [1951] 1969. *The Monarch of Wit*. London: Hutchinson University Library.

Machiavelli, Niccolò. 2009. *The Prince*, edited and translated by Tim Parks. Harmondsworth: Penguin.

Marotti, Arthur F. 1986. *John Donne, Coterie Poet*. London: The University of Wisconsin Press.

―――. 2006. "The Social Context and Nature of Donne's Writing: Occasional Verse and Letters". In *The Cambridge Companion to John Donne*, edited by Achsah Guibbory, 35–48. Cambridge: Cambridge University Press.

Maurer, Margaret. 1980. "The Real Presence of Lucy Russell, Countess of Bedford, and the Terms of John Donne's 'Honour is So Sublime Perfection'". *ELH* 47(2): 205–34.

Maus, Katharine Eisaman. 1995. *Inwardness and Theater in the English Renaissance*. Chicago, IL: Chicago University Press.

Milgate, Wesley (ed.). 1967. *John Donne. The Satires, Epigrams and Verse Letters*. Oxford: Clarendon Press.

Montaigne, Michel. 1603. *The Essays*. Translated by John Florio. London: Val. Sims for Edward Blount.

Mucci, Clara. 2010. "Allegory". In *A New Companion to English Renaissance Literature and Culture*, edited by Michael Hattaway, vol. 2, chapter 55, 214–24. Oxford: Wiley-Blackwell.

Newbold, W. Webster. 2007. "Letter Writing and Vernacular Literacy in Sixteenth-Century England". In *Letter-Writing Manuals and Instruction From Antiquity to the Present*, edited by Carol Poster and Linda C. Mitchell, 127–40. Columbia: The University of South Carolina Press.

Pebworth, Ted-Larry. 1989. "John Donne, Coterie Poetry, and the Text as Performance". *Studies in English Literature 1500–1900* 29(1): 61–75.

Perry, Curtis. 2010. "Court and Coterie Culture". In *A New Companion to English Renaissance Literature and Culture*, edited by Michael Hattaway, vol. 1, chapter 20. 304–19. Oxford: Wiley-Blackwell.

Porter, Roy. 1997. "Introduction". In *Rewriting the Self: Histories from the Renaissance to the Present*, edited by Roy Porter, 11–14. London and New York: Routledge.

Proffitt, M. (ed.) (2016). *The Oxford English Dictionary Online*. Available online at www.oed.com (accessed 15 May 2016).

Puttenham, George. 1589. *The Arte of English Poesie*. London: Richard Field.

Sawday, Jonathan. 1997. "Self and Sefhood in the Seventeenth Century". In *Rewriting the Self: Histories from the Renaissance to the Present*, edited by Roy Porter, 29–48. London and New York: Routledge.

Schneider, Gary. 2005. *The Culture of Epistolarity: Vernacular Letters and Letter Writing in Early Modern England, 1500–1700*. Newark: University of Delaware Press.

Smith, Roger. 1997. "Self-Reflection and the Self". In *Rewriting the Self: Histories from the Renaissance to the Present*, edited by Roy Porter, 20–57. London and New York: Routledge.

Stubbes, Philip. 1877–79. *Anatomy of the Abuses*, edited by Frederick J. Furnivall. London: Traübner, The New Shakespeare Society.

Stubbs, John. [2006] 2008. *John Donne. The Reformed Soul. A Biography*. New York and London: W. W. Norton & Company.

Tertullian. 1977. *De Spectaculis*. In Tertullian, *Apology and De Spectaculis*. Translated by T.R. Glover and Minucius Felix. Cambridge, MA: Harvard University Press-London: Henimann.

Thomson, Patricia. 1949. "John Donne and the Countess of Bedford". *The Modern Language Review* 44(3); 329–40.

Vincent, Susan J. 2003. *Dressing the Elite. Clothes in Early Modern England.* Oxford: Berg.

Weightman Stewart, Patricia. 1992. *Hypocrisy and Heresy: Language and Concepts in Early Modern England.* PhD diss., British Columbia, Faculty of Graduate Studies, Department of History, University of British Columbia.

Zagorin, Perez. 1990. *Ways of Lying: Dissimulation, Persecution, and Conformity in Early Modern Europe.* Cambridge, MA; London: Harvard University Press.

3 Religious Hypocrisy in Performance

Roman Catholicism and The London Stage

Lucia Nigri

From the Medieval period to the Restoration, the hypocrite remained a remarkably popular figure, proving its resilience as an object of fascination not only in literature but in theological, political, and social debates. In the Tudor and Stuart period more specifically, fictional and non-fictional discourses coalesce into a popular dramatic motif which, by engaging with false-seeming characters on a metatheatrical level, operates both to conceal and to reveal concerns relating to the true or false application of religious doctrine. Early modern representations of hypocrisy on stage significantly reify this general anxiety about the often ambiguous and deceitful behaviour displayed by some clergymen of the time. Despite the many representations of hypocritical Puritans on stage (see Walsh 2016, 46–9), it is in the specific charge against the representatives of the Roman Catholic Church that the elusiveness of the term 'hypocrisy' recurs – unsurprisingly – with its most powerful material, religious, and cultural resonances.

A notable early English example, which begins a trend by associating hypocrisy with the Roman Catholic religion, is Chaucer's character of the Pardoner. Described as "a noble ecclesiast" who "knew that when that song [an Offertory] was sung / He'd have to preach and tune his honey-tongue / And (well he could) win silver from the crowd" (Chaucer 1960, 36; see also Fletcher 1990; Kruger 1994, 121), the Pardoner is a brilliant simulator of virtue. As he openly boasts in *The Pardoner's Prologue*,

> priestlike in my pulpit, with a frown,
> I stand, and when the yokels have sat down,
> I preach...
> And tell a hundred lying mockeries more.
> I take great pains, and stretching out my neck,
> To east and west I crane about and peck
> Just like a pigeon sitting on a barn.
> My hands and tongue together spin the yarn
> And all my antics are a joy to see.

58 *Lucia Nigri*

...

For my exclusive purpose is to win
And not at all to castigate their sin.
Once dead what matter how their souls may fare?
They can go blackberrying, for all I care!

(1960, 258–9)

In the Pardoner's lucid self-evaluation, hypocrisy is associated with wittiness, the adoption of a refined language, and an ability to deceive others through a carefully 'targeted' representation of the self. The emphasis here is on the acting of a part whose success depends on the congregation's naiveté ("yokels") and the trust placed in the performer (on the topic of trust and hypocrisy, see Vickers 1979). However, in *The Pardoner's Prologue* he also details the immoral and psychological "motive[s]" which drive the play of hypocrisy:

Believe me, many a sermon or devotive
Exordium issues from an evil motive.
Some to give pleasure by their flattery
And gain promotion through hypocrisy,
Some out of vanity, and some out of hate;
...

And so I take revenge upon our foes
And spit my venom forth, while I profess
Holy and true – or seeming holiness.
...

I preach for nothing but for greed of gain.

(1960, 259)

What is here confessed with remarkable candidness – the Pardoner's greed, his evil motives, and his desire for revenge – constitutes, in the character's words, the necessary prerequisites (and justification) for the ecclesiastic's cover of holiness.

Chaucer's insistence on the hypocrite's false piety, which serves dishonourable purposes by manipulating the audience, is here loaded with specific biblical allusions. From the more general meaning of impious men in the Old Testament, the word 'hypocrite' recurs more prominently in the New Testament with reference to the simulators of piety, the Pharisees: "hypocrites... that be like to sepulchres whited [that be like to sepulchres made white], which withoutforth seem fair to men; but within they be full of bones of dead men, and of all filth" (Matthew 23:27, Wycliffe Bible; see also the Introduction to this volume). Chaucer thus positions his own anticlerical polemic against hypocritical Roman Catholic ecclesiastics within the biblical charge against Pharisees whose

Religious Hypocrisy in Performance   59

actions and prayers demand to be seen (Matthew 6:2; 6:5; 6:16, Wycliffe Bible).

Even applying fairly strictly Chaucer's description of the Pardoner as a self-conscious hypocrite, one is faced with a plethora of hypocrites in Elizabethan and Jacobean literature, as well as many characters with sufficient 'hypocritical' qualities to be enlisted in the group. Importantly, however, what distinguishes this type from the troops of villains and rogues, which populate early modern works, is the character's "seeming holiness" achieved through the "priestlike" show.

The medieval representation of sin dressed up as Christian righteousness in fact carries through to the later period when Elizabethan and Jacobean hypocrites were still portrayed in a recognisable fashion as it appears in the description of "The Hypocrite" offered by Joseph Hall in his *Characters of Virtues and Vices* (1608). Hall purposefully places the hypocrite as the first character amongst "The Vices" and the one directly following "The Virtues" because, as he acknowledges in *The Proem* of his second book, "hypocrisy shall lead this ring [of vices]: worthily, I think, because both she cometh nearest to Virtue, and is the worst of Vices" (1837, 104; see also Knutson 1994). Reminiscent of the etymology of the term *hypocrite*, recorded in the *Oxford English Dictionary* as deriving from the "Greek ὑποκριτής an actor on the stage, pretender, dissembler" (Proffitt 2016), Hall's description reiterates the performative nature of a character who is "the worst kind of player, by so much as he acts the better part... in whose silent face are written the characters of religion, which his tongue and gestures pronounce, but his hands recant" (Hall 1837, 104). In a similar fashion to the Pardoner's, this hypocrite's performance necessitates an audience in order to be validated:

> At church, he will ever sit where he may bee seen best; and in the midst of the sermon, pulls out his tables in haste, as if he feared to loose that note; when he writes, either his forgotten errand, or nothing: then, he turns his Bible with a noise, to seek an omitted quotation; and folds the leaf, as if he had found it; and asks aloud the name of the preacher, and repeats it; whom he publicly salutes, thanks, praises, invites, entertains with tedious good counsel, with good discourse, if it had come from an honester mouth.
>
> (Ibid., 105)

In this description, Hall delineates the stereotypical features which identify this type of hypocrite: a self-conscious character who is able to master the psychology of the churchgoers and who acknowledges the importance of 'being seen' by them.

The public gaze and the pretence of being holy emerge, too, in Robert Bolton's *Discourse about the State of True Happinesse* (1611) where the English preacher provides a classification of different kinds of hypocrites: those who deceive only themselves (*Privie*); those deceiving others but not themselves (*Grosse*); and those deceiving themselves and others (*Formal*). It is the latter who presents

> a shew of piety and outward forme of religion [and] a false conceit and persuasion that he is in a happie state, when as in truth his soule was never yet seasoned with saving grace and the power of religion.... To all these he may adde a glorious profession of the Gospell, a performance of all outward duties and exercises of religion, many workes of charity and monuments of his rich magnificence.
>
> (Bolton 1611, 34; see also Bryn Roberts 2016, 94–120)

Once again, Bolton seems to assume that the difference between real and hypocritical faith can be 'seen' in the person's manner, precisely because the behaviour obviously follows a pattern of role learning.

If in cultural and literary discourses of early modern England public performances of holiness are associated with hypocrisy, then it comes as no surprise that Roman Catholic clergymen who, to borrow Bolton's words, paraded their "outward duties and exercises of religion" are also charged with the accusation of hypocrisy by their Anglican opponents. Specifically during the second half of the sixteenth century and into the first decade of the seventeenth century a renewed surge of anti-Catholic feelings spread across the country as a direct and intensely political response to the many plots attempting to remove from the English throne Anglican monarchs in favour of their Catholic counterparts. Protestants, in fact, began to use Roman Catholic intervention in the country's internal affairs as an effective way of promoting their own political cause through an unremitting propaganda, which saw a new momentous turn in 1570 with the papal excommunication of Elizabeth I. The bull *Regnans in Excelsis* was actually meant to embolden the Rising of the North (1569), a rebellion initiated by noble Catholic families in the north of England who had been resisting the religious repressions which followed Elizabeth's coronation. Ironically, the much-anticipated papal condemnation of Elizabeth as heretic reached England too late, the rebellion having already been repressed. The failure of the Northern uprising was to play a crucial role in what was a foreseeable intensification of Anglican resentment against Catholics, who were now publicly (and more vehemently) accused with the charge of hypocrisy and strictly forbidden to disguise themselves as "merchants, gentlemen and students" in order to practice their faith (Hyland 2011, 128; see also Beier 1985, 102). Coupled with Tudor homilies focusing on private devotion against public show, this anti-Catholic attack contributed to the establishment of an early modern discourse of hypocrisy designed to attack Roman Catholicism and its representatives.

The historical context provided here lays the basis for a more comprehensive understanding of what then occurs in the theatre. Despite the

Religious Hypocrisy in Performance 61

fact that non-theatrical discourse tradition had in fact developed independently of drama, early modern playwrights were quick to fashion generic conventions and categories of representation which could play out these religious and political conflicts. London theatres then consistently staged the heated debates of the time, using performance itself to illuminate the issue of hypocritical performance, thus arising the question of how the stage engaged with hypocrisy on a metatheatrical level: if it focussed on multiple and diverse representations of authentic or insincere performances, there was the obvious charge of destabilising the basis of both private and public identities. Moreover, in dramatising the complex range of hypocrisy in the Tudor and Stuart period, the dramatists needed to take account of concerns relating to social status and religious doctrine: social status and one's religious practice could not be separated easily in terms of identity. Thus, together with representations of the evil of hypocrisy and the means for achieving hypocrisy, comes suspicion of all identities.

If, arguably, the 'stage hypocrite' occurs only partly as a feature in theatrical traditions (see, for example, 'Doctor Hypocrisy' in Wilson's 1592 *The Three Ladies of London* and 'Hypocrisy' in the anonymous' *New Custom*) he could and often did express the sense of deception and incoherence experienced in specific forms by members of the audience who watched these plays and who would be inclined to associate hypocrisy with the clergy's behaviour and, more generally, with their public exhibition of faith perceived as a way to fulfil political aspirations. As Brian Vickers claims, in drama

> the pretense of good is not merely a cover for the continuing practice of one's own faults, whether grave or trifling, but is the method by which a person breaks out new ones, tries to reach some clearly defined goal.
>
> (1979, 45)

Religious hypocrisy on stage, then, unavoidably intersects with political corruption.

The value of how this ambivalent and often intensely emotional material could be transformed into compelling and fascinating characterisation can be seen in the play of *Richard III*, which provides an extraordinary representative case of a layman who, by affecting "zealous contemplation" and devoutness in order to gain and secure power (3.7.93), drives the process of misinterpretation of his immoral conduct as authentic devotion. Significantly represented in a history play, Shakespeare explores the paradigm of the religious hypocrite through Richard's public performance of holiness. In the third act the audience – on stage and off stage – is a witness to Buckingham's "holy descant" (3.7.48) and Catesby's portrayal of a most devout Richard who is

62   *Lucia Nigri*

"within, with two right reverend fathers, / Divinely bent to meditation; / And in no worldly suit would he be moved / To draw him from his holy exercise" (3.7.60–3). Assumed by others to be in a state of rapture in the privacy (on the privacy and the spiritual life see McKeon, 2005, 225–8; Rambuss 1998, 103–36), Richard is physically separated from the public space where those who can legitimately endorse his power through audible approval, the Lord Mayor and Citizens, are met. Richard's absence from the scene serves his accomplices' portrayal of the man's piousness and disinterest with the material world altogether ("in no worldly suit would he be moved"). The whole evocative scene, in fact, is designed to play upon Richard's conspirators' and their audience's shared understanding of what a meditative exercise 'should' entail: a space "within", spiritual guides, and physical and moral subjugation to God ("divinely bent"). However, the construction of visible privacy attained through words is insufficient to fulfil Gloucester's plan and only functions as a preparation for what is going to follow publicly. For his play of hypocrisy to work and meet his designs, Richard knows that he needs to be 'seen' in the act of zealous contemplation; he knows that he must put religious practice on display through the adoption of the theatrical gestures of the pious man. Richard's 'show' of his counterfeited virtue demands in fact the reiteration of private physical gestures ("on his knees at meditation"; 3.7.72), the presence of an audience which includes the constituents of the civic power, the presence of props for the enactment of hypocrisy ("two props of virtue for a Christian prince" (3.7.95) namely, "two deep divines"; 3.7.74), and "a book of prayer in his hand, / True ornaments to know a holy man" (3.7.97–8).

What happens here involves a *mise en abyme* of hypocrisy: the actor's sin – what Matthew H. Wikander describes as "the malicious charge that an actor must necessarily be a hypocrite" (2002, 11) – is re-duplicated in the character's pretension to goodness. Obviously, the audience on stage does not share in the exposure of hypocrisy which is, instead, revealed to, and intended for, the audience off-stage. The presence of the friars in *Richard III* serves a double purpose here because, while signalling – off-stage – Richard's 'false' holy nature, it works as a validation for the characters on stage of what they believe is the necessary 'condition of coincidence' of one's 'true' virtuous nature with the external demonstration of it. Not only is Richard's (feigned) holiness prompted by the 'use' of material forms of devotion, which recognisably anchor people's faith (see Williamson 2009) but it is also reinforced by the necessary objectification of religious figures in props which, dramaturgically identified by their simple, inexpensive garments, stand external to Richard. The friars operate in fact to heighten Richard's success at appearing sincerely pious: with their consecrated authority, they adorn him as "true ornaments". In other contemporary plays, however, these "props of virtue" complicate the discourse of hypocrisy when internalised in the mask

Religious Hypocrisy in Performance 63

of the ecclesiastic – a popular disguise for rulers or revengers on the London stages.

Measure for Measure provides another noteworthy example of how Shakespeare complicates the audience's response to hypocritical behaviours: in addition to the insincerity of Angelo who feigns holiness in order to maintain power, the dramatist introduces Vincentio, the legitimate Duke who disguises himself as Friar Lodowick:

> I will, as 'twere a brother of your order,
> Visit both prince and people. Therefore, I prithee,
> Supply me with the habit, and instruct me
> How I may formally in person bear
> Like a true friar.

> (1.3.44–8)

Shakespeare thus explores holy false-seeming on stage through the representation of the corrupted Angelo, but he also duplicates and complicates the motif in Vincentio's usurping of the "true friar['s]" clothing, which results in the successfulness of the 'bed trick' and the 'head trick' and in the accomplishment of a restored political order. Clearly, the goal here appears to be a noble one: to 'observe' the city's affairs and gain a better understanding of how to end corruption. In this context, hypocrisy gains legitimacy through the robe of the clergyman but also in terms of the figure who wears that disguise: the Duke himself, who functions as both a political and spiritual ruler, though the ambivalence which many spectators and readers feel at the close of the play testifies to the ambivalence of the performance of hypocrisy as a dramatic trope.

As in *Richard III*, in *Measure for Measure* Shakespeare does not intend a criticism of Catholic representatives – at least not overtly. The friar's clothing here is important because it can demonstrate its potential to be '(ab)used' in rather ambiguous businesses (Hwang 2016), as done by Vincentio. This particular use of the robe of morality significantly complicates the problem of semiotic interpretation of the codes of moral truth. The Duke's moral function should not require him to don the robe of the clergy since he already carries in his political function the role of moral leader of his society, and we know that divine right meant precisely the role of moral leader. So, if the Duke must go disguised, it tells the audience something about the folly of simplistic assumptions about who can be deemed a moral leader.

The adoption of the mask as a device to accomplish one's plan also occurs in John Webster's *The White Devil*, where Lodovico and Gasparo pretend to be Capuchin monks in order to murder Brachiano and revenge Isabella's death. Acting the part of "two noblemen of Hungary [who] entered into religion, into the strict order of Capuchins" (5.1.13–6), these two characters' deceitfulness – and consequently their victims' naiveté – is

64 *Lucia Nigri*

exaggerated by the fact that they wear "coats of mail" (5.1.25) – a legacy of their knighthood and, as described by Flamineo, a "strange" mark of their ambiguous past:

> being not well settled in [the Order of Capuchins'] undertaking they left their order and returned to court: for which being after troubled in conscience, they vowed their service against the enemies of Christ; went to Malta; were there knighted; and in their return back, at this great solemnity, they are resolved for ever to forsake the world, and settle themselves here in a house of Capuchins in Padua.
>
> (5.1.16–21)

Lodovico's and Gasparo's public performance of holiness is not exhibited through religious garments but is, instead, marked by the pronouncement of the characters' association with the order and by their adoption of Latin, the language of the Church:

> *Si nunc quoque probas ea, quæ acta sunt inter nos, flecte caput in lævum.*
> He is departing: pray stand all apart,
> And let us only whisper in his ears
> Some private meditations which our order
> Permits you not to hear.
>
> (5.3.142–7)

Clearly, in this passage, Latin language functions as a dramatic device that allows these churchmen to win the trust of those who should participate in the prayer of the dying man and who are, instead, asked to leave. The request to remain alone with Brachiano in order to "whisper in his ears / Some private meditations" is accepted by the others because, once again, it complies with the necessary privacy which accompanies 'true' religious exercises. The audience off-stage, instead, is aware of the inner motives of the performers of prayer and they can thus judge the sincerity of their demand and expect, once the mask is discarded in the solitude of the room, the now unpreventable fulfilment of the two noblemen's revengeful plans. Webster here seems to reflect on the generic benefits of this oscillation between the theatrical representation and the audience's need to assess and judge the types of speech and behaviour represented on stage, not only in terms of the moral implications but also in terms of the theatrical expectations being built into the structure of the representation. Moreover the interpretation of this passage is further complicated because of possible intertextual resonances which enliven the play of hypocrisy. As Christina Luckji correctly points out in her edition of the play,

> The whole passage is based on Erasmus, *Funus*, an account of the death of Georgius Balearicus, a corrupt and wealthy man, whose

Religious Hypocrisy in Performance 65

death is described by Erasmus as 'last acte of the comedie'. After purchasing papal remission of sins (and justifying all his goods 'goten by extorcyon and robbery'), Georgius himself, 'lyke a man of warre', delivers the first two speeches which Webster gives to the assassins. Erasmus emphasizes the corruption and hypocrisy of the dying man; Webster uses the same ceremony to highlight the villainy and hypocrisy of the dying man's assassins.

(Webster 2014, 528)

In *The White Devil*, then, Webster interconnects the theme of revenge with the visual-audible power of devotional practices, which generally mark hypocritical discourses. If the disguise cannot 'justify' the characters' performance of holiness for personal goals, the play suggests the legitimacy of using the disguise to serve a righteous end: the honourable murder in return for the injury suffered.

In order to entangle his investigation of false-seeming holiness, Webster also introduces with the character of Monticelso 'the' representatives of the Roman Catholic Church, the Cardinal, and the Pope. Different from Lodovico's and Gasparo's enactments of holiness, Cardinal Monticelso's "scarlet" robe marks his feigned virtue, a point noticed by Vittoria: "O poor charity / Thou art seldom found in scarlet" (3.2.72). Vittoria is here using personification in order to criticise the hypocritical and deceptive nature of the Catholic ecclesiastic. The Cardinal's sumptuous religious garments become the target of her desperate plea for innocence while representing at the same time for the audience the very visual sign of Catholic corruption that was at the heart of Protestant propaganda. As noted by Su-kyung Hwang, "among other clothes carrying symbolic meaning, what makes the vestments seem more hypocritical is ironically their strong attachment to what they were once supposed to symbolize" (2016, 305). Monticelso's duplicitous attitude is here made even more obvious by the fact that he is first introduced as a righteous advisor, which is what his role should actually entail. At the beginning of the second act, we assist to the Cardinal's scolding of Brachiano who is catechised on his moral conduct: "Should in your prime age / Neglect your awful throne, for the soft down / Of an insatiate bed" (2.1.30–2). Of course, the ecclesiastic's pretension to goodness emerges quickly when he asks Camillo, his nephew and Vittoria's husband, to leave Rome and go fight the pirates. The stratagem, as we are told, serves the Cardinal's plan to "give violent way / To Duke Brachiano's lust" (2.2.371–2). Not only does Monticelso operate systematic inversions of the truth (as with Camillo's trick) but he also fails to show the charitable understanding and guidance one would associate with his role. As an unscrupulous intelligencer, the Cardinal participates in Brachiano's and Vittoria's downfall, which thus adds to his performance as a religious hypocrite a Machiavellian ability to manipulate other characters and to devise

66 *Lucia Nigri*

successful conspiracies, as suggested by his possession of a book, which lists the names of possible knaves to be employed:

> It is reported you possess a book
> Wherein you have quoted, by intelligence,
> The names of all notorious offenders
> Lurking about the city.
>
> (4.1.29–32)

This presentation of a duplicitous clergyman might have possibly reinforced the audience's negative perception of Catholic authorities, a perception shared by Flamineo who claims that "Religion; oh how it is commeddled with policy" (3.3.35). The fact that Monticelso's first public act as Pope Paulus IV is the excommunication of Vittoria and Brachiano can be read as a crowning manifestation of religious power – and intervention – in temporal matters:

> Now, though this be the first day of our seat,
> We cannot better please the divine power
> Than to sequester from the holy church
> These cursed persons. Make it therefore known,
> We do denounce excommunication
> Against them both: all that are theirs in Rome
> We likewise banish. Set on.
>
> (4.3.64–70)

While operating on a dramatic level, Monticelso's deceitfulness reinforces the hypocritical stigma attached to Roman Catholic representatives by casting doubts on papal integrity. After all, Webster's choice of dramatising a conflict between characters belonging to the republican Venice and those representing non-secular Rome cannot be taken as a mere coincidence here (see Luckyj 2016). As James Doelman claims in his *King James I and the Religious Culture of England*, "The English saw the quarrel between Venice and Rome as the counterpart to their own struggle: in both cases the civil government was challenging what they saw as the intrusion of the pope into matters of secular authority" (2000, 105). Thus, Webster interweaves his tragedy with anti-Catholic sentiments, which find in the figure of the Roman Cardinal/Pope the best representative of duplicitous and insincere behaviour and in the figure of the Venetian Vittoria an embodiment of the Protestant theatre audience's opposition to the Roman Catholic Church. After all, as Luckyj argues, Vittoria's pressing petitions to "this auditory" and "all this assembly" in the trial scene (3.2.15 and 19) precisely point towards the audience's participation in a process of distrust and suspicion of religious conduct (2016).

Religious Hypocrisy in Performance   67

Ironically, towards the end of the play the dramatist seems to tone down the anticlerical criticism by showing a more cautious Pope who, in the fourth act, warns Lodovico against damnation, the direct consequence of his revenge:

> If thou persist in this [revenge], 'tis damnable.
> Dost thou imagine thou canst slide on blood
> And not be tainted with a shameful fall?
>
> (4.3.117–19)

If Webster's characterisation of the Cardinal focuses on his political meddling, his treatment of the Roman Catholic leader, the Pope, is definitely mitigated through the image of a religious mentor whose words now stand for a (somewhat implausible) virtue. The fact that the dramatist portrays in this scene a corrupt individual who passes the correct judgement on a moral situation indeed complicates the whole issue of hypocrisy by exposing the seeming disjunction between the corrupt and the virtuous. But the tragedy is about to end and Webster must have felt the dramaturgical urgency to focus on those characters whose actions would naturally lead towards the final catastrophe required by the genre. At this point in the play, the Cardinal is in fact removed from the plots that follow (and which require the death of those involved).

This positive portrayal of Catholic representatives at the end of the tragedy is not unique on the early modern stage. Webster's Pope seems indeed to conform to the more popular, "exceptionally sympathetic" stage treatment conceded to friars, especially Franciscans (Beauregard 2001, 249. See also Holland 2001, in particular pp. 57–70). Indeed, if in *Richard III* "the two props of virtue" are not given any dialogue, even when a friar plays a more substantial role in a play, as in the case of Friar Laurence in *Romeo and Juliet*, the sanctity of their spiritual guide is never doubted. Friar Laurence, for example, admits his responsibilities in the tragic events of the lovers – "and if aught in this / Miscarried by my fault, let my old life / Be sacrificed" (5.3.266–68) – but he is never accused of hypocrisy by any of the other characters in the play. His devotion is never questioned, even when Juliet momentarily calls in doubt his integrity: "What if... and yet methinks it should not, / For he hath still been tried a holy man" (4.3.24–9). Laurence's responsibility in the tragic outcome of the lovers' story is then legitimised by his good intention "to turn [the lovers'] households' rancour to pure love" (2.3.88). Together with Friar Laurence, portrayals of Franciscans in *Romeo and Juliet* are generally positive, thus significantly diverging from what is considered the tragedy's most immediate source, Brooke's poem. In *Romeus*

68 *Lucia Nigri*

and Juliet, the narrator sharply criticises Friar Laurence's Order in his moralistic preface "To the Reader":

> And to this end, good Reader, is this tragical matter written, to describe unto thee a couple of unfortunate lovers, thralling themselves to unhonest desire; neglecting the authority and advice of parents and friends; conferring their principal counsels with *drunken gossips and superstitious friars (the naturally fit instruments of unchastity)*; attempting all adventures of peril for th' attaining of their wished lust; *using auricular confession the key of whoredom and treason, for furtherance of their purpose*; abusing the honourable name of lawful marriage to cloak the shame of stolen contracts; finally by all means of unhonest life hasting to most unhappy death.
>
> (Brooke 1908, np, my emphasis)

Brooke's gloss on the narrative holds strictly to patriarchal values, and his portrayal of abusing friars raises the threat of radical Christian sects to the political status quo of patriarchy. The negative description of the friars recurs once more in the very introduction of the good Friar Laurence, a "barefoot friar girt with cord his gravish weed, / For he of Francis' order was, a friar, as I rede. / Not as the most was he, a gross unlearned fool" (ibid., ll. 565–7). Brooke describes Romeo and Juliet's confidante as very different from those adhering to the same Order: he is a learned "Doctor of Divinity" (ibid., l. 568) and a wise counsellor, not an "unlearned fool". This characterization of Friar Laurence provides a useful antecedent for the likeable rendering of Shakespeare's friar's devoutness, wisdom, and prudence (this latter in marked contrast to the rashness of the lovers). In *Romeo and Juliet*, in fact, the dramatist recuperates the positive representation of Brooke's friar while departing from the portrayals of the superstitious and untrustworthy ministers found in the play's source and, more generally, in the well-established satirical and anti-fraternal tradition. Franciscan friars are in Shakespeare charitable and merciful characters, as emphasised in act 5, scene 2 by Friar John's narration of the "barefoot brother": "One of our order, to associate me, / Here in this city visiting the sick" (5.2.5–7). Their honourable reputation is in fact confirmed once more by the Prince at the end of *Romeo and Juliet*: "we still have known thee for a holy man" (*Romeo and Juliet*, 5.3.270).

Similarly, in *Measure for Measure*, Shakespeare chooses to include the presence of two helpful and reliable friars, Peter and Thomas, who must 'instruct' Vincentio in his religious performance and who are, similar to Friar Laurence, the only authoritative narrators who are able to resolve for the audience on stage the mysteries in the story of the protagonists (*Romeo and Juliet*, 5.3.229–69; *Measure for Measure*, 4.5.1–6 and 5.1.152–64). Once again, the friars' acceptance in helping the Duke

Religious Hypocrisy in Performance 69

deceive the Prince and the citizens is endorsed by the righteousness of their reputation and by the nature of the affair at stake.

Significantly, despite the many allusions to friars' hypocrisy in early modern cultural and literary discourses (see, amongst others, Marlowe's *Doctor Faustus* 1.3.23–6 and John Foxe's Latin religious play *Christus Triumphans* 5.1.16–8 and 22), friars on stage are generally not represented as hypocrites. In a marked difference from higher members of the ecclesiastical order such as Cardinals, the lowly friar cannot aspire to become more than what he is. Their theatrical portrayals are not tainted with hypocrisy and corruption precisely because the fixity of their place in the social structure guarantees stability and, most importantly, the impossibility of jeopardising or subverting any order.

Spurred on by anti-Catholic feeling, clerical and non-clerical hypocrites on the London stages both discuss and enact how religious duplicity can function to achieve (illegitimate) political and personal goals in the future, as Angelo, Richard or the Cardinal do, or, through the mask of the ecclesiastic, re-address crimes and difficulties from the past, as manifested by Vincentio, Gasparo, and Lodovico. Through their strategic (mis)use of clerical vestments and religious objects, these plays mostly reflect contemporary social anxiety about religion and its relationship to theatricality. However, instead of endorsing a straightforward Protestant antipathy for the Roman Catholic Church, the dramatists of the period are prone to demonstrating the dangers of the politics of religion when 'used' for personal gain and advancement. Significantly, even when Franciscans intervene in matters of secular affairs, their hypocrisy is not dramatised on stage by either Shakespeare or Webster, both of whom portray these religious figures in a more positive light. The friars' intervention in temporal matters cannot in fact result in any possible re-positioning on the social ladder. Moreover, as maintained by Jean MacIntyre and Garrett P. J. Epp, clothes worn on the early modern stage clearly identified the character's social standing (1997, 270) and, arguably, particularly in terms of the character's generic function, his potential to villainy. In this context, the friars' simplicity of their garments is received by dramatists and theatre audience as codified metaphors of the Franciscans' commitment to a moral, rather than a political, system. Their inoffensiveness clears them from the charge of hypocrisy.

Early modern representations of theatrical characters are driven by a range of complex and not always easily mapped factors. A dramatist may or may not wish to pursue the accepted doctrinal line, may not want to follow the official view but also may not want to run the danger of being hung for heresy, may be torn between ideological commitments, may be interested in pushing the generic possibilities of characterisation (as in *Richard III*), or may be playing with other representations found in other plays. Arguably there are inevitable conflicts between the demands of the larger genre (tragedy, for instance) and the 'life' that a character comes to represent, which may push generic conventions. In this context, the development of hypocrisy from a literary and cultural convention to a prevalent commercial product on the London stage is evidence of the anxiety that surrounds devotional life and practices in England. In the hands of early modern dramatists a new character type emerges whose complexity and dynamism delivers as entertainment and as food for thought. The important thing to note here is the clear connection between drama and the prevailing social reality: in this more diverse religious and social environment the hypocrite does operate at deeper levels of cultural power than simply as a character in a drama.

Works Cited

Anonymous. 1906. *Anonymous Plays: 3rd Series, Comprising Jack Juggle, King Darius, Gammer Gurton's Needle, New Custom, Trial of Treasure, Note-Book and Word List*. London: Early English Drama Society.

Beauregard, David. 2001. "Shakespeare on Monastic Life. Nuns and Friars in *Measure for Measure*". *Religion and the Arts* 5(3): 248–72.

Beier, A. Lee. 1985. *Masterless Men: The Vagrancy Problem in England, 1560–1640*. London: Methuen.

Bolton, Robert. 1611. *A Discourse about the State of True Happiness*. London: Imprinted by Felix Kyngston, for Edmund Weaver, and are to be sold at his shop, at the great North-gate of Pauls Church.

Brooke, Arthur. 1908. *Romeus and Juliet. Being the Original of Shakespeare's 'Romeo and Juliet'*, newly edited by J. J. Munro. New York: Duffield and Company; London: Chatto & Windus.

Bryn Roberts, S. 2016. "'Milke and Honey': Puritan Happiness in the Writings of Robert Bolton, John Norden and Francis Rous". In *Puritanism and Emotion in the Early Modern World*, edited by Alec Ryrie and Tom Schwanda. 94–120. Basingstoke, Hampshire: Palgrave Macmillan.

Chaucer, Geoffrey. 1960. *The Canterbury Tales*. Translated by Neville Coghill. London: Penguin Books.

Doelman, James. 2000. *King James I and the Religious Culture of England*. Cambridge: D. S. Brewer.

Fletcher, Alan J. Fall 1990. "The Topical Hypocrisy of Chaucer's Pardoner". *The Chaucer Review* 25(2): 110–26.

Foxe, John. 1973. *Two Latin Comedies by John Foxe the Martyrologist: Titus et Gesippus, Christus Triumphans*. Edited by John Hazel Smith. Ithaca, NY: Published in Association with the Renaissance Society of America by Cornell University Press.

Hall, Joseph. 1837. *The Works of Joseph Hall, with Some Account of His Life and Sufferings*. A new Edition, revised and corrected, Vol. VI. Oxford: D. A. Talboys.

Holland, Peter. 2001. *Shakespeare and Religion* in *Shakespeare Survey*, Vol. 54. Cambridge: Cambridge University Press.

Hwang, Su-kyung. Spring 2016. "From Priests' to Actors' Wardrobe: Controversial, Commercial, and Costumized Vestments". *Studies in Philology* 113(2): 282–305.

Religious Hypocrisy in Performance   71

Hyland, Peter. 2011. *Disguise on the Early Modern Stage*. Farnham: Ashgate.

Knutson, Harold C. Summer 1994. "Three Characters in Search of a Vice: The Hypocrite in Theophrastus, Joseph Hall and La Bruyère". *Dalhousie French Studies. Réflexions sur le genre moraliste au dix-septièmesiècle* 27: 51–63.

Kruger, Stephen. 1994. "Claiming the Pardoner: Toward a Gay Reading of Chaucer's Pardoner's Tale". *Exemplaria* 6: 115–39.

Luckyj, Christina. 2016. "New Directions: Boy Prince and Venetian Courtesan – Political Critique in The White Devil". In *The White Devil: A Critical Reader*, edited by Paul Frazer and Adam Hansen, 155–172. London: Bloomsbury Arden.

MacIntyre, Jean and Garrett P. J. Epp. 1997. "'Clothes Worth All the Rest': Costumes and Properties". In *A New History of Early English Drama*, edited by John D. Cox and David Scott Kastan, 269–85. New York: Columbia University Press.

Marlowe, Christopher. 2008. *Doctor Faustus*. Oxford: Oxford University Press.

McKeon Michael. 2005. *The Secret History of Domesticity: Public, Private, and the Division of Knowledge*. Baltimore, MD: Johns Hopkins University Press.

Proffitt, M. (ed.). 2016. *The Oxford English Dictionary Online*. Available online at www.oed.com (accessed 15 May 2016)

Rambuss, Richard. 1998. *Closet Devotions*. Durham, NC: Duke University Press.

Shakespeare, William. 2006. *Measure for Measure*. Edited by J. W. Lever. London: Arden Shakespeare.

———. 2009. *King Richard III*. Edited by James R. Siemon. London: Arden Shakespeare.

———. 2012. *Romeo and Juliet*. Edited by René Weis. London, New Delhi, New York, Sydney: Bloomsbury Arden Shakespeare.

Vickers, Brian. Summer 1979. "Shakespeare's Hypocrites". *Dedalus. Hypocrisy, Illusion, and Evasion* 108(3): 45–83.

Walsh, Brian. 2016. *Unsettled Toleration: Religious Difference on the Shakespearean Stage*. Oxford: Oxford University Press.

Webster, John. 2014. *Four Revenge Tragedies: The White Devil*. Introduced by Janet Clare and edited by Christina Luckji. London: Methuen.

Wikander, Matthew H. 2002. *Fangs of Malice: Hypocrisy Sincerity and Acting*. Iowa City: University Of Iowa Press.

Williamson, Elizabeth. 2009. *The Materiality of Religion in Early Modern English Drama*. Farnham and Burligton: Ashgate Publishing Company.

Wilson, Robert. 1592. *A Right Excellent and Famous Comedy, Called the Three Ladies of London*. Written By Robert Wilson. As It Hath Been Publiquely Plaied at London: Printed By Iohn Danter, Dwelling in Ducke Lane, Neere Smithfield.

Wycliffe Bible. 2001. *Wycliffe's New Testament Translated by John Wycliffe and John Purvey: A Modern-Spelling Edition of Their 14th century Middle English Translation, the First Complete English Vernacular Version, with an Introduction by Terence P. Noble*. Vancouver, BC: T.P. Noble.

4 Flattery, Hypocrisy, and Identity in *Thomas of Woodstock*

Rossana Sebellin

Often included in the Shakespeare apocrypha, *Thomas of Woodstock*, also known as *King Richard II part 1*, discusses flattering as a form of dissimulation and self-representation in a specific political context. The only surviving manuscript (contained in MS Egerton 1994) is incomplete, lacking the first and the last page; it is anonymous and has no title. Hence the different titles chosen by the editors (Corbin and Sedge 2002, 3). It deals with the first part of the reign of King Richard the Second, and with the episode of the murder of the King's uncle, Thomas of Woodstock, Duke of Gloucester, also called Plain Thomas in the play, for his plain clothes and straightforward speech. Still unattributed, (amongst the possible candidates to its paternity, Thomas Dekker and Samuel Rowley have been quoted), the tragedy's date of composition has been debated amongst scholars since the manuscript was found, varying from as early as the 1590s to 1610 and even later. According to the preferred date, then, the close verbal and thematic similarities with Shakespeare's *Richard II* have been alternatively attributed to reciprocal influences, and many authoritative scholars have considered *Thomas of Woodstock* as a text Shakespeare knew and somewhat employed as a source for his own play (see, for example, the introductions to Shakespeare's *Richard II* in the Arden Series by Peter Ure in 1956, and Charles R. Forker in 2002, or the introduction to the Cambridge edition by Andrew Gurr in 1984). In recent years, though, on the basis of linguistic analysis (lexicon, rhyme pattern, feminine, and masculine endings, expletives, and so on) MacDonald P. Jackson has argued that the text is certainly Jacobean, possibly dating around 1607–1610, therefore "*Woodstock* was written in the seventeenth century and must... echo Shakespeare's *Richard II*, rather than the other way around" (Jackson 2001, 17). In 2012, Donatella Montini also proposed a seventeenth-century attribution, based on similar considerations, in particular on the use of 'ye' in the text (Montini 2012). A further confirmation for a later date of composition is the presence of a masque as a turning point in the development of the plot: masques became fashionable after 1605, with Ben Jonson's and Inigo Jones' works, and were often used as metatheatrical devices after that date. The later dating of the play can contribute

Flattery, Hypocrisy, and Identity in Thomas of Woodstock   73

to the analysis of the different aspects of dissimulation and hypocrisy in the context of courtly life in Jacobean England, such as the ongoing debate around dissimulation, equivocation, and mental reservation, which began in Elizabethan times but took new strength after Father Garnet's episode during the Powder Plot and King James I's Oath of Allegiance of 1606.

The text presents us with an investigation on a complex and problematised idea of truthfulness and its absence from courtly life. There are several levels of hypocrisy displayed in the play, which take the form of flattery, duplicity, simulation and dissimulation of self, and lying. Equivocation is also mentioned and evoked, but not truly employed in the text in its precise historical sense, as it will be briefly discussed later. Flattery is the main sin throughout the whole play: it is a form of lying adopted by characters who utter false praise in order to obtain advantage or, indeed, advancement. In the debate on courtly life, this kind of lying is not necessarily seen as negative: even though the two most influential conduct books on courtly life at the time (*Il libro del Cortegiano* by Baldassarre Castiglione, 1528, and *Il Principe* by Niccolò Machiavelli, 1532) both strongly condemn flattery, a certain amount of dissimulation is not only admitted, but even encouraged. This is true to a certain extent of *Thomas of Woodstock*, whose characters' behaviour and speech towards the King can be seen as epitomising their understanding and adherence to notions of honesty and truthfulness in courtly life. In the context of this play, we can in fact identify three different groups of characters: (1) the King's favourites, young and ambitious, who represent the new fashion (both literally and metaphorically) establishing itself at Court; (2) the King's old uncles and their noble entourage, who represent the old set of values superseded – at least temporarily – by the new courtesans; and (3) the commoners, who are represented as morally and ideologically linked to the second group, that of the ancient nobility.

The Flatterers

Declinations of the word flatter (flatterer, flattering, flatter) occur twenty-three times in the text. Flattery appears as early as in the opening scene: the King's uncles have just discovered they had almost been poisoned, and immediately identify the King's minions as the true minds behind the scheme, thus directly establishing the Court as a natural environment for false display of loyalty and affection. The King's new favourites, in fact, are depicted in the text as a cohesive group of young people who surround the King, elevated by him to the rank of councillors and, later in the play, to more prominent offices. One of the Monarch's upstart favourites, Tresilian, is presented as a "sly machiavel" (1.1.63), thus reinforcing the idea of a King surrounded by people accustomed to lying.

74 *Rossana Sebellin*

The terms "flatterer" and "flattering" are usually coupled with defining words such as "minions" (four times), "sycophants" (twice), "hateful", "polling" (in the sense of greedy), "smooth-faced", "hound", "harmful", "cursed", and finally "pernicious", and these terms are employed to describe the group composed by Greene, Bagot, Bushy, Scroop, and Tresilian (1.1; 1.3; 2.2; 2.3; 3.3; 4.1; 4.2; 5.1; 5.3). This set of characters parade themselves in outward display of false loyalty towards the King. From the very beginning of their appearance on stage, they show a language which is suggestive of a sophisticated manipulation of facts, as when they discuss the discovery of their plot to kill Richard's uncles but put blame on the Carmelite friar, who revealed the poison scheme to the Lords, and who is now labelled as a traitor and a villain to be cursed (1.2.7–12).

It is also worth noticing that these characters are fully aware of their duplicity, and in act 4 explicitly mention their attitude as such: in order to push the hesitant King towards signing the act for the "farming of the land", Bushy tells Tresilian that "we have left that smooth-faced flattering Greene to follow him close, and he'll never leave till he has done it" (4.1.45–7). The recognition of their own flattering nature, which also recurs a few lines later, is reinforced when the King enters the scene: "*Bushy*. See, see, he comes, and that flattering hound, Greene, close at's elbow. / *Scroop*. Come, come, we must all flatter if we mean to live by it" (4.1.64–7).

With the exception of Tresilian, the favourites of the King are given no soliloquies for us to measure the distance between their inner self and their public *personae*: but when left to talk amongst themselves, they are ready to discuss their attitude towards Richard and his noble uncles. There is only one aside given to the flatterers, and this goes again in the direction of the flatterers manipulating their King and directing the topic of conversation: "*Bushy*. [*Aside to Greene*] 'Sfoot, urge our suit again, he will forget it else" (4.1.130–31). The guilt and the intent of the flatterers are therefore immediately clear to the audience: they do not lie in order to survive in a hostile environment, nor to protect themselves when facing a cruel tyrant. They lie solely for material gain and social advancement: "Had they [Richard's uncles] been dead, we'd ruled the realm and him [Richard]" (1.2.19). Later, when they tell Tresilian that he is to be Lord Chief Justice, they appear to have directed the King into such a (poor and tragic) choice:

Cheer thee, Tresilian, / Here's better news for thee: we have so wrought / With kingly Richard that by his consent / You are already mounted on your footcloth / Your scarlet or your purple, which you please, / And shortly are to underprop the name... / Of Lord Chief Justice of England.

(1.2.23–8)

Flattery, Hypocrisy, and Identity in Thomas of Woodstock   75

The King, on the other hand, is portrayed as a weak ruler, victim of a pack of unscrupulous social climbers, a Monarch who fails to recognise them for what they are and who is unable to refuse them anything. The "farming of the land" is clearly perceived as immoral by the King, who cannot bring himself to oppose the schemes of his favourites. Richard is not the prudent prince described by Machiavelli in chapter 23 of *Il Principe*, where the author details with how to avoid flatterers and their dangers. According to Machiavelli, the prince should be surrounded only by wise men, but should grant them freedom of speech only when he wants to know more about specific, ambiguous subjects. King Richard is here depicted (as in Shakespeare's play) as preferring the company of sycophants, who lead and rule him. Richard is a king who is unable to lead his courtiers both on a personal level and as a group.

Tresilian, described by Cheney as the "sly machiavel", is the only character to pronounce soliloquies, which reveals the distance between public respectable self and inner corruption, as in the following example: as soon as he is appointed Lord Chief Justice, he resolves to "fashion" the law according to his patrons, the King's nearest friends, and assures them he will act in deference to their wishes: "It shall be law what I shall say is law, / And what's most suitable to all your pleasures" (1.2.47–8). But when left alone on stage he shows his true nature, which is of course to pursue his own good:

> But yet until mine office be put on
> By kingly Richard, *I'll conceal myself,*
> Framing such subtle laws that *Janus-like*
> May with *double face* salute them both.
> I'll search my brain and *turn the leaves* of law:
> Wit makes us great, greatness keeps fools in awe.
>
> (1.2.63–8; my emphasis)

The law is thus pictured as easily bent to one's wishes, rather than as the dam which shields people from abuse of power (Schott Syme 2012). The character of Tresilian represents the new man, the upstart of humble origins, who is driven by ambition and who reaches a high place in the newly mobile society of early modern England. His cunning and social ability enable him to fit perfectly in the new Court, and place him in direct contact with the King. It is in the court that he becomes the mind behind the many schemes that will be deployed: he is the inventor of the blank charters that enrage the commoners to the point of mutiny, and which are a masterpiece of deceit (*"Tresilian.* See here, my lord, only with parchment, innocent sheepskin. Yet see here's no fraud, no clause, no deceit in the writing. / *All.* Why, there's nothing writ! / *Tresilian.* There's the trick on't." 3.1.11–3). And he is the one who suggests the stratagem of the masque through which Thomas of Woodstock will

76 *Rossana Sebellin*

be apprehended from his residence. He is also the one who thinks of disguise as an indirect course of action against the King's uncles: "[i]t must be done with greater policy / For fear the people rise in mutiny" (2.1.44–5).

The manipulative intent of the flatterers is of course carefully hidden from the King, towards whom they show a mixture of deference (as due to his role) and youthful camaraderie. By playing a role in front of the King, they impersonate hypocrisy, thus alluding to the close connection, invoked by Prynne, between hypocrisy and playing as 'one and the same in substance' "by breaking down the potential correspondence between insides and outsides, the theatrical performer refuses all possibility for a transparent and readable self" (Targoff 1997, 51).

Like a mimetic animal merging with its background, the flatterers are a paradigm of liquid, unstable identity, which changes according to the environment. As Herzig and Eliav-Feldon remind us, "early modern obsession with false identities emerged from repeated confirmations that an ever growing number of individuals were not who they claimed to be" (2015, 1). The King has no means to discover the flatterers' true nature, which is only apparent from an external vantage point, by people outside the circle of courtesans surrounding the King like a cocoon: his uncles, who are aware of the growing discontent caused by the new Court, and the audience who is admitted to the revealing soliloquies or dialogues. It is precisely the dialogic relation between nature and culture which constitutes the basis for the early modern debate on dissimulation in the Court: to what extent is dissimulation or simulation admissible, and even advisable, in a space where candid characters barely survive? The many early modern publications on the subject try to find a balance between a theoretically preferable, but practically unattainable, complete truthfulness and an acceptable level of self-preserving ability to recognise when and how truth not only should, but can be told. (Castiglione's *Il libro del Cortegiano*, translated by Thomas Hoby in 1561 as *The Book of the Courtier*; Stefano Guazzo's *La civil conversatione*, 1574, book 1 to 3 translated by George Pettie as *Civile Conversation* in 1581, and book 4 by Bartholomew Young in 1586. See Richards 2003.) An effective example of this dichotomy is in 1.3.3, when the new courtesans clash with the old ones at the King's wedding. After having exchanged nice pleasantries and compliments in the manner of perfect courtesans, an argument arises between Thomas of Woodstock and the King and his minions, starting off around the topic of clothes, and quickly escalating in the level of verbal conflict. To honour the King's wedding, Woodstock has left his customary plain way of dressing in favour of a courtlier attire. The King praises him, mocking his usual humble

Flattery, Hypocrisy, and Identity in Thomas of Woodstock   77

"hose", and receives in exchange a typical criticism of courtly squandering and dissipation:

> A hundred oaks upon these shoulders hang
> To make me brave upon your wedding day,
> And more than that, to make my horse more tire,
> Ten acres of good land are stitched up here.

(1.3.95–9)

The term "plain" here is doubly applied to clothes and words, and the character of Woodstock – though in elegant dress – reverts to his usual direct and unsophisticated address mode, accusing the King of giving too much power to his favourites. The Lord Protector (a title theatrically effective, but historically inaccurate) cannot restrain himself in front of the clearly unhappy choices of the King, and – unable to recur to policy and political concealment – "talks no riddles. Plain Thomas / Will speak plainly" (1.3.114–5). He calls the flatterers "cankers" and later the Lords add "caterpillars" (1.3.155–7): a term that is strongly reminiscent of Shakespeare's *Richard II*. The strong contrast between Woodstock and the flatterers is reinforced by the open and direct way in which the King's uncle speaks as opposed to Greene and Bagot's more ambiguous sentences (the only ones uttered in this scene): the latter's lines are in fact provocative, yet pronounced in jest, and they are perceived as either apparently defending the King's honour (1.3.189–93), or as veiled threat to the Lords (1.3.205–7). The Lord Protector here is depicted as lacking the qualities of restraint or self-command, which he had previously tried to instil in his brothers ("*York. [to Lancaster]* 'Sfoot, he forewarned us and will break out himself", 1.3.113–4): both restraint and self-command are necessary to survive at Court, but Woodstock is incapable of policy. On the contrary, the ability to recognise when and if to speak the truth is a constant preoccupation of the courtesans, who are perfectly able to command the art of dissimulation.

It is certainly not coincidental that the first attempt at killing the King's uncles that the favourites deploy is through the use of poison, an obvious choice to be preferred to an open battle. Poison (so frequent in Jacobean authors, from Webster to Middleton) can be considered here as the metaphorical representation of flattery: something outwardly appearing good and palatable, but which is essentially venomous and lethal. Poison is therefore the perfect means for flatterers to kill, as it stands for lying and duplicity. And the noxious atmosphere at Court brought about by the new courtesans is certainly strongly felt by the old ones, who express the discomfort they felt at Court as soon as they are removed from it: "I lived with care at court, I now am free" (3.2.6) and "I ne'er slept soundly when I was amongst them" (3.2.8).

78 *Rossana Sebellin*

The favourites of the King all profess their love for the Monarch, who in turn appears sincerely affectionate to them all. But the Court, represented by both Richard and the flatterers, is not a place for true loyalty and is instead portrayed as a place of vanity and frivolous discourse, where people are preoccupied with external appearance rather than with true nobility of mind and behaviour. The King himself, in fact, is more concerned with fashion and a display of lavishness rather than with exerting power: "Your youths are fitting to our tender years / And such shall beautify our princely throne" (2.1.4–5).

In Act 2 the King is seen trying to find a way to limit the power of his uncles (all bearing leading roles in the care of the realm), and especially to be rid of the Lord Protector, who can effectively constrain the King and rule him. This decision is prompted by Greene, Bushy, Bagot, and Scroop, who, in their lust for power and wealth, calumniate the King's uncles and convince Richard to act against them. Endowed with political cunning, the caterpillars bend history to their purpose and devise a stratagem to lead the King into believing he is already of age and his uncles are deliberately concealing this fact from him, thus depriving him of his rights (the text mentions the *English Chronicles* in 2.1.55): historical truth is questioned and appears unstable, when the flattering courtiers are concerned. The King readily believes the flatterers and wishes to have his uncles accused of treason, arrested and, following Greene's suggestion, executed. It is evident here that the two groups of characters, the noble lords and the king's false friends, have opposing ideas of power: for Woodstock his role as Lord Protector is a burden, because power is seen as service and, though furious at the attitude of the King, he is clearly relieved to be discharged from his role ("The right I hold, even with my heart I render / And wish your grace had claimed it long ago. / Thou'dst rid mine age of mickle care and woe, /... A heavy burden hast thou ta'en from me", 2.2.96–8 and 104); for the flatterers, power is a privilege to be exploited to the uttermost level.

Hypocrisy, which is an attribute of the flatterers as such, is then infected into the King, who is convinced by them to use nice words in the face of his uncles, while he prepares his trap to divest Thomas of Woodstock of his role as Lord Protector: "Give them fair words, and smooth awhile: / The toils are pitched, and you may catch them quickly" (2.2.30–1). The "toil" is in the traditional form of the parable according to which a poor son, after his father's death, is robbed of his meagre revenue amounting to only "three crowns" by a rich man, who is in fact the guardian of the young man. Here the use of the parable is distorted, because the king represents himself in the figure of the robbed young man, and instead of promoting the advancement of truth, as parables normally do, the small narrative works as a trick to fool the noble and honest uncles, who in their straightforwardness praise the King for his interest in such a legal case, before they realise the real aim of the story.

Flattery, Hypocrisy, and Identity in Thomas of Woodstock   79

The display of falseness and the double standards of behaviour between public display of bounty, of virtue, and the actual political scheming and imposture of the Court stand as strongly critical of the true nature of power as opposed to its public appearance. As soon as the King ascends the throne and officially discharges the Lord Protector, the Parliament is dismissed and the King's uncles leave in outrage as the new Monarch has divested them of their political roles, now bestowed on his minions. As soon as the wise counsellors have left, the new elite busy themselves in fashioning new laws which are completely centred on exterior appearances: "It shall be henceforth counted high treason for any fellow with a grey beard to come within forty foot of the court gates" (2.2.174–6) or, "We'll not have a beard amongst us; we'll shave the country and the city too, shall we not, Richard?" (2.2.179–80). This entails a disparagement of old age and an emphasis on male beauty, but there is also a pun on the polysemy of the term "shave", as they are clearly planning to exploit the citizens with harsher taxes, stripping them of their money or possessions (this figurative sense is attested as early as 1399 according to *OED*).

Clothes too are amongst the first preoccupations of the new Court, and the long description of the extravagant new fashion is given prominence in the text, both in the words of the characters themselves (2.2.206 and 210) and in the descriptions of their occupations: "they sit in council to devise... wild and antic habits / Such as this kingdom never yet beheld.... Their plumed tops fly waving in the air / A cubit high above their wanton heads" (2.3.87–95). Clothes appear then as outward revelation of the characters' values: in the eyes of the courtesans, their roles and identity are displayed and confirmed in their outward appearance as if in a performance (see MacIntyre and Garrett 1997), while Woodstock represents the opposite stance, someone whose true nobility is interiorised and does not need external validation. Woodstock can dress like a humble man (and be mistaken for one) because his integrity and deepset belonging to the ancient nobility cannot be shaken. The flatterers need to be seen and admired as the courtiers they have become ("If our fashion be not published, what glory's in the wearing?" 3.1.79–80), and that is the reason why they decide to parade through London in order "to be gazed at" (3.1.81). The ostentation of wealth and extravagance is in fact a poor political choice and reinforces the idea of power as empty theatricality and lack of husbandry in the state. The ten thousand men fed at Richard's court are the same mentioned by Shakespeare in his *Richard II*, but here the description of the waste is even heightened ("I daily spend / Thirty fat oxen and three hundred sheep, / With fish and fowl in numbers numberless", 3.1.87–8).

The full display of hypocritical conduct and corruption of power at Court (the latter as a consequence of the first) reaches its maximum expression in act 4 scene 1, where the audience is faced with two horrifying

80 *Rossana Sebellin*

patterns of behaviour: the manipulative use of words and cunning which lead the king to agree with the flatterers (a subversion of the natural order of things), and the subsequent division of the kingdom, the obvious outcome of the careful and effective schemes orchestrated by the villains as a group.

At the beginning of act 4, Tresilian is counting the sum of money of the new tax revenues. Tresilian is here depicted as a miser-like figure, obsessed by greed. From the total amount he receives, he keeps four thousand pounds for himself and gives three thousand to the King, surpassing even the boldest of dishonest tax collectors: "Let fools make conscience how they get their coin, / I'll please the King and keep me in his grace, / For prince's favours purchase land apace" (4.1.13–5). The truth is hidden, and all is theatre and acting, in the pejorative sense of the word. Later on, Tresilian assures Bushy that he has "set a trick afoot for ye, and ye follow it hard and get the king to sign it, you'll be all kings by it" (4.1.38–40): it is the infamous farming of the kingdom also highly censured in Shakespeare's *Richard II*. When the moment comes for Richard to sign away his kingdom to his courtiers, he appears aware of the future reprimands and disapproval his actions will be subject to, but again the flatterers' words are powerful enough to shift the balance in their favour once again: "*Greene.* 'Sfoot, what need you care what the world talks? You still retain the name of king, and if any disturb ye, we four comes presently... to assist you" (4.1.151–54). Again, appearance is what counts, not the essence. Greene also threatens Richard to "turn traitor" and join the King's uncles, to which the Monarch responds: "they did well to choose you for their orator that has King Richard's love and heart in keeping" (4.1.161–3). The Court is shown as so debased that, after the King has signed, Greene addresses him in a familiar and extremely informal way: "Thou never didst a better deed in thy life, sweet bully. Thou mayst now live at ease, we'll toil for thee and send thy money in tumbling" (4.1.218–20).

The division of the kingdom (4.1.221–60) is strongly reminiscent of the similar scene in Shakespeare's *Lear*, also from the staging point of view and props employed. The king has a map brought in on stage and proceeds in allotting portions of the land to his friends, including the detail of the last and better part kept for his favourite: "I keep thee last to make thy part the greatest. See here, sweet Greene... thou here shalt lie i'th' middle of my land" (4.1.246–9). The visual power of this scene, together with the effective display of a perverted Court where low level individuals are elevated to the highest ranks (displacing their betters) reinforces once more the play's strong criticism of power.

The flatterers' duplicity in their professed love for King Richard is also evident in the event of the Queen's death and the imprisonment of Plain Thomas. Act 4 ends with the sudden death of Queen Anne (O'Beame) and with Woodstock kept prisoner at Calais, unaware he is awaiting to

Flattery, Hypocrisy, and Identity in Thomas of Woodstock   81

be murdered at the King's orders. The departing of such a positive female figure, modest, virtuous, and charitable, makes a clear parallel with the imprisonment of Plain Thomas: the two unstained characters disappear almost at the same time. The effect on the King is deeply felt, and he repents his decision to kill his uncle and tries to stop the assassination, but the flatterers disregard the King's wishes and appear to be more preoccupied with the sudden change in the King's stance, which may harm their position of privilege, than with his heart-felt distress. When the King enters the scene, they all rush in to comfort him with perfunctory expressions of condolences: "My dearest friend, forsake these sad laments. / No sorrows can suffice to make her live" (4.3.141–2). And later on: "Let not one loss so many comforts drown" (4.3.155), and also: "Dear liege, all tears for her are vain oblations. / Her quiet soul rests in celestial peace; / With joy of that let all your sorrows cease" (4.3.169–71). Their professed affection for the King is unsubstantial and they are totally unable to take part in the king's suffering.

Thomas of Woodstock and the King's Uncles

As a perfect contrast to the new flattering courtesans, the main character, Thomas of Woodstock, is presented as "good", "plain", "simple", and "unsophisticated" (1.1.98, 100, 103), all terms semantically and metaphorically connected with the idea of unadulterated sincerity. The use of "plain" for both his appearance and his inner self is the opposing metaphor to the use of disguise and elaborate dressing adopted by morally deplorable flatterers to convey a moral negative stance. Woodstock's decision not to conform to the norms dictated by sumptuary laws or courtly conduct book in his style of clothing is perceived as a political stance by the other characters, who feel the need to comment on this behaviour amongst each other, and so to explain it to the audience ("Plain Thomas, for by th'rood so all men call him / for his plain dealing and his simple clothing", 1.1.99–100). Simplicity and plainness of attire and of speech are one and the same in the character of Woodstock, who chooses not to comply with the established modes of the fashionable courtier ("Scoff ye my plainness, I'll talk no riddles. Plain Thomas / Will speak plainly" 1.3.115–16). The unvarying attitude of this character is somewhat made problematic in the words of another character, Cheney, who describes him as "homely and plain, both free from pride and envy, / And therein will admit distrust to none" (1.1.107–8): the weakness of this Lord is in his own inability to use any form of disguise and in his unsuspecting attitude which make him unable to cope with the shifting values and manners of the Court. The Duke's brothers, Lancaster and York, and the Earls of Arundel and Surrey appear as equally noble, but possibly less blind. When Woodstock enters the scene immediately after the plot has been revealed, he warns them to be careful as "[m]ischief

82   *Rossana Sebellin*

hath often double practices; / Treachery wants not his second strata-gem" (1.1.115–16), but later quenches their rage by assuring them that the King "loves you all;... the princely gentleman is innocent / Of this black deed, and base conspiracy" (1.1.134–6), and suggests that they proceed gradually in their attempt to set apart the King from his flat-tering minions. After his long and subtle speech, the Lords agree to attend amicably the King's nuptials the following day, but Lancaster's line shifts the balance of Woodstock's position when he affirms that "[t]o hide our hate is soundest policy" (1.1.193), thus establishing their behaviour as stemming from political calculation rather than affection for the young King, as in Woodstock's case. The Duke of Gloucester is portrayed in the text as a figure never stained or touched by the other characters' thirst for power, nor by their hypocrisy. He remains truthful to the point of naiveté and at times appears as a salvific figure: "I will re-move those hinderers of his [the King's] health, / Though't cost my head" (1.1.189–90). This religious allusion is made more explicit in the parallel of Woodstock to a Christ-like figure: "How I have nightly waked for England's good, / And yet to right her wrongs would spend my blood. / Send thy sad doom, King Richard, take my life: / I wish my death might ease my country's grief" (5.1.124–7).

The main character in the play certainly stands for old values in contrast with new fashions and manners, but is also occasionally given a less obvious role. In the above-mentioned scene of the wedding, the main characters are all on stage and the conflict between the oppos-ing parties can be visualised and enacted: after having welcomed the new Queen with highly rhetorical language, Woodstock addresses her and – in the name of truth – describes her newly wed husband as "young and wanton", "wild headed, "unsettled", "hare-brain", and a "wag" (1.3.24–8). Even though these adjectives are softened by as many praises ("kingly gentleman", "princely bred", "royal'st bloods in Europe", "a king loving and kind"), the King accuses Woodstock of having given him a "double praise" (1.3.33), thus adding falseness and duplicity to the words of the character who is less likely to display any.

The treatment of this character is made less obvious in act 3, when Woodstock is at Plashy House and the King sends one of his minions to summon Plain Thomas to Court. The scene is definitely comic, though extremely meaningful in the dialectics between outward appearance and inner essence. The "spruce", "very fantastically" attired courtier (3.2.127, 131) meets Woodstock at the gate of Plashy House and fails to recognise him as the Lord of the castle because of his plain dressing, treating him as a groom and offering him a tester (sixpence) to walk his horse. The courtier is obviously a *nouveau riche*, who has never seen nor met the King's uncle. His attire clearly identifies him as a nobleman but this outward look does not correspond to any inner quality, nor to ancient nobility. On the other hand, Woodstock's lack of the customary

Flattery, Hypocrisy, and Identity in Thomas of Woodstock   83

respect for the sumptuary laws shows his disregard for appearance in favour of an interest for more substantial matters. Even a small detail is evidence of his true nobility and liberality as opposed to the squandering of the Court: he does not feel diminished by the offer of a small sum of money to perform a menial task, but then doubles the sum to his own servant to do the same (3.2.186–97).

The scene of the kidnapping of Plain Thomas via the stratagem conceived by Tresilian and readily agreed upon by the King and his followers is also meaningful in terms of the characterisation of Woodstock, and in the treatment of the theme of dissimulation. From *The Spanish Tragedy* in 1588, to *Hamlet,* to *The Revenger's Tragedy* in 1606 up to *Women Beware Women* in 1621, the play within-the-play or the masque is a device to punish the guilty and reveal the truth: this is why this metatheatrical solution has been seen as validation of theatricality, in that it helps to resolve the plot. In this case, instead, we have a complete reversal of the stratagem of the play within-the-play: the villains contrive a masque in order to approach the Duke of Gloucester in his home. In a multiplication of disguises, members of the Court pose as a group of country gentlemen who have come to give homage to Woodstock in such dire times. In a sort of frenzy of dissimulation, where reality is completely blurred, the audience is faced with: the actors who play the King and the nobles who play the role of the country squires, who in their turn pose as Cynthia and the Hunters. Concealment of the truth is so deeply embedded in the mindset of the new courtesans, that even after Woodstock has been apprehended and asks if the King is present because he has recognised his voice, they deny and conceal the truth, even if there is no practical reason to do it any more. The subtle cruelty of the formulation on the masque adds to the duplicity enacted: Cynthia's lines, "there lies / A cruel tuskèd boar, whose terror flies / Through this large kingdom" (4.2.107–9), refer to the emblem of the Duke of Gloucester, who fails to recognise the implicit threat and – as he had already done when presented with his wife's ominous dream (the Duchess of Gloucester is "troubled with sad dreams" (4.2.6) in which she saw her husband being attacked by a lion and a pack of wolves) – again misinterprets reality: "ye come like knights to hunt the boar indeed; / And heaven he knows we had need of helping hands, / So many wild boars roots and spoils our lands / That England almost is destroyed by them", 4.2.138–41. The old, noble, and trusting Woodstock interprets the verses in the opposite sense – *omnia munda mundis* – and is thus betrayed by the young courtiers and King.

Even in his final moments Plain Thomas is a victim of dissimulation, as his murder is made to appear as a natural death: "smooth down his hair and beard; close his eyes and set his neck right. Why so, all fine and cleanly. Who can say that this man was murdered now?" (5.1.243–5).

84 *Rossana Sebellin*

The Commoners

Political themes are also embedded in the comic scene in 3.3, which is entirely focused on the lower classes (see Tipton 1998). The effect of the growing power of the courtesans and diminished authority of the King is the immediate misery of common people, who suffer from the oppression and heavy taxation imposed upon them by the new rulers. Civil unrest grows amongst the citizens, and Nimble is sent to spy on them in order to find traitors. In this context, law is still perceived as a guarantor of commoners' rights against the abuse of power but when people try to appeal to the law they are immediately rebuked by Nimble or by Tresilian, as in 4.3. When two prisoners, the Shrieve of Kent and the Shrieve of the North, protest against unfair taxation and unlawful imprisonment, Tresilian opposes their claim with his idea of royal authority: "Is not the subject's wealth at the King's will?... Will you set limits to the King's high pleasures?" (4.3.30 and 40). For the new courtier, power means privilege and liberty to commit abuse. In such circumstances, counterfeiting the words becomes, even for commoners, a matter of survival, as they have to hide their libels against the King and his new favourites so that they sound like innocent songs. The Schoolmaster is the only character who openly says that he "covered [these verses] rarely... for this last line helps all, wherein with a kind of equivocation I say 'God bless my Lord Tresilian'" (3.3.167–8, 192–3). The figure of speech the Schoolmaster employs is irony rather then equivocation, but the use of the term is significant in this context because it clearly supports the hypothesis for a Jacobean dating: as known, the word became more prominent after the Gunpowder Plot of 1605 and the already mentioned Oath of Allegiance of 1606: the Jesuit Father Garnet, who employed it, ended up condemned to death in spite of it.

Self-defence against an oppressive power, therefore, is evoked in the Schoolmaster's words, as "[e]quivocation was the doctrine designed to prevent this undesirable outcome [torture and execution]. The aim was for the speaker to be able to preserve their status as a truth-teller before God, while deliberately misleading the authorities, keeping the torturers of this world from your door" (Berensmeyer and Hadfield 2015, 134). The lyrics the Schoolmaster quotes from the ballad he himself has composed as a libel against the Lord Chief Justice appear nonetheless more as an ironic use of language, as already stated, rather than equivocation. But it appears meaningful that the character considers his song a potential threat to power and considers equivocation the suitable defence against an accusation of treason.

The commoners are described by the words of the nobles (Woodstock and his brothers) as oppressed, heavily taxed and offended by the Court, and in those of the flatterers as an unidentified mass to be exploited. The old lords are the only ones to show preoccupation for the destiny of the

Flattery, Hypocrisy, and Identity in Thomas of Woodstock   85

people under rapacious rulers, and they protest in front of the King more vigorously than the citizens themselves (1.3.123–9, 138–40, 232–46; see also 3.2.82–9). The people's protest, on the other hand, is aimed at the flatterers and personally at Tresilian and never to the King, as when a Butcher, a Farmer, and a grazier blandly remonstrate about their treatment and about the blank charters. The connection between the commoners and the old nobility is also established when the people lament the banishment of the old lords (3.3.69–73 and 76–9). When all these characters are arrested for "whispering", their reaction is a harmless exclamation of distress "Now out alas, we shall all to hanging, sure!" (3.3.155). The Schoolmaster and Serving man are slightly less meek and more skilful, when they face accusation, and here a trace of equivocation is possibly discernible:

> *Schoolmaster.* Treason? *Patientia*, good sir. We spoke not a word. / *Ignorance.* Be not so pestiferous. Mine ears have heard your examination, wherein you uttered most shameful treason, for you said, 'God bless my Lord Tresilian'. / *Schoolmaster.* I hope there's no treason in that, sir,
>
> (3.3.213–18)

and later "Well, sir, if we be, we'll speak more ere we be hanged in spite of ye" (3.3.222–3).

Conclusion

As Corbin and Sedge state in their Introduction to the Revels Plays edition,

> the play as a whole allows its audience to look beneath the façade of 'establishment' ceremony and public relations iconography to examine the naked ambition and jockeying of power and influence which characterize the *realpolitik* [sic] and falsehood of stagecraft.
>
> (Corbin and Sedge 2002, 36–7)

The play investigates the constant dissimulation of one's real intentions and enacts a multilayered display of hypocrisy and questionable identities: false words and legal dubious technicalities with which the character of Tresilian often twists the truth are an example of hypocritical behaviour, meant to fool people, Lords and commoners alike. Devious and duplicitous language goes together with the display of extravagance in the new dress code devised by the King and his Council, who are focused on outward appearance as validation of their perceived identities, and who despise traditional values (3.3.220–5). This extravagance is in strong contrast with Thomas of Woodstock's style, his plainness in

86 *Rossana Sebellin*

clothes and in speech, his direct and unceremonious style; his expressions of unpalatable truths in front of the King cost him his favours. If the flatterers' language is double, the Lord Protector's language is unguarded in its directness, and, because of this, is shown to be inadequate to the way politics works in this new ethical surrounding. Both attitudes are problematised in the text, testifying to the shift of values in early modern society and to the (im)possibility of an achievable compromise between a "true heart" and the fear "of no wrong", as shown in one of the last significant speeches of the tragedy:

> Alack, good man,
> It was an easy task to work on him,
> His plainness was too open to their view:
> He feared no wrong because his heart was true.
>
> (5.3.5–8)

Works Cited

Anonymous. 2002. *Thomas of Woodstock or Richard the Second, Part One.* Manchester: Manchester University Press (The Revels Plays).

Berensmeyer, Ingo, and Andrew Hadfield. 2015. "Mendacity in Early Modern Literature and Culture: An Introduction". *European Journal of English Studies* 19(2): 131–47.

Corbin, Peter, and Douglas Sedge. 2002. Introduction to *Thomas of Woodstock or Richard the Second, Part One*, by Anonymous, 1–46. Manchester: Manchester University Press (The Revels Plays).

Herzig, Tamar, and Miriam Eliav-Feldon. 2015. Introduction to *Dissimulation and Deceit in Early Modern Europe*, 1–8. New York: Palgrave.

Jackson, MacDonald P. 2001. "Shakespeare's *Richard II* and the Anonymous *Thomas of Woodstock*". *Medieval & Renaissance Drama in England* 14: 17–65.

MacIntyre, Jean, and Garrett P. J. Epp. (1997). "'Clothes Worth All the Rest': Costumes and Properties". In *A New History of Early English Drama*, edited by John D. Cox and David Scott Kastan, 269–85. New York: Columbia University Press.

Montini, Donatella. 2012. "Grammatica, stile e politica: il pronome 'ye' in *Thomas of Woodstock*". *Memoria di Shakespeare* 8: 335–50.

Richards, Jennifer. 2003. Introduction to *Rhetoric and Courtliness in Early Modern Literature*, 1–19. Cambridge: Cambridge University Press.

Schott Syme, Holger. 2012. "(Mis)representing Justice on the Early Modern Stage". *Studies in Philology* 109(1): 63–85.

Targoff, Ramie. 1997. "The Performance of Prayer: Sincerity and Theatricality in Early Modern England". *Representations* 60: 49–69.

Tipton, Alzada J. 1998. "'The Meanest Man ... Shall be Permitted Freely to Accuse': The Commoners in 'Woodstock'." *Comparative Drama* 32(1): 117–45.

5 "Come buy Lawn Sleeves"
Linen and Material Hypocrisy in Milton's Antiprelatical Tracts

Naya Tsentourou

In 1641 the anti-episcopal satire, *Lambeth Faire: wherein you have all the Bishops Trinkets set to Sale*, was published anonymously displaying on its frontispiece the woodcut of a colossal bishop in extravagant dress collapsing on his chair. The pamphlet, reprinted in 1642 under the name of its author, the Leveller Richard Overton, is representative of publications that flourished after the collapse of press censorship in July 1641; these were often directed against Archbishop of Canterbury, William Laud, his Arminian liturgical practices, and his alleged involvement in the dissolution of the Parliament by Charles I, a few days before exasperated Londoners attacked Lambeth Palace, the episode which inspired the satire (Zwicker 2002, 189). The word "trinket" in the title captures the deceitful nature characteristic of trade and idolatry, as both practices are firmly rooted in the paradoxical combination of faith – in the word of the Church and of the merchant – and profit, or else in the interdependence between material and immaterial negotiations. Locating exchanges of faith for profit in a "fair" selling "trinkets", post-Reformation authors satirised the materialistic spirit of the established church in England by associating it with Catholic practices. As David Kaula writes with reference to the famous Shakespearean peddler, Autolycus, "again and again such words as 'trumpery' and 'trinkets' appear in the Protestant diatribes against what were considered the mercenary and idolatrous practices of selling indulgences, crucifixes, rosaries, medals, candles and other devotional objects" (Kaula 1976, 289; on trinkets see Kearney 2000). According to Kirste Milne, "the fair was a well-worn metaphor, fit for a sententious sermon or a swipe at Catholicism", but in the 1640s "re-animated to attack the hierarchy of the Laudian church" (Milne 2015, 53). In the case of *Lambeth Faire*, the trinkets for sale dominating the frontispiece are the large, lavish ecclesiastical garments worn by the archbishop who has sunk with grief into his ostentatious popish seat ("S. Peters Chaire") lamenting the assault on his estate.

The bishop's garments are luxuriously exaggerated in size and style, as they appear to be completely swamping a body whose actual corporeal shape is lost under the sumptuous folds of the dress. In the spirit of many anti-episcopalian tracts, satires, and dramatic dialogues, Overton's verse

88 Naya Tsentourou

criticises the materiality of devotion promoted by Laud's church government in the 1630s, denouncing its fixation with garments, crosses, cro-
siers, and other ceremonial paraphernalia by paralleling episcopacy to a
mercantile culture keen on maximising profits. The bishops are depicted
in the narrative as pedlars trading in Lambeth, loudly, and desperately,
asserting the glamorous quality of their products and the religious authority that comes with wearing them:

> Come buy *lawn sleeves*. I have no money took,
> Here, try them on, you'l like a *Bishop* looke.
> ...
>
> Come hither friend, and buy this silken Gowne,
> I'm sure you cannot match't in *Lambeth* Towne:
> In this same Gown, did *Canterburies Grace,*
> At *High-Commission* shew his gracelesse face;
> Many a storme, and shower it will abide,
> Yea, and a world of knavery 't will hide.
>
> (Anon. 1641a, sig.A3r)

Ecclesiastical dress, in the shape of the "lawn sleeves" and the "silken
Gowne", captures the imagination of the satirist and emerges as an appropriate emblem for the hypocrisy of the church, covering the bishops'
moral degeneration with a lavish exterior. Denouncing the commodification of religion, the pamphlet derides the fact that a spiritual human
activity (worshipping) has been compromised by Laud and his prelates
and it has been replaced by a predominantly material one (trading).

In this chapter I seek to examine how debates of hypocrisy in antiprelatical writing are a combination of the metaphorical and the literal, of
texts and textiles. Drawing on John Milton's early prose and examples in
which he concentrates on the materiality of clerical garments, and in particular their linen fabric, the chapter explores linen as part of Milton's efforts to fragment and destabilise the uniformity that Laud's ecclesiastical
regime strived for. In ridiculing the vestments Milton exposes them as
trinkets, as disjointed commodities whose uniformity he resists by tear-
ing the garments apart and examining them not as a meaningful whole
but as components to be traded. Critics have long established Milton's
rhetorical strategy in these tracts as one of excess, fraught with images
of disease and fleshly appetites, physical violence, and vitriolic humour,
all part of his attempt to confine rationality and historical reality in
memorable images that form what Lana Cable terms "carnal rhetoric"
(Cable 1995, 2). When it comes to discussing the references to church
vestments, however, scholarship often privileges a reading of what the
garments stand for, rather than what they actually are and what they
are made of. Milton's references to clothing are viewed as predominantly
concerned with the bishops' manipulative authority over their subjects

"Come buy Lawn Sleeves" 89

and less concerned with clothes as physical items. Marcus K. Harmes, for instance, writes that "the often satirical comments on episcopal vestments by Prynne, Milton and others were less concerned with the vestments as physical items and more with how they revealed prelatical deceit and manipulation of power" (Harmes 2013, 103). Similarly, Roze Hentschell has argued that "when Milton talks about clothing in these pamphlets he spends little time on the particulars of clerical vestments, opting instead to emphasise the way in which any such vestments – physical, rhetorical, or liturgical – make plain the mental manipulations pursued by England's prelacy" (Hentschell 2008, 115).

These approaches are indicative of a wider trend in Milton studies: clothing is either interpreted in largely metaphorical terms or is absent. Milton critics have traditionally focused on nakedness; for instance, Dennis Danielson's study examines Milton next to Bunyan and uses their clothing metaphors to prove that their writing becomes a cloak of art and imagination for their theology, while Judy Kronenfeld refers to Milton and the idea of the naked truth but again the focus is on clothing as a metaphor rather than actual clothes (Danielson, 1995; Kronenfeld 1998, 26–8). Kristen Poole's work departs from such views and studies *Paradise Lost* in the context of the sect of the Adamites and their insistence on perceiving the state of nakedness as the closest to prelapsarian linguistic perfection. Her view is that, contrary to Adamites and Quakers, for Milton, "clothing... is an integrated element of the essence of creation' and he 'rejects nakedness as paradigm to re-enter the past Eden" (Poole 2000, 180–1). More recent approaches to Milton and clothing have highlighted further the materiality of the garments or even of the hair of some of Milton's characters. For instance, Ann Rosalind Jones and Peter Stallybrass read God's act of clothing Adam and Eve in *Paradise Lost* as following the livery system (Jones and Stallybrass 2000, 20–1), while Will Fisher examines *Paradise Lost* and *Samson Agonistes* as examples of Milton's engagement with early modern debates about hair, ornamentation, and gender identity (Fisher 2006, 129–58).

Applying similar methodologies to the polemical tracts, I propose that it is the particular materiality of the vestments that Milton exploits and adapts to his style in order to expose Laudian practices as hypocritical and spectacular merchandise. Milton's argument against the embodied religion of the liturgical dress relies on referring to the prelates as dismembered articles of worship and reducing priests to sleeves, socks, and hats, highlighting in the process the hollowness and disintegration of the unified body of episcopacy. Such evocative imagery serves Milton's purpose of undressing the clergy from their excessive and tyrannical layers both literally (by seeking reform of church practices and abolition of episcopal garments) and metaphorically (by exposing the perils and hypocrisy of a material-only devotion). Linen dress, then, is not only Milton's target, but his tool as well; through dress Milton adopts a

90 Naya Tsentourou

material strategy to counter the threat of Laudianism, which he sees as re-animating the practices of popery. In this respect, the chapter serves to place Milton, and Milton studies more generally, within the parameters of material culture studies and to argue that the study of hypocrisy in the context of 1640s religious controversies requires a multi-disciplinary model of investigation, one that pays as much attention to fabrics as to print culture.

Ground-breaking work by social historians, such as John Styles and Alice Dolan, has demonstrated the centrality of linen in the early modern period and its importance for national and international commercial, as well as domestic, bonds (see Styles 2007; Dolan 2014). "Touching linen was a universal experience in daily life" (Dolan 2015, 19), and in the form of dress, linen came in direct and intimate contact with the body, covering it, and endowing it with a sense of decency and respectability that became most prominent in the eighteenth-century use of the fabric. As Linda Levy Peck's work has shown, linen's significant value is evident from the period's inventories that catalogue it straight after silver plate (Levy Peck 2005, 222), while Harmes suggests that "white linen was an expensive commodity, expensive to produce and to keep clean and was thus a statement of reasonable wealth and status" (Harmes 2013, 101). The import of linen in the years leading up to the Reformation consti-tuted a major portion of the English trade and it was one of the main activities of the Mercers of London, the company that dominated the English import and export operations from the early Middle Ages up to the end of the sixteenth century (see Sutton 2005; Jack 1977). The large extent of linen's commercial and industrial use was due to the fabric's adaptability: "Without it [linen]", argues Leslie Clarkson, "the range of textile materials to clothe the body, to keep it warm, comfortable and fashionable, would have been much restricted" (Clarkson 2003, 492). Linen's versatile character and the long-standing tradition of its trade and exploitation made it an important asset for the English state.

Church vestments were made predominantly of linen, thus ecclesiasti-cal apparel was one of the luxurious goods on display in the context of early modern worship. If linen and its trade were seen as a profitable na-tional enterprise, however, the continuation of the fabric's prominent use in church was unwelcome. In post-Reformation England, liturgical dress became a regular point of disputation between the established church and those disappointed by the church's reluctance to dispense with cer-emonies and accessories. The 1559 Book of Common Prayer reinstated the special apparel for the priests (of alb and cope or chasuble) that its 1552 predecessor had sought to suppress (Mayo 1984, 129), meaning that the visual status of the priest as separate from the laity was re-stored by Elizabeth I's injunctions which aimed to control the clerical elite (Hayward 2009, 255). As Graeme Murdock suggests, "in establish-ing appropriate standards of dress for Protestant ministers in daily life,

"*Come buy Lawn Sleeves*" 91

synods and clergy hierarchies set out their wish for ministers to be highly visible within their local communities" (Murdock 2000, 195).

The controversy over vestments remained unresolved during the reign of Charles I, and the clergy's high degree of visibility was maintained and emphasised further after the succession of William Laud to the office of Archbishop of Canterbury in 1633. According to Peter Lake, the programme instigated by Laud required "that awe, fear, and reverence (that God's presence in church demanded) had to take a directly physical form" and the Laudians exhibited "an intense concern with the material fabric of the church and a heightened sense of the value of ecclesiastical ornament and decoration" (Lake 1993, 165). Laud's reforms, promoting the "beauty of holiness", stemmed from an anxiety that the rejection of the rituals and visual ornamentations of the church denied liturgy its sacred character. Responding to the charge of high treason shortly before his execution in 1645, Laud's reply contained his vision:

> But all that I laboured for in this particular was, that the external Worship of God in this *Church,* might be kept up in Uniformity and Decency, and in some Beauty of Holiness. And this the rather, because first I found that with the Contempt of the Outward Worship of God, the Inward fell away apace, and Profaneness began boldly to shew it self.
>
> (Laud 1695, 157)

For Laud, external, physical forms of faith, such as episcopal vestments, were necessary conditions to uphold the inward belief and participation in God's worship. "Uniformity and Decency" were essential elements in the liturgy, securing the believers' spiritual commitment, as well as the social rank and recognition of God's representatives. Integrity, dignity, and visibility within the local community were the indispensable benefits of linen church vestments. The distinction which the garments were called on to signify and assert was much debated by reformers who denounced the special status of priests and argued that such material ceremonies reinforced rather than severed the church's bonds with its idolatrous Catholic past. Clause XIV of the 'Root and Branch' petition expressed the people's suspicion of vestments:

> XIV. The great Conformity and likenesse both continued and encreased of our Church to the Church of *Rome,* in vestures, postures, Ceremonies and Administrations, namely as the Bishops Rochets, and the Lawne sleeves, the 4. cornerd Cap, the Cope and Surplisse, the Tippit, the Hood, and the Canonicall Coate, the Pulpit clothed, especially now of late with the Jesuites Badge upon them every way.
>
> (Anon. 1641b, sigB3v)

92 Naya Tsentourou

Milton participated in the controversy not through satirical verse like Overton, but via polemical writing, and from May 1641 to April 1642 he produced five tracts castigating the state of the English church for cultivating a disparity between the letter and the spirit of worship, and calling for the abolition of the bishops and any form of customary worship which spiritually impoverished the people driving them to idolatrous piety. Scholars have argued that Milton's prose in these tracts is fraught with images of disease and fleshly appetites, and that his vehement rhetoric is excessive, appealing to the senses instead of engaging with doctrinal matters. Tom Corns, for instance, suggests that Milton "is almost silent on doctrinal divisions within the church" and he "seems committed to a redefinition of the term 'doctrine' so as to remove it from the theoretical to the practical level" (Corns 1998, 41–2). Milton is indeed preoccupied with the excesses of the body, yet his language also betrays a fixation with what covers the body and how this body is displayed.

In the opening of his tract *Of Reformation* Milton rails against the state of the Church before the Reformation. By avoiding to explicitly name the Catholic church, he implicitly draws similarities with Laud's party:

> They hallow'd it (the body), they fum'd it, they sprincl'd it, they be deck't it, not in robes of pure innocency, but of pure Linnen, with other deformed, and fantastic dresses in Palls, and Miters, gold, and guegaw's fetcht from *Arons* old wardrope, or the *Flamins vestry*.
>
> (Milton *CPW*, 1:521)

"They" is left ambiguous, implicating both Catholic and England's bishops in a model of worship where the spiritual enlightenment of priest and individual, the "robes of pure innocency", is replaced by the accessories of ceremony, "pure Linnen". The covering of the body of the church in linen debases it to a concrete and highly spectacular form. "Arons old wardrope" is a sarcastic reference to the bishops' claims that ecclesiastical hierarchy and its visualisation in the liturgical dress were founded in the Scriptures, in God's appointment of Aaron as the first priest, which Milton explicitly denounces in his *Reason of Church Government*, stating that "it is impossible to found a Prelaty upon the imitation of this Priesthood" (Milton *CPW*, 1:767). For Milton it is only on a metaphorical level that the finery of the robes is to be celebrated; purity can only be immaterial whereas the external material form contaminates what it seeks to dress. As is evident in this passage, when attacking liturgical garments, Milton often lists items and value one after the other, adopting the style of an inventory and mirroring the accounts of the material possessions of the church. The church's commodification of worship provides Milton with a material vocabulary, which resembles the fascination with images he seeks to undo. Later in the same tract he

"Come buy Lawn Sleeves" 93

lists again items and prices, evoking the images of luxury and sensual appeal he seeks to suppress.

> Now I appeale to all wise men, what an excessive wast of Treasury hath beene within these few yeares in this Land not in the expedient, but in the Idolatrous erection of Temples beautified exquisitely to out-vie the Papists, the costly and deare-bought Scandals, and snares of Images, Pictures, rich Coaps, gorgeous Altar-clothes.
>
> (Milton *CPW*, 1:589–90)

In this respect, the linen dress of the Bishops alternates between two realms of display in the seventeenth-century: the realm of ecclesiastical spectacle, and the realm of trade. Consider for instance this quote:

> They would request us to indure still the russling of their Silken Cassocks, and that we would burst our *midriffes* rather then laugh to see them under Sayl in all their Lawn, and Sarcenet, their shrouds, and tackle, with a *geometricall rhomboides* upon their heads.
>
> (Milton *CPW*, 1: 611–12)

Milton vividly recreates the experience of witnessing the clergy in church by drawing attention to our senses and exposing the parade of prelates as a feast for the eyes, an extravagant performance devoid of internal faith. While elsewhere he attacks the church for setting "an Enterlude to set out the pompe of Prelatisme" (Milton *CPW*, 1:526) here he stages such interlude for us. We can almost hear the russling of the Cassocks and the invitation not to laugh actually highlights the absurdity of the scene. The bishops' garments are again anatomised and inventoried one by one, items of clothing that seem to acquire an agency of their own and to obscure the presence of an actual body underneath them. By the time we arrive at the "geometrical rhomboids" the bishops' ridiculous appearance is complete with caps as measured and disciplined as the study of geometry would require. All we see and hear is the linen dress.

The accumulated effect of terms such as lawn, sayl, sarcenet, shrouds, and tackle, is to position the spectacle not only in the field of church clothing, but in the wider maritime industry as well, since the items listed designate the equipment of ships. Reducing prelates to the fabric of their episcopal garments conjures in Milton's mind images of sailing, the other sphere of activity where linen was central. As Leslie Clarkson has shown, "the industrial uses of linen were large, particularly for shipping where it was in demand for sails, ropes, and hatch covers and the like" (Clarkson 2003, 475). Milton then humorously, and effectively, extracts the linen garments from the church and places them within the commercial context of shipping, transforming in the process the prelates from human beings to vessels of commercial wealth.

94 *Naya Tsentourou*

Such rhetorical strategies connect Milton to anti-episcopalian satires which often visually dramatised the church as a ship, such as the pamphlet by Thomas Stirry, whose *A Rot Amongst the Bishops*, published in 1641, portrays Laud as the captain of a ship navigated towards hell. Helen Pierce, who has studied the visual culture of anti-episcopacy, lists the image of the church as ship as an established motif in the vernacular art of satirical convention: "established motifs with roots in vernacular art – the gateway to Hell as the jaws of a monster, the church imagined as a great ship, the dark she-devil accompanying Bishop Wren – are fused with topical images such as the cannons, and a flag raised by Laud tied to a papal staff, which point to, and raise concerns about, current, contentious issues" (Pierce 2004, 845). Milton's description, therefore, of the bishops as sailing boats and their garments as sailing equipment provides the reader with an image as detailed and imaginative as satirical woodcuts, underscoring the clergy's corruption, their ostentation, and their obsession with the display of their linen garments. Milton's strategy of condemning the uniformity of Laud's programme, "the crust of Formalitie" as he calls it (Milton *CPW*, 1.522), by dissecting its ceremonial appearance into clothing items highlights their absurdity and satirically unravels the prelates' hypocrisy. Most importantly, however, it exposes the bishops as goods for display and reduces them to commodities whose gloss and beauty fascinate the observers.

In *An Apology against a Pamphlet*, Milton again employs attention to visual detail for the commodification, and implicit dehumanisation, of the bishops:

> A Bishops foot that hath all his toes maugre the gout, and a linnen Sock over it, is the aptest embleme of the Prelate himselfe. Who being a pluralist, may under one Surplice which is also linnen, hide foure benefices besides the metropolitan toe, and sends a fouler stench to heaven, then that which this young queasinesse reches at.
> (Milton *CPW*, 1:894)

The diseased foot of the bishop is an example of Milton's metaphor of the corrupt body politic that requires amputation of its contaminated limbs to recover its health. A memorable instance of this is found in *Of Reformation* where the bishops are paralleled to a "diseased tumor" which needs to be severed from the public body: 'We must first of all begin roundly to cashier, and cut away from the publick body the noysom, and diseased tumor of Prelacie' (Milton *CPW*, 1:598). The image of the afflicted foot in *An Apology* reiterates the idea that bishops are an ailment to the state, yet it is the detail of the foot's cover that heightens the effect of Milton's attack. References to the bishop's foot are recurrent in Milton's antiprelatical tracts and constitute part of his Martin-esque rhetoric (see King 2002; also Black 1997; Egan 1975 for the Marprelate

"Come buy Lawn Sleeves" 95

Tracts). In Milton's imagination the diseased foot is covered by "a linen sock" and "linen surplice", combining luxurious church ceremonies with stage practices. Since "sock" is the conventional image for comedy in the period and a visual reminder of popery, the "aptest emblem" for a bishop is one that joins stage conventions of dress with ecclesiastical vestments. The linen sock embodies the theatrical and insincere presence of the prelates in public life and accentuates the difference between the ugly, smelly, diseased foot, and its misleading cover. In this striking and memorable image the bishop is seen as merely a lower and deformed part of the body covered in fancy footwear.

The above examples are characteristic of Milton's polemic strategy in his antiprelatical tracts: he resists the hypocritical conformity sought by the ceremonies of religious observance by lifting clothing items out of context, out of the decent and uniform performance of liturgy as a whole, and exposing them as empty of any devotional value. By making linen sleeves, socks, caps, stand out, the materiality and greed of Laudian church is underscored and "the crust of Formality" is constantly broken to show its foundation on disjointed commodities and body parts. Milton reacts to homogeneity by focusing on parts, on individuals, by fragmenting and by constantly dismembering the form – the linen garments allow him to deny essence to custom and to expose the Church as physically decadent under its clothing.

Milton is aware that for the reformation to be successful in its aim to liberate individuals from the spiritual bondage of ceremonies, attack on ecclesiastical garments is not enough. In his 1649 *Eikonoklastes*, his response to *Eikon Basilike*, attributed to Charles I as the king's meditations and circulated shortly after his execution, he concludes that

> it is not the unfrocking of a Priest, the unmitring of a Bishop, and the removing him from off the Presbyterian shoulders, that will make us a happy Nation, no, if other things as great in the Church, and in the rule of life both economicall and politicall be not lookt into and refom'd.
>
> (Milton *CPW*, 2: 550)

By 1649 it seems that Milton comes to acknowledge the futility of rhetorically seeking to restructure the church if that is not part of a broader agenda for national reform, but in his early 1640s pamphlets his style aims exactly at such acts of undressing, of stripping off both garments and power, by particularising the bishops' clothes and exposing the layers of ostentation of the church establishment.

For the last part of this chapter I want to consider Milton's crucial comment on linen dress as found in his 1644 pamphlet, *Areopagitica*, a treatise against the material regulations on print that for Milton could have unbearable internal consequences on national and individual level.

96 Naya Tsentourou

Areopagitica was published in November 1644 as Milton's response to the Parliament's Licensing Order of June 1643, which sought to secure the monopoly on printing held by the Company of Stationers. Here Milton famously calls for the permission of the publication of all books and for the readers' trial, meaning the exercise of their reason and choice between beneficial and pernicious books.

In *Areopagitica*, books and the intellectual labour of the author are examined next to metaphors of trade, meat, disease, and architecture in order to highlight their differences to solely commercial and tangible goods. A reference to the clothing industry is used to juxtapose commodities to the unregulated search for knowledge and truth:

> Truth and understanding are not such wares as to be monopoliz'd and traded in by tickets and statutes, and standards. We must not think to make a staple commodity of all the knowledge in the Land, to mark and licence it like our broad cloath, and our wooll packs.
>
> (Milton *CPW*, 2: 535–6)

The clothing trade, strictly regulated and monopolised, is similar yet different to the field of intellectual pursuit and writing. Blair Hoxby explains that truth and understanding are "vital wares of public use and necessity whose production and exchange must not be driven into the hands of a few men" (Hoxby 2002, 40). In other words, following Milton's argument, books and authorial labour are understood as products to be used, and truth and knowledge become physical items to be exchanged, yet such products cannot be restricted by the monopolies imposed on the circulation of other merchandise. As in the antiprelatical tracts, the commodification of worship finds its way into Milton's style, turning his tracts into an imaginary catalogue of church vestments and body parts anatomised and paraded in their luxury, in *Areopagitica* the market ideology which controls human activity infiltrates Milton's vocabulary. According to Christopher Kendrick, "the commodity places its shadowy print on much of the imagery on the tract...as a result, market ideology comes to be inscribed most intimately within Milton's argument, and to motivate its figuration" (Kendrick 1986, 40).

Restricting truth and knowledge via material monopolies carries for Milton the stigma of popish practices. Linking pre-publication censorship to Catholicism, Milton writes:

> How many other things might be tolerated in peace, and left to conscience, had we but charity, and were it not the chief strong hold of our hypocrisie to be ever judging one another. I fear yet this iron yoke of outward conformity hath left a slavish print upon our necks; the ghost of a linnen decency yet haunts us.
>
> (Milton *CPW*, 2:563–4)

"Come buy Lawn Sleeves" 97

Clothing features in this example, not as the material commodity we are familiar with, but as a supernatural reappearance of the spirit of popery. The matter of pre-publication censorship is for Milton a tyranny equivalent to that of the imposition of custom worship in Church. He associates freedom of press with religious freedom, defending in the process the right of sectarian beliefs against a uniform model of devotion.

Milton's rhetorical gestures in this passage move between the material and the immaterial: the images of the "iron yoke" and the "linnen decency" work together to establish the real and inescapable materiality of the church, whereas the images of "slavish print" and the haunting "ghost" testify to the internal subjection produced by idolatry. From a material culture perspective, the tangibility of these images resonates with the process of producing paper from linen rags. Milton fears that the prelates are attempting to transmit on the printing press the memory of Catholicism implicit in their garments; that uniform religious worship which controls private faith corresponds to political absolutism, which controls public expression. Earlier, Milton had argued that licensing of the press is a traditionally Catholic practice: "this project of licencing crept out of the Inquisition, was catcht up by our Prelates, and hath caught some of our Presbyters" (Milton *CPW*, 2:493). "The slavish print upon our necks" becomes doubly significant, signalling not just metaphorical tyranny, but denouncing the linen-clad bishops for imposing material restrictions on print. In a treatise foregrounding the physical properties of books by imagining books as men, full of blood and life, the bishops are imagined as printers whose censorship is grafted on the people's bodies.

Although in *Areopagitica* Milton has moved away from the satirical demarcation of bishops as items of clothing and members of the body, linen emerges as the haunting reminder of the underlying threat of material forms on individual conscience. What is at stake here is memory, memory transcribed on linen clothes, the constant visual and material reminder of Catholic bondage that cannot be erased. Milton, and the English people, cannot escape this memory and in his attack against the clergy's clothing, Milton tries to declare Catholic ceremonies dead, only to acknowledge in the process that they might not be, that the ghost of linen is still haunting England. Read from a Derridian perspective, the ghost of linen decency becomes a spectre, the "becoming-body" (Derrida 1994, 6). Seen as spectres, the linen garments in Milton's imagination are both material and immaterial, at the same time disappearing while becoming. Dress stands between the metaphysical (or else the spiritual degeneration of the people) and the physical presence of ceremonies and conformity.

Engaging, therefore, with the physicality of dress and not just its symbolism, and paying attention to the cultural contexts linen occupies, can open up fresh investigations into Milton's works and the vestment controversy, investigations that focus on the material considerations of Milton's

98 *Naya Tsentourou*

polemical rhetoric. Such directions demonstrate how invested Milton is in what Jones and Stallybrass have called the "animatedness of clothes":

> To understand the significance of clothes in the Renaissance (they write), we need to undo our own social categories, in which clothes are prior to objects, wearers to what is worn. We need to understand the animatedness of clothes, their ability to 'pick up' subjects, to mould and shape them both physically and socially, to constitute subjects through their power as material memories.
>
> (Jones and Stallybrass 2000, 2)

It is the materiality of the garments, which Milton picks on and magnifies in order to remove any potential spiritual meaning from them. His attack against the whole is to focus on the parts and to treat linen garments as commodities, describing and ridiculing them as such, and resisting their appeal to a uniform model of devotion. By the time he writes *Areopagitica*, however, the parts seem to have united back into a haunting presence.

In Milton's early prose, when the linen vestments do not alternate between the realm of ecclesiastical spectacle and the realm of trade, they might occupy the realm of the theatrical stage, such as the "linen Sock" he accuses Bishop Hall of wearing, or even the supernatural realm, such as the 'ghost of linen decency' in *Areopagitica* which acquires further meaning when we consider that woodcut illustrations of ghosts, such as one of Cardinal Wolsey, depicted them predominantly in linen winding sheets (see Handley 2007, 76). After all, Milton fashions his response at the start of *An Apology* in terms of a stripping act:

> With me it fares now, as with him whose outward garment hath bin injur'd and ill bedighted; for having no other shift, what helpe but to turn the inside outwards, especially if the lining be of the same, or, as it is sometimes, much better.
>
> (Milton *CPW*, 1: 888–9)

The lining of a male dress in the early seventeenth century was indeed often finer and more valuable than the exterior (Patterson 2009, 54) making Milton's stripping and reversing act all the more steeped into the material culture of his day, and his attack against the bishops all the more concrete and practical in its call for reformation.

Works Cited

Anon. 1641a. *Lambeth Faire, Wherein You Have All the Bishops Trinkets Set to Sale*. London: s.n.
———. 1641b. *The First and Large Petition of the Citie of London and Other Inhabitants Thereabouts: For a Reformation in Church-Government, as Also for the Abolishment of Episcopacie*. London: s.n.

Black, Joseph. 1997. "The Rhetoric of Reaction: The Martin Marprelate Tracts (1588–89), Anti-Martinism, and the Uses of Print in Early Modern England". *Sixteenth Century Journal* 28: 707–25.

Cable, Lana. 1995. *Carnal Rhetoric: Milton's Iconoclasm and the Poetics of Desire*. Durham, NC: Duke University Press.

Clarkson, Leslie. 2003. "The Linen Industry in Early Modern Europe". In *The Cambridge History of Western Textiles*, edited by David Jenkins, vol. 1, 473–92. Cambridge: Cambridge University Press.

Corns, Thomas N. 1998. "Milton's Antiprelatical Tracts and the Marginality of Doctrine". In *Milton and Heresy*, edited by Stephen B. Dobranski and John P. Rumrich, 39–48. Cambridge: Cambridge University Press.

Danielson, Dennis. 1995. "Milton, Bunyan, and the Clothing of Truth and Righteousness". In *Heirs of Fame: Milton and Writers of the English Renaissance*, edited by Margo Swiss and David A. Kent, 247–69. London: Associated University Presses.

Derrida, Jacques. 1994. *Spectres of Marx: The State of Debt, the Work of Mourning, and the New International*, translated by Peggy Kamuf. London; New York: Routledge.

Dolan, Alice. 2014. "The Fabric of Life". *Home Cultures* 11(3): 353–74

———. 2015. "The Fabric of Life: Linen and Life Cycle in England, 1678–1810". PhD diss., University of Hertfordshire.

Egan, James. 1975. "Milton and the Marprelate Tradition". *Milton Studies* 8: 103–23.

Fisher, Will. 2006. *Materializing Gender in Early Modern English Literature and Culture*. Cambridge: Cambridge University Press.

Handley, Sasha. 2007. *Visions of an Unseen World*. London: Pickering and Chatto.

Harmes, Marcus K. 2013. *Bishops and Power in Early Modern England*. London; New York: Bloomsbury Academic.

Hayward, Mary. 2009. *Rich Apparel: Clothing and the Law in Henry VIII's England*. Farnham: Ashgate.

Hentschell, Roze. 2008. *The Culture of Cloth in Early Modern England: Textual Constructions of a National Identity*. Farnham: Ashgate.

Hoxby, Blair. 2002. *Mammon's Music: Literature and Economics in the Age of Milton*. New Haven, CT: Yale University Press.

Jack, Sibyl M. 1977. *Trade and Industry in Tudor and Stuart England*. London: Allen & Uhwin.

Jones, Ann Rosalind, and Peter Stallybrass. 2000. *Renaissance Clothing and the Materials of Memory*. Cambridge: Cambridge University Press.

Kaula, David. 1976. "Autolycus's Trumpery". *Studies in English Literature 1500–1900* 16: 287–303.

Kearney, James J. 2000. "Trinket, Idol, Fetish: Some Notes on Iconoclasm and the Language of Materiality in Reformation England". *Shakespeare Studies* 28: 257–61.

Kendrick, Christopher. 1986. *Milton: A Study in Ideology and Form*. New York; London: Methuen.

King, John N. 2002. "'The Bishop's Stinking Foot': Milton and Antiprelatical Satire". *Reformation* 7: 187–97.

Kronenfeld, Judy. 1998. *King Lear and the Naked Truth: Rethinking the Language of Religion and Resistance*. Durham, NC: Duke University Press.

100 *Naya Tsentourou*

Lake, Peter. 1993. "The Laudian Syle: Order, Uniformity and the Pursuit of the Beauty of Holiness in the 1630s". In *The Early Stuart Church, 1603–1642*, edited by Kenneth Fincham, 161–85. Basingstoke: Palgrave Macmillan.

Laud, William. 1695. *The History of the Troubles and Tryal of the Most Reverend Father in God and Blessed Martyr, William Laud, Lord Arch-Bishop of Canterbury Wrote by Himself during His Imprisonment in the Tower.* London: Printed for Ri. Chiswell.

Levy Peck, Linda. 2005. *Consuming Splendor: Society and Culture in Seventeenth-Century England.* Cambridge: Cambridge University Press.

Mayo, Janet. 1984. *A History of Ecclesiastical Dress.* London: Batsford.

Milne, Kirsty. 2015. *At Vanity Fair: From Bunyan to Thackeray.* Cambridge: Cambridge University Press.

Milton, John. 1641–42. *Complete Prose Works of John Milton*, general edited by Don M. Wolfe, 8 vols, 1953–82. New Haven, CT: Yale University Press.

Murdock, Graeme. 2000. "Dressed to Repress?: Protestant Clerical Dress and the Regulation of Morality in Early Modern Europe". *Fashion Theory* 4: 179–200.

Patterson, Angus. 2009. *Fashion and Armour in Renaissance Europe: Proud Lookes and Brave Attire.* London: V&A Publishing. Available online at http://collections.vam.ac.uk/item/O110590/doublet-and-breeches-unknown/ (accessed 15 August 2016).

Pierce, Helen. 2004. "Anti-episcopacy and Graphic Satire in England, 1640–1645". *The Historical Journal* 47: 809–48.

Poole, Kristen. 2000. *Radical Religion from Shakespeare to Milton: Figures of Nonconformity in Early Modern England.* Cambridge: Cambridge University Press.

Styles, John. 2007. *The Dress of the People: Everyday Fashion in Eighteenth-Century England.* London: Yale University Press.

Sutton, Anne F. 2005. *The Mercery of London: Trade, Goods and People, 1130–1578.* Farnham: Ashgate.

Zwicker, Stephen N. 2002. "Habits of Reading and Early Modern Literary Culture". In *The Cambridge History of Early Modern English Literature*, edited by David Lowenstein and Janel Mueller, 170–98. Cambridge: Cambridge University Press.

6 "Much like the Picture of the Devill in a Play"

Hypocrisy and Demonic Possession

Jacqueline Pearson

On 20 January 1573, in a Puritan household in Suffolk, Alexander Nyndge was "grievously tormented with an evil Spirit". This was demonstrated by the way his body contorted and became so swollen that "he seemed to be twice so big as his naturall body" and he made "such strange and idle kinds of gestures... that he was suspected to be mad": even his identity tottered as the demon was heard within him, speaking in a "hollow voyce" not his own (Nyndge 1616, sigs. A3v-A4r). Demonic possession was in the early modern period defined in opposition to other conditions likely to cause the same symptoms, like "naturall" disease on the one hand and hypocrisy on the other. Although the latter term is never used, the account of Nyndge's possession seems energised by anxieties that the victim might be a hypocrite in all three of its original senses: a speaking respondent (the demon entered into dialogue with Nyndge and his brother), an actor (Nyndge was "monstrously transformed... much like the picture of the Devill in a play"), and a deceiver (Nyndge 1616, sig. B).

In early modern constructions of religious experience, hypocrisy was always an important issue. Anxieties that one might unknowingly be a hypocrite were agonisedly expressed in puritan life-writings (e.g. Booy 2007, 51; Davy 1670, 9), with believers all too aware that Christ had attacked the apparently godly Pharisees as "hypocrites" and "whited sepulchres" (Matthew 23:27, King James Bible). The performance of "outward workes" did not add up to godliness, for these "an hypocrite may doe, onely hee failes in the Heart" (Adams 1626, 75). Hypocrisy, moreover, sometimes becomes a vital issue in accounts of the supernatural. The "hipocrisie" of civic officers might be punished through the birth of monsters (Batman 1581, 408); "Hypocrisy and Theft" might be exposed by poltergeist phenomena in the house of the guilty man (R. B. 1688, 97); and witches were especially terrifying because of the "Hypocrisie" (Davenport 1646, titlepage) by which they "made outward shews, as if they had been Saints on earth" (Stearne 1648, 39), while being in reality in league with the Devil. The culturally urgent question about the relation between outward acts and inward realities proved especially acute in the case of demonic possession, since it radically problematised issues of agency and even identity, of who is acting, and who an individual truly is.

102 *Jacqueline Pearson*

Hypocrisy and anxieties about hypocrisy, and about fraud, the point where legal authority concerns itself with hypocrisy, were endemic in early modern stories of demonic possession, unsurprisingly since the Devil "knows too well how to play the Hypocrite" (Anon. 1683, 64). "*Hypocrisie...* were iustly called the *White Devill*" (Adams 1615, 6), "an hypocrite... is a Devil incarnate" (Anon. 1664a, 110), and Satan, the master hypocrite, could easily appear like an angel of light (2 Corinthians 11:14, King James Bible). The "evill Spirit" who manifested at Macon displayed a troubling versatility in "acting" alternative identities, including a man engaged in a lawsuit, the servant of the demonic entity, a would-be apprentice, and the ghost of a woman who had recently died in the house (Perrault 1658, 3, 18, 15, 16, 21). While "God is a creator", however, the Devil is only "God's ape", hypocritically "counterfetting" the divine creation (James VI 1597, 22–3) and exploiting the fact that "hypocrisie... possesseth the hearts of all the sonnes of Adam" (Abbott 1600, 81), just as the Devil possesses demoniac victims.

While hypocrisy was an issue both implicit and explicit in accounts of demonic possession, accusations of hypocrisy are more complex and, sometimes, hypocritical than may at first appear, and no statement can safely be taken at face value. Too much was at stake for the possessed persons, their communities, church leaders and the authors of published accounts, and texts as well as individuals may be hypocrites. The account of Alexander Nyndge I quote above is taken not from the original pamphlet of, perhaps, 1573, written by the brother of the demoniac and published very shortly after the possession itself, but from a revision of 1615, not necessarily by the same author, whose motives are unknown but who clearly aims, perhaps hypocritically, to ratchet up the suspense by increasing the time that Nyndge was possessed from a day to six months, and by adding striking similes ("like the picture of the Devill in a play") not present in the original.

Demonic possession was, apparently, at epidemic proportions in early modern England. Alexander Nyndge's experiences were typical of more than a hundred individuals who displayed telltale symptoms of fits, bodily and facial distortions, superhuman strength, animalistic noises, disorderly speech, and, sometimes, demonic voices from within. Later the vomiting of strange objects, especially pins, would be added to the repertoire. This was dramatic but easy to simulate: observers noted that the "Hypocrite" demoniac Richard Hathaway was only able to vomit pins after "putting his hands to his pocket", where it was found he had "great quantities of Pins" (Anon. 1702, 13, 26). However, contemporary attitudes to this epidemic were remarkably diverse, ranging from sceptical to superstitious, though recent scholars have emphasised the complexity of both these positions, and that they may not in any case be the binary oppositions they once appeared (Clark 1999).

"*Much like the Picture of the Devill in a Play*"   103

The period is bookended by two episodes in which the Church of England struggled to define its identity and assert its authority in the face of competition from both Catholics and nonconforming Protestants. Both episodes produced contending published accounts, and the Church of England's spokesmen – Samuel Harsnett, the Bishop of London's trouble-shooter and later Archbishop of York, in the 1590s and Zachary Taylor, Lancashire Tory and Anglican minister, in the 1690s – used narratives of demonic possession and charges of hypocrisy to accomplish this. While both episodes can only be fully understood in the context of their specific times and locations (Westaway and Harrison 1996), they also show remarkable similarities around the issue of hypocrisy.

Both Harsnett and Taylor, for instance, elided the two very different oppositional groups, Catholics and puritan dissenters, insisting that they were both equally hypocrites and political subversives. For Harsnett, John Darrell's puritan dispossessions were "hypocriticall sleightes" indistinguishable from the "hypocriticall dissimulation" of Catholic exorcists (Harsnett 1599, 5; 1603, "To the Seduced Catholiques of England", n.p.). Satirising Darrell's alleged success in dispossessing Nottingham apprentice William Somers in 1597, Harsnett attacked him as a "counterfeiting hypocrite", who coached Somers until the boy became equally adept in "*hypocrisie*", "as *Roscius* himself could not have done it better"; this was not materially different from the Catholic exorcists he also accused of being "Pharisaical hypocrites" (Harsnett 1599, 79, 118; 1603, 171). For Taylor, Lancashire nonconformists were political subversives fomenting civil dissension under the "*Hypocrisy*" of claims to religion and motivated by an unholy mix of "Hypocrisy and Enthusiasm" (Taylor 1683, 20; 1698, 24). In their attempt to emulate the famous local Catholic exorcism of Thomas Ashton of Wigan by dispossessing Richard Dugdale of Surey, the nonconformists, Taylor accused, had demonstrated they were guilty of "Hypocritical Pretences" (Taylor 1698, 10) equal to the "*Hypocrisie*" (Taylor 1696, 14) of the Catholics, and were merely "Tools of Popery" (Taylor 1698, 4) who "agreed" with the Catholics on all material points (Taylor 1697, 5).

The Church of England in the late Elizabethan and early Jacobean period – and also in the 1690s as it defined itself as moderate and reasonable as opposed to the superstition of Catholics and the enthusiasm of dissenters – officially took a sceptical line on the supernatural generally and possession in particular. "Miracles are nowe ceased" (G. Co. 1598, sig. B4v), superseded by the all-sufficient scriptures, and "[t]here is, in these days, neither possession nor dispossession of demons" (Swan 1603, 323–4). To claim otherwise was "an opinion dangerous" (I. D. 1597, 26), smacking of popish or puritan attempts to destabilise government and the established church, and the holder of such views was in danger of being labelled not only subversive but "hypocritical" (G. Co. 1598, sig. B4v).

104   *Jacqueline Pearson*

In 1585–6 there was a high-profile series of Catholic exorcisms in Kent and Essex, which Harsnett sought to discredit, his key strategy to accuse those involved of hypocrisy, especially through an exuberant use of theatrical imagery (Greenblatt 1989, 94–128). The Pope's church is a "play-house" (Harsnett 1599, Epistle to the Reader, n.p.), a "pageant of Puppits", Catholic exorcists tour the country "as your wandring Players use to doe", the demoniac is an "actor" playing "his part *extempore*", and those involved in the exorcism fall into theatrical stereotypes, the "young gallant", the Sycophant, the Merchant, the Leno (Harsnett 1603, 20, 11, 18–19). He used exactly the same strategies to discredit puritan John Darrell, although his supporters insisted they used only strategies legitimised by the Gospels, "the holy exercise of Prayer and Fasting" (I. D. 1597, 33). Somers' possession, Harsnett argues, alluding to type-characters from the Tudor moral interlude, was "pure play, containing two principall parts, of a vice and a devill" (Harsnett 1599, Epistle to the Reader, n.p.). For Harsnett, this story – perhaps every story – of possession is one of hypocritical theatricality rather than the supernatural.

A hundred years later Zachary Taylor in Lancashire faced exactly the same dilemma and adopted analogous solutions. In 1696, the Catholic priests who claimed to have exorcised Thomas Ashton in Wigan had reported that the Devil had cooperatively confirmed many aspects of Catholic belief before being banished: for Taylor this is simply "*Hypocrisie*", a "Scene" with an "Epilogue" acted "upon the Stage" (Taylor 1696, 14), a "*Play... more like Burlesque*" (Taylor 1696, "To the Right Reverend Father in God", n.p.), a "*Show*", a "Game", "a Gambol to end *Christmas* with" (Taylor 1698, 2), and, no doubt quoting Harsnett, "*a Pupet-Show*" (Taylor 1696, 14). When a year later Surey gardener Richard Dugdale became possessed, after a drunken revel when he (perhaps) "had offer'd himself to the Devil, on condition the Devil would make him a good Dancer" (Jollie 1697, 2), a number of dissenting clergymen led by Thomas Jollie and John Carrington eventually (perhaps) succeeded in dispossessing him through fasting and prayer, but Taylor challenged their claims, charging them with "Insincerity" and the use of absurdly over-dramatic "Rhodomantado Dialogues", and again emphasising the theatricality with which they appeared "openly upon the Stage, play[ing] the sanctified Buffoon" (Taylor 1697, 9, 3, 1). These accusations of hypocrisy were perhaps especially troubling to the nonconformists, for the devil possessing Richard Dugdale had also accused them of being "*Hypocritical*", and Dugdale himself, however genuine, "would sometimes pretend that a good Spirit was in him" rather than the devil, and so might be suspected of hypocrisy even by his supporters (Jollie 1697, 7; 1698, 63).

Both Taylor and his dissenting opponents were very aware of the history of Harsnett and Darrell. Taylor begins his 1698 pamphlet with

"Much like the Picture of the Devill in a Play"   105

a letter in which he offers a detailed analysis of the *"fearful story"* of the *"Devil-monger"* Darrell and praises the church convocation of 1603, which attempted to control such "Hypocritical Pretences" (Taylor 1698, 9–10). The nonconformists' account of the dispossession of Richard Dugdale "reproduces some highly unusual evidences" also found in the account of Darrell's exorcisms (Westaway and Harrison 1996, 221) and uses biblical citations "noticeably similar" (Lea 2011, 198). The century-old controversy, and especially its scatter-gun accusations of hypocrisy, to a surprising degree set the agenda in the late 1690s for attacking, or defending, the authenticity of possession experiences and the sincerity of dispossessors.

Neither Harsnett nor Taylor was, of course, motivated by Enlightenment scepticism. At both periods, possession was "a politically sensitive idea", as the Church of England asserted its authority over Catholic and dissenter claims (Newton 2008, 15). In the 1590s Catholic exorcisms, Harsnett emphasises, one alleged demoniac, Anthony Marwood, was the servant of "Babington the traytor", who was executed for conspiring with Mary Queen of Scots, so that treason, possession, and hypocrisy become parallel forms of inauthenticity (Harsnett 1603, 11). Similarly, his attack on Darrell represents the puritans as traitors intent on "dismantling the hierarchical organization of the established Church" (Gibson 2006, 3): the dysfunctional body of the demoniac thus serves as a graphic metaphor for the puritans' attack on the body of the true church and state. For Taylor, too, the Catholic exorcists are covertly in league with the Devil they claim to have power over, while the dissenters, whose unity in Lancashire was crumbling, have no organisation whatever, but only disparate "Personal" ambitions and "a studied Design of Popularity and Vain-glory" (Taylor 1697, 1), which leads inevitably to hypocrisy.

Harsnett, Taylor and their church had a good deal invested in representing demonic possession as fraud and identifying puritans and Catholics as dangerous hypocrites. But on the margins of the Church of England, and in dissenting groups beyond it, demonic possession remained a live issue. In the civil wars and interregnum, as the authority of the episcopal Church of England was dismantled, stories of the supernatural supplied ways of understanding "the breakdown of government" (Johnstone 2006, 248), and with the draconian measures taken against nonconforming Protestants by the Clarendon Code after the Restoration, possession again became part of the struggle between the established church and its critics. While for Harsnett and Taylor it was strategic to employ accusations of hypocrisy, for nonconforming ministers seeking to establish their own personal authority and the truth of their ecclesiological beliefs, it was important to emphasise the authenticity of their possessed persons. Narratives of hypocrisy are thus assiduously avoided, denied, or raised only to be expelled. God told possessed

106 Jacqueline Pearson

Thomas Darling that someone had been spreading rumours that he was a "dissembler", but promised to punish this slander (I. D. 1597, 42). "If some be Cheats and Counterfeits, must all be so?", one nonconforming minister asked, answering in the negative (Petto 1693, Preface to the Christian Reader, n. p.), and another pamphlet author insisted on the authenticity of his subject: "there is no room... for the Surmises of the incredulous, it being impossible she or any of her Relations could imagine any advantage to themselves by counterfeiting or pretending a Possession" (Anon. 1677, 2).

The symptoms of possession were remarkably consistent, "stereotyped and patterned" (Sharpe 1996, 192), which to some commentators proved their authenticity: "[n]ow this harmonie & consent in signes and actions... doth make it evident, that they were all really... possessed" (More 1600, 46–47). Conversely, though, the same evidence could equally prove the easy availability of an imitable script which any hypocrite could master. If possession was "learned behaviour" (Almond 2004, 40), Harsnett argued that it was learned as a deliberate fraud by William Somers from a literal script "in writing" prepared by his exorcist (Harsnett 1599, 81–2). Possession was infectious, perhaps because the Devil moved nimbly from victim to victim, but perhaps because others learned by example how to perform the role of demoniac: in London in 1574, Rachel Pindar learned to perform possession from Agnes Brigges, who had herself, probably, learned it from Robert Brigges; all three were treated by John Foxe, so information could have circulated freely in his circle (Sands 2004, 57–89). The influential account of the possession of the Throckmorton children by the "witches" of Warboys (Anon. 1593) scripted a whole generation of performances: William Somers (Almond 2004, 243), Anne Gunter (Sharpe 2000, 135), and thirteen-year-old Edward Smith in Leicester in 1616 (Pickering and Pickering 2010, 116), whose performance of possession led to the execution of nine women before he confessed fraud, all had access to the earlier story of possession and perhaps copied some aspects of it.

Hypocrisy may well, then, be part of some possession experiences, but it would be ill-advised to propose a single "one-size-fits-all" model, and it is possible to tease out a number of different ways possession was understood and practised. Some cases, it is clear, were hypocritical in the sense of organised and conscious fraud. In 1622 Katharine Malpas confessed, before the Star Chamber, of inciting her daughter, of the same name, "to counterfeite and fayne her selfe to be bewitched and possessed with a evill spirite" in order to "gaine and gett money" (Raiswell 1999, 29–30), and in 1698 Susanna Fowles also confessed to falsifying possession symptoms, "upon some Discontent arising between her self and Husband", and *"to get Money"* (Howson 1698, 20–1). One of the most notorious demoniacs, the "Boy of Bilson", twelve-year-old William Perry, the son of an "Honest Husbandman" who in 1622 developed

"Much like the Picture of the Devill in a Play" 107

"extreme fits", the vomiting up of strange objects, black urine, and other classic symptoms, was also, perhaps, a skilled and organised fraud. The Bishop of Lichfield and Coventry, into whose household he was taken, began to suspect "he did but counterfeit", and close surveillance demonstrated that he produced the black urine to order by hiding ink in his foreskin. He confessed to a fraud he claimed was masterminded by Catholic priests, his motive simply "that he was not willing to goe to schoole again" (R. B. 1622, 58, 26, 61, 64, 70). This case in many ways reruns Harsnett's narratives, with possession the result of hypocrisy and Catholic conspiracy.

Or rather, this was one of the narratives told about the boy. The pamphlet, *The Boy of Bilson* (1622), is a palimpsest of seven different texts by diverse authors with different beliefs about possession. It includes vigorous anti-Catholic propaganda, "A Discourse Concerning Popish Exorcizing" which attacks Catholic exorcists in twenty-three separate "advertisements", and a sceptical, Protestant account arguing that the boy was a "notable fraud", his symptoms wholly "counterfeit" (R. B. 1622, 1–57, 59, 61). However, the book also includes a first-person account, by one of the priests involved, of the exorcism, supporting the authenticity of the case and the validity of Catholic procedures, and attacking "*Puritans*" for their "lacke of beliefe", and another convinced deposition by a "Recusant" gentleman (R. B. 1622, 50, 52, 74–5). Thus, while the pamphlet overall is edited to offer a story of hypocrisy, "Popish delusions", "notable fraud", "*impostures*", "counterfeiting" and "*dissimulation*" (R. B. 1622, 1, 59, 47, 9, 60), it also makes visible other ways of reading it. This story, like possession in general, "was a site of conflicting interests" (Almond 2004, 333), and the two-facedness of the hypocrite can be carried over into the organisation of the text itself.

Some cases generated elaborate charges and counter-charges of fraud and hypocrisy: it may be "unwise to take at face value confessions of fraud by demoniacs", since confessions of hypocrisy may themselves be strategically hypocritical (Almond 2004, 39). William Somers confessed to fraud, but an ecclesiastical commission refused to accept this (the Devil possessing him could have been lying), while the Archbishop of Canterbury, who had a good deal invested in controlling would-be exorcists, in turn rejected their verdict. The case of thirteen-year-old Thomas Darling, in which John Darrell was also involved, was almost equally complex. Darling, a member of a devout puritan family, developed symptoms that were defined as possession or bewitchment. While, as in many possession cases, crises took place when prayers were said and the Bible read, Darling fought the Devil heroically, protecting the Bible from attack. Later he confessed to fraud, and testified against Darrell, but this was (according to Darrell) the result of intimidation, since the boy was imprisoned, beaten and starved until he capitulated, and he later withdrew his confession. Darling's experiences were, perhaps, not completely

108   *Jacqueline Pearson*

out of line with what was expected of puritan conversion, and his sense that he *"had the spirit of God in me"* which *"resisted Sathan"* (Harsnett 1599, 290), is reminiscent of a number of more extreme puritan conversion narratives (e.g. Jessey 1647, 19). Moreover, Darling (according to Harsnett) did not think of himself as possessed until Darrell put the idea into his head (Harsnett 1599, 272). Perhaps cooperating with a narrative of possession was "the only way [he] could fulfil [his] own desire for holiness" (Ferber 2004, 29), and the episode shows a crisis of terminology rather than hypocrisy. Later Darling found other, equally risky, ways of expressing this desire, in 1603 being tried before the Star Chamber for accusing the Vice-Chancellor of the University of Oxford and a number of privy councillors of being crypto-catholics. Despite his confession of fraud, the idea of hypocrisy is much too blunt an instrument for understanding the case of Thomas Darling.

If possession symptoms were not caused by hypocrisy or by miracles, early modern observers also considered the possibility that they were the result of "natural causes" rather than "supernaturall" (Jorden 1603, 2): natural diseases like "Epilepsie, Mother, Crampe, Convulsion, Sciatica or Gowt" rather than "a devill", it was alleged by some physicians and clergymen, created the performances misidentified as possession (Harsnett 1603, 28). Some narratives do invite medical explanations. Sarah Bower, a "Brisk and Lively" teenager who became "possess'd with an evil Spirit" in Wapping in 1693 may, despite her youth, have suffered a stroke: after a blow on her back, "the greater part of one side of her Body was all benumm'd", which led to "Lameness", "strange and unaccountable Fits" and hallucinations (Kirby 1693, 2, full title, 3). James Barrow, possessed in 1664, perhaps shows symptoms of obsessive-compulsive or autistic-spectrum disorders, like his inability to perform routine tasks without first singing (Barrow 1664, 5, 6, 7). Samuel Petto, nonconforming minister, chronicled the possession of Suffolk Congregationalist Thomas Spatchet, insisting that only *"Atheistical* and Irreligious Persons" would believe it was the result only of a "Natural Cause" (Petto 1693, "A Preface to the Christian Reader", n.p.). And yet Petto subverts his own narrative by providing enough information to suggest that natural causes are the most plausible. Spatchet was an unusual demoniac, an elderly man with a history of civic responsibilities. In infancy he suffered a catastrophic brain injury when a servant dropped him, fracturing his skull on a stone (Petto 1693, 2–3), and it is hard not to read his symptoms of fits, shaking, and disorderly behaviour as the effects of neurological damage rather than the witchcraft-mediated demonic possession which Petto advocates.

Demonic possession, then, raised a range of explanatory and diagnostic models, from outright fraud and hypocrisy through natural illnesses to genuine and momentous supernatural events; but perhaps even these distinctions are too crude, since the "boundary between simulation

"Much like the Picture of the Devill in a Play" 109

and authenticity in the possessed can be opaque" (Almond 2004, 41). Hannah Allen, for instance, was no hypocrite, and her symptoms were clearly genuine, in the sense that she was really suffering agonies of terror, loneliness, suicidal thoughts, anger and self-loathing, and attributed these to the agency of the devil. Modern accounts (Hodgkin 2007) tend to diagnose her symptoms as madness, but this explains little more than the seventeenth-century terms. However, even at the most critical moments, there is for Allen an element of detachment and even pleasure at the effectiveness of her performance and her linguistic creativity: at one desperate point, convinced that she is "the Monster of the Universe", she is "much delighted" with this verbal formulation (Allen 1683, 59). For Allen neither hypocrisy (too conscious) nor madness (too unconscious) seems quite the right term. Like many stories of demonic possession, Allen's raises questions about the nature and limits of human agency and identity.

Like Allen's, where a story of family tension and neglect and the resentment of an abandoned and then widowed wife underlies the narrative of demonic assault, and where remarriage puts an end to her symptoms, some accounts of possession hint at the "half-unacknowledged meanings" (Purkiss 1996, 76) which possession had for its sufferers and their communities. Such texts, like other life-writings, may thus inadvertently give the reader "enough evidence to make interpretations which the writer is unaware of" (Watkins 1972, 65), or at least does not fully endorse, through their "anxieties, inconsistencies, and gaps" (Martin 2005, 155). These counter-narratives may suggest buried stories about identity, family, community, or nation.

What, for instance, are we to make of the story of the "Devil of Glenluce"? An evil spirit targeted the home of weaver Gilbert Campbell in Galloway in 1654, destroying his work and the family clothes, burning beds, throwing stones and other objects, and establishing an intimate relationship with the family children which approaches possession (Sinclair 1685, 75–92). Academic mathematician George Sinclair sees this as indubitably an infestation by the *"Foul Fiend"* (77), *"Satan"* (79, 87), "the Devil" (87–8); indeed, the entity frankly defines itself as *"an evil Spirit, come from the bottomless Pit of Hell"* (84). And yet the narrative enables dissenting readings too. The first sign of demonic activity was a mysterious whistling, and when Campbell's daughter Jennet said "I would fain hear thee speake, as well as Whistle", it threatened, "I'le cast thee *Iennet* into the *Well*". The most remarkable thing is that "The voice was most exactly like the Damsels voice, and did resemble it to the life"; and the whistling too was "such, as Children use to make, with their small slender *Glass Whistles*" (77). Later when the voice of the "Devil" is heard, it apparently *"speaks out of the Children"* (84). If the children left home the demonic phenomena ceased, but resumed when they returned (78–9): the "Devil" seems to have no existence, or voice, separate from theirs.

110 *Jacqueline Pearson*

Are the Campbell children hypocrites, fabricating the phenomena with their own voices, bodies, and knowledge? The devil quotes "the first words of the *Latine Rudiments*, which Schollars are taught, when they go to the *Grammar School*" (79), which would be well known to Sinclair's source, "*Gilbert Campbels Son*", probably Thomas, "then a student of Philosophy in the *Colledge* of *Glasgow*" (76). When the devil knows the names of the family, speaks "in the proper Countrey Dialect" (80), and evinces a schoolboy brand of humour, it seems to have no information or tastes not readily available to the children. Some modern commentators have suggested the real story is one of fraud: Thomas Campbell fears being taken out of university to contribute to his father's weaving business, and so systematically destroys that business using the alibi of demonic assault (Robbins 1959, 224–6). P. G. Maxwell-Stuart, however, considers the evidence for this "flimsy" and urges that we put aside modern prejudices and consider what the episode meant to "Gilbert Campbell and his community" (Maxwell-Stuart 2011, 128–9). This however may underestimate the range of views available within Campbell's community: even Sinclair, while strongly arguing for the authenticity of the phenomena, also supplies the bare bones of a counter-narrative which emphasises the involvement of the children, and hints at a backstory involving Thomas that is never quite spelled out. Why is there "evil" (79) in the weaver sending the children away? Why is Gilbert Campbell so keen to get Thomas out of the house? Is Thomas suspected of fraud, or is it feared he is a special focus for demonic malice? What does the minister mean when he says that the weaver "*would find himself deceived*" (78) if he sends Thomas away? It is possible that the Campbell children are conscious hypocrites, who become trapped in a fiction that rapidly spirals out of control, or unconscious hypocrites, who have internalised their community's narratives and its "language of demonology", like some who confessed to witchcraft, because this was the only language available to them to express everyday "guilt", desire, and anger (Jackson 1995, 70, 74). Or perhaps they were genuinely involved in inexplicable phenomena: it has become a cliché that poltergeist phenomena tend to centre on "adolescents, especially girls" (Gauld and Cornell 1979, 16), and may be generated (or fabricated) consciously or unconsciously by the creativity and frustration of adolescence and its experimentation with individual identity. Hypocrisy may, in the context of demonic encounters, be a more complex phenomenon than Harsnett and his confederates can acknowledge, only one part of a complex tangle of conscious and unconscious motivations.

As we have seen, some writers insisted on the authenticity of their accounts because demoniacs and their communities can have no "advantage to themselves" in "pretending a Possession" (Anon. 1677, 2). But of course it depends what kind of "advantage" we are imagining. Of the sixty-four possessed persons considered by Philip Almond, fifty-six

"Much like the Picture of the Devill in a Play" 111

were under twenty years old, and of sixty-two, forty-four were female (Almond 2004, 22–3). Possessed individuals were thus often "disempowered" (Oldridge 2000, 119), and possession offered many potential advantages, allowing demoniacs to challenge hierarchies of age, gender and status; protest against the demanding disciplinary expectations of Protestant culture; take central place in their own dramas; and gain the rare opportunity of access to a public sphere and its language to tell their own stories. Possession is always "fundamentally concerned with questions of authority", especially authority over language and narrative (Ferber 2009, 216).

With possessed servants or apprentices like William Somers (G. Co. 1598), Jane Ashton (More 1600), Margaret Gurr (Skinner 1681–4), Elizabeth Burgiss (Anon. 1681), Mary Webb (Anon. 1687), Thomas Sawdie (Anon. 1664b) and Jane Stretton (M. Y. 1669), possession had the "advantage" of allowing some escape from a service role, and it is easy, probably too easy, to blame a "mischievous and idle youth... a knavish servant" (Baring-Gould 1908, 174) for (fraudulent) demonic manifestations. Servants, or possessed children and adolescents like the five Throckmorton girls at Warboys (Anon. 1593) or the Starkie children in Lancashire (More 1600), or unhappy wives like Hannah Allen (Allen 1683), Margaret Cooper (Anon. 1584), Joan Drake (Hart On-Hi 1647) and Susanna Fowles (Howson 1698), must have found that their relationships with their family and position in the local community changed in marked, and at least partly positive, ways. Such performances may have been conscious, hypocritical fraud but are more likely to have been less clear-cut. They may speak, quite directly or in coded ways, of the needs and desires of the young or subaltern in early modern society, for more money, less work, something fashionable to wear, "fine Suits of Head-Cloths, and very high Top-knots" (Kirby 1693, 4), for colour, excitement, attention, or simply for someone to listen or recognise their grievances.

Mary Glover's possession in 1602–3 brought together the full range of opinion. Like the Somers and Darling cases, it exposed the tensions between official Church of England and puritan attitudes, aroused the ire of the Bishop of London leading to the loss of office of at least one clergyman, and raised counter-narratives about witchcraft on the one hand and natural disease on the other. In addition, possession may have functioned strategically for Glover herself. Through the alibi of the devil, her social and family position changed. While in normal reality she showed "seemly and proper reverence" (Swan 1603, 300), through possession she can express forbidden emotions, "fierce... scornfully disdaining... threatening" (315), forbidden bodily functions, belching and spitting (317), forbidden gender transgression (317), forbidden actions, "violently... resist[ing]" adult authority (321), and forbidden language. Her mouth became "excessively wide", her tongue "black and curled

112 *Jacqueline Pearson*

inward", "Her voice loud, fearful, and very strange" (315–16): most sinisterly an aggressive demonic voice issued out of her nostrils (Almond 2004, 288), While possession appeared to deprive her of "freedom of speech" (303) and agency, it also paradoxically allowed her "free liberty of speech" and a new and reinforced agency since she alone can "procure her own deliverance" (307).

In particular, she seizes a role in the community, and family, narrative. At the climactic moment of her dispossession, Mary, previously unable to speak, appropriates the heroic dying words of her Marian martyr grandfather (Swan 1603, 318), writing herself into a central place in her community's master-narrative of Protestant victory over the forces of evil. A family narrative is also clearly involved, though we lack the information to flesh this out in detail. Possession gains her more of her mother's time and attention, and by appropriating her grandfather's words, she reasserts a family as well as a community identity; a kinsman greets her with "you are now again one of us" (320), and she re-enters her community and family but in an improved position, as she is welcomed back by her weeping mother and father. Glover may have been the innocent victim of a demonic attack, a hypocrite, or a hysteric – all three positions were vigorously argued in 1603 – but it is more likely that no single diagnosis is adequate. For her, and others like her, possession was a resource, providing "strategies for being heard", which may suggest hypocrisy but need not be confined to it (Clark 2001, 12).

Possession behaviour may constitute a strategy for avoiding familial neglect or abuse, and for revealing household tensions, which cannot be directly admitted in normal ways. Edward Nyndge, Oxford 'Master of Arts' (Nyndge 1616, sig. A3), used the occasion of his brother's possession to assert both his own authority – the "evill spirit" admitted being "marvellously afraid" of his learning and godliness – and that of his puritan community, rebuking Catholic neighbours who invoke the Virgin Mary, and insisting on austere Protestant scripturalism as the only proper way to achieve Alexander's "deliverance" (sig. B3r). From Alexander's perspective, the story may, as it chronicles an extraordinary tale of demonic possession, imply a much more mundane narrative of family tensions and a young man's struggle to find a place amongst competing siblings, especially in relation to the smug Edward who places such emphasis on his MA.

The Starkie children used possession performances to bring about the arrest and execution of the cunning man Edmond Hartley, who was first employed to cure their alarming symptoms and was then accused of bewitching them. While contemporary observers probably supposed that Hartley persistently, and against their will, kissed the children and the maids as a way of bewitching them, we could also read the story as one of sexual harassment decisively punished (More 1600, 16–17). Katherine Wright, long abused by her stepfather, found he treated her better when

"*Much like the Picture of the Devill in a Play*"   113

she was possessed, so her possession spoke of and moderated his abuse of her (Sands 2004, 109–26). Hannah Crump, when possessed, burned her sister's arm with a brand from the fire "the breadth of a shilling that the skin shrivelled off presently", which also suggests that possession removed inhibitions about acting on family tensions and rivalry (Barrow 1664, 19). Such performances may be in part consciously hypocritical, but it may be more plausible to read them as inventive but not fully self-conscious attempts to resolve otherwise insoluble family conflicts.

On 29 June 1663, twelve-year-old servant boy Thomas Sawdie went to the fair near his master's house in Cornwall, and was "very importunate with his Mother for money", but she "did deny him". Moreover, he had to leave the fair early to work. Sawdie was, perhaps, resentful at his poverty and pressures of work, and the immediate consequence was an encounter with "a Woman very gawdy, all in white", who offers him money. A demonised version of the mother who refused him, this "*spectrum*" morphs into a "great Black Dog" with "fiery eyes" which gives him money (Anon. 1664b, 1–2). This is only the beginning of a full-scale episode of demonic possession which lasts for seven weeks, marked by "several sorts of Fits" (3), bodily distortions and animalistic noises, superhuman strength and agility, violent behaviour, and claims to see the Devil in the shape of "a little man, with long fingers and great eyes, clad all in black" (5). In particular, Sawdie "would bellow, roar, and whistle" when the scriptures were read or during religious services (5), and insults the clerics who come to help him, calling them fools and "Black Rogues" (8–9), safe in the alibi of demonic possession.

The dissenting clergymen who minister to him and the pamphlet author are convinced that Sawdie is no hypocrite, but at the same time his possession is clearly scripted by those things that concern him most at that moment, his quarrel with his mother, his desire for money, and tensions over the restrictions of nonconformist religiosity and his servant role. Diane Purkiss argues that for another possessed adolescent, Margaret Muschamp, the performance of possession "allowed a range of fantasy ways out of the impasses of the mother-daughter bond" (Purkiss 1998, 247) and the story of Thomas Sawdie suggests that it may offer fantasy ways to evade other social and familial "impasses", here involving both mother–son and master–servant bonds. Possession also expresses and supports the twelve-year-old servant's reluctance to grow up and enter the adult male world of work and responsibility. While possessed he speaks in a "childish fawning voice" (6), "making a Childish noise" (9), and acts out childish fantasies involving unlimited noise and defiance of his so-cial superiors. The episode is brought to an end not so much by the dis-possessing power of the clergymen as, like Mary Glover's, by the child's decision to end it by announcing that the devil has left. At this point the boy still "could not stand alone, nor had strength to feed himself, but was fed on a Womans knees as a child" (12). The narrative that begins with

114 *Jacqueline Pearson*

a quarrel between mother and son ends with his achieving an extended period of mothering. Moreover, his master now "keeps him to School", so he receives an education and is allowed to remain a child (14). In an age where masculinity was by definition "anxious" (Breitenberg 1996) and "unstable" (Van Dijkhuizen 2007, 188), this retrogression to childhood, through the means of demonic possession, may be a good solution for a twelve-year-old servant who dreams of leisure, wealth, irresponsibility, and endless mothering. The mechanisms through which this is achieved, though, seem more complex, less under conscious control, than hypocrisy.

It was in the interests of Harsnett, Taylor, and their masters to convict demoniacs of hypocrisy, and in the interest of their ministers and communities to deny those charges. But interpreting possession requires a more complex approach than the simple binary of mere hypocrisy or authentic supernatural occurrence. Thomas Darling did not define his experiences as possession until this word was put into his mind, and what might have seemed to one observer a legitimate spiritual experience like conversion, looked to another like hypocrisy, to a third like a natural illness such as hysteria, to a fourth like the results of witchcraft. As Tom Webster has reminded us, if we are to understand possession texts and the culture that produced them, we should "accept the reality of the discourse of possession", and above all be sensitive to "the positioned nature" (Webster 2008, 110–11) of all early modern accounts. Harsnett's, or Taylor's, charges of hypocrisy should not be equated with scientific rationalism, but understood as one self-interested political position amongst many. Possession might be "learned behaviour", and therefore easy to equate with hypocrisy, but the same is true of a number of social behaviours which are "carefully scripted performances" (Almond 2004, 40–1) without necessarily being inauthentic or hypocritical. Demoniacs may have been "performers in religious dramas who were following scripts they learned from others", but that they by definition "assumed dramatic roles" does not necessarily equate with hypocrisy (Levack 2013, viii–ix). Narratives of the devil permitted people "to talk about things they could not say or that could not be said" (Clark 2001, 12) in any other way, and if, to some suspiciously, "experience coincided with the narrative tradition" (Hall 1989, 85), this may have less to do with hypocrisy than with the ways individuals use stories "to interpret existence, make judgements, and solve problems" (Gaskill 2001, 56) in ways which are culturally legible.

Works Cited

Abbott, George. 1600. *An Exposition upon the Prophet Ionah*. London: Richard Field.
Adams, Thomas. 1615. *The Blacke Devil or the Apostate*. London: William Jaggard.

"Much like the Picture of the Devill in a Play" 115

———. 1626. *Fiue Sermons*. London: Aug. Matthewes and John Norton for John Grismand.

Allen, Hannah. 1683. *A Narrative of God's Gracious Dealing with that Choice Christian Mrs Hannah Allen*. London: John Wallis.

Almond, Philip C. 2004. *Demonic Possession and Exorcism in Early Modern England*. Cambridge: Cambridge University Press.

Anon. 1584. *A True and Most Dreadfull Discourse of a Woman Possessed with the Devill*. London: J. Kingston for Thomas Nelson.

———. 1593. *The Most Strange and Admirable Discovery of the Three Witches of Warboys*. London: Thomas Man and John Winnington.

———. 1664a. *Advice of a Father*. London: Printed for the Author.

———. 1664b. *A Return of Prayer: Or a Faithful Relation of Some Remarkable Passages of Providence Concerning Thomas Sawdie*. London: s.n.

———. 1677. *Wonderful News from Buckinghamshire, or, a Perfect Relation How a Young Maid Hath Been for Twelve Years and Upwards Possest with the Devil*. London: D. M.

———. 1681. *Strange and Wonderful News from Yowel in Surry*. London: J. Clarke.

———. 1683. *A Whip for the Devil or, the Roman Conjurer*. London: Thomas Malthus.

———. 1687, *News from Pannier-Alley: or, a True Relation of Some Pranks the Devil Hath Lately Play'd*. London: Randal Taylor.

———. 1702. *The Tryal of Richard Hathaway, Upon an Information for Being a Cheat and Impostor*. London: Isaac Cleave.

Baring-Gould, Sabine. 1908. *Devonshire Characters and Strange Events*. London: J. Lane.

Barrow, John. 1664. *The Lords Arm Stretched Out in an Answer of Prayer*. London: s.n.

Batman, Stephen. 1581. *The Doome, Warning All Men to the Judgement*. London: Ralph Nubery assigned by Henry Bynneman.

Booy, David (ed.). 2007. *The Notebooks of Nehemiah Wallington, 1618–1654: A Selection*. Aldershot and Burlington: Ashgate Press.

Breitenberg, Mark. 1996. *Anxious Masculinity in Early Modern England*. Cambridge: Cambridge University Press.

Clark, Stuart. 1999. *Thinking with Demons: The Idea of Witchcraft in Early Modern Europe*. Oxford: Oxford University Press.

———. 2001. Introduction to *Languages of Witchcraft: Narrative, Ideology and Meaning in Early Modern Culture*, edited by Stuart Clarke, 1–18. Basingstoke: Macmillan.

Davenport, John. 1646. *The Witches of Huntingdon*. London: W. Wilson, for Richard Clutterbuck.

Davy, Sarah. 1670. *Heaven Realized, or, the Holy Pleasure of Daily Intimate Communion with God*. London: Printer unknown.

Ferber, Susan. 2004. *Demonic Possession and Exorcism in Early Modern France*. London: Routledge.

———. 2009. "Possession and the Sexes". In *Witchcraft and Masculinities in Early Modern Europe*, edited by Alison Rowlands, 214–38. Basingstoke: Palgrave Macmillan.

116 *Jacqueline Pearson*

G. Co. 1598. *A Breife Narration of the Possession, Dispossession and Repossession of William Sommers*. Amsterdam: s.n.

Gaskill, Malcolm. 2001. "Witches and Witnesses in Old and New England". In *Languages of Witchcraft: Narrative, Ideology and Meaning in Early Modern Culture*, edited by Stuart Clarke, 55–80. Basingstoke: Macmillan.

Gauld, Alan, and Anthony D. Cornell. 1979. *Poltergeists*. London: Routledge Kegan Paul.

Gibson, Marion. 2006. *Possession, Puritanism and Print*. London: Pickering and Chatto.

Greenblatt, Stephen. 1989. *Shakespearean Negotiations: The Circulation of Social Energy in Renaissance England*. Berkeley: University of California Press.

Hall, David. 1989. *Worlds of Wonder, Days of Judgement: Popular Religious Belief in Early New England*. New York: Alfred A. Knopf.

Harsnett, Samuel. 1599. *A Discovery of the Fraudulent Practises of Iohn Darrel*. London: John Wolfe.

———. 1603. *A Declaration of Egregious Popish Impostures*. London: James Roberts.

Hart On-Hi. 1647. *Trodden down Strength, by the God of Strength, or, Mrs Drake Revived*. London: R. Bishop for Stephen Pilkington.

Hodgkin, Katharine. 2007. *Madness in Seventeenth-Century Autobiography*. Basingstoke: Palgrave Macmillan.

Howson, Robert. 1698. *The Second Part of the Boy of Bilson: Or, a True and Particular Relation of the Impostor, Susanna Fowles*. London: E. Whitlock.

I. D. 1597. *The Most wonderfull and true Storie, of a certaine Witch named Alse Gooderige*. London: I. O.

Jackson, Louise. 1995. "Witches, Wives and Mothers: Witchcraft Persecution and Women's Confessions in Seventeenth-Century England". *Women's History Review* 4: 63–84.

James VI. 1597. *Daemonologie in Forme of a Dialogue*. Edinburgh: Robert Waldegrave.

Jessey, Henry. 1647. *The Exceeding Riches of Grace Advanced by the Spirit of Grace, in an Empty Nothing Creature, viz. Mris. Sarah Wight*. London: Matthew Simmons for Henry Overton and Hannah Allen.

Johnstone, Nathan. 2006. *The Devil and Demonism in Early Modern England*. Cambridge: Cambridge University Press.

Jollie, Thomas. 1697. *The Surey Demoniack, or an Account of Satan's Strange and Dreadful Actings, in and about the Body of Richard Dugdale of Surey*. London: Printed for Jonathan Robinson.

———. 1698. *A Vindication of the Surey Demoniack as No Impostor, or, a Reply to a Certain Pamphlet Publish'd by Mr. Zach. Taylor*. London: Printed for Neville Simmons and sold by A. Baldwin.

Jorden, Edward. 1603. *A Briefe Discourse of a Disease Called the Suffocation of the Mother*. London: John Windet.

King James Bible. 1613. *The Holy Bible Containing the Old Testament, and the New: Newly Translated Out of the Original Tongues... By His Majesties Speciall Commandement*. London: Robert Parker.

Kirby, Richard. 1693. *Dreadful News from Wapping: Being a Further Relation of the Sad and Miserable Condition of Sarah Bower*. London: W. D.

"*Much like the Picture of the Devill in a Play*" 117

Lea, Deborah. 2011. "Witchcraft, Possession and Confessional Tension in Early Modern Lancashire". PhD diss., University of Liverpool.

Levack, Brian P. 2013. *The Devil Within: Possession and Exorcism in the Christian West*. New Haven, CT and London: Yale University Press.

M. Y. 1669. *The Hartford-Shire Wonder: or, Strange News from Ware*. London: John Clark.

Martin, Randall. 2005. "Henry Goodcole, Visitor of Newgate: Crime, Conversion, and Patronage". *The Seventeenth Century* 20: 153–85.

Maxwell-Stuart, P. G. 2011. *Poltergeists: A History of Violent Ghostly Phenomena*. Stroud: Amberley.

More, George. 1600. *A True Discourse Concerning the Certaine Possession and Dispossessio[n] of 7 Persons in one Familie in Lancashire*. Middleburg: Richard Schilders.

Newton, John. 2008. "Introduction: Witchcraft; Witch Codes; Witch Act". In *Witchcraft and the Act of 1604*, edited by John Newton and Jo Bath, 1–28. Leiden and Boston: Brill.

Nyndge, Edward. 1616. *A True and Fearefull Vexation of one Alexander Nyndge*. London: W.B.

Oldridge, Darren. 2000. *The Devil in Early Modern England*. Stroud: Sutton, 2000.

Perrault, François. 1658. *The Devil of Mascon*, translated by Peter du Moulin. Oxford: Hen. Hall for Rich. Davis.

Petto, Samuel. 1693. *A Faithful Narrative of the Wonderful and Extraordinary Fits which Mr. Tho. Spatchet (Late of Dunwich and Cookly) was under by Witchcraft*. London: John Harris.

Pickering, Andrew, and David Pickering. 2010. *Witch-Hunting in England*. Stroud: Amberley.

Purkiss, Diane. 1996. *The Witch in History: Early Modern and Twentieth-Century Representations*. London: Routledge.

———. 1998. "Invasions: Property and Bewitchment in the Case of Margaret Muschamp". *Tulsa Studies in Women's Literature* 17: 235–53.

R. B. 1622. *The Boy of Bilson: or, a True Discovery of the Late Notorious Impostures of certaine Romish Priests in their Pretended Exorcisme, or Expulsion of the Diuell out of a young boy, named William Perry*. London: F. K. for William Barret

———. [i.e. Nathaniel Crouch]. 1688. *The Kingdom of Darkness*. London: Nathaniel Crouch.

Raiswell, Richard. 1999. "Faking It: A Case of Counterfeit Possession in the Reign of James I". *Renaissance and Reformation* 23: 29–48.

Robbins, Rossell Hope. 1959. *The Encyclopedia of Witchcraft and Demonology*. London: Spring Books.

Sands, Kathleen R. 2004. *Demon Possession in Elizabethan England*. Westport: Praeger.

Sharpe, James A. 1996 "Disruption in the Well-Ordered Household: Age, Authority, and Possessed Young People". In *The Experience of Authority in Early Modern England*, edited by Paul Griffiths, Adam Fox and Steve Hindle, 187–212. Basingstoke: Palgrave Macmillan.

———. [1999] 2000. *The Bewitching of Anne Gunter*. London: Profile Books.

118 *Jacqueline Pearson*

Sinclair, George. 1685. *Satan's Invisible World Discovered*. Edinburgh: John Reid.

Skinner, John. 1681–84. *A Strange and Wonderful Relation of Margaret Gurr*. London: I.W., I.C., W. T. and C. P.

Stearne, John. 1648. *A Confirmation and Discovery of Witch-Craft*. London: William Wilson.

Swan, John. 1603. *A True and Brief Report, of Mary Glovers Vexation*. In *Demonic Possession and Exorcism in Early Modern England* by Philip C. Almond, 2004, 291–330. Cambridge: Cambridge University Press.

Taylor, Zachary. 1683. *A Disswasive from Contention*. London: John Gain for William Cadman.

———. 1696. *The Devil Turn'd Casuist or the Cheats of Rome*. London: Peter Buck.

———. 1697. *The Surey Impostor Being an Answer to a Late Fanatical Pamphlet, entituled the Surey demoniack*, London: John Jones and Ephraim Jonston.

———. 1698. *Popery, Superstition, Ignorance and Knavery, Confess'd, and Fully Proved on the Surey Dissenters*. London: John Jones and Ephraim Jonston.

Van Dijkhuizen, Jan Frans. 2007. *Devil Theatre: Demonic Possession and Exorcism in English Renaissance Drama, 1558–1642*. Cambridge: D. S. Brewer.

Watkins, Owen C. 1972. *The Puritan Experience*. London: Routledge Kegan Paul.

Webster, Tom. 2008. "(Re)Possession of Dispossession: John Darrell and Diabolical Discourse". In *Witchcraft and the Act of 1604*, edited by John Newton and Jo Bath, 91–112. Leiden and Boston, MA: Brill.

Westaway, Jonathan, and Richard D. Harrison. 1996. "'The Surey Demoniack': Defining Protestantism in 1690s Lancashire". In *Unity and Diversity in the Church*, edited by Robert Norman Swanson. *Studies in Church History* 32: 263–82.

7 Abject Hypocrisy
Gender, Religion, and the Self

Katharine Hodgkin

In 1628 John Earle's *Micro-cosmographie* presented a series of fifty or so contemporary character types, satirising the vices and follies of his age. All but two of these were male. Women, defined by their social roles as daughters, wives, and mothers, could not be readily incorporated into a list of types such as "a mere dull physitian", "an Alderman", or "an upstart knight". The two female characters who make it into the catalogue are "A Handsome Hostess" and a religious woman: "A Shee precise Hypocrite", who "is so taken up with Faith, shee ha's no roome for Charity, and understands no good Workes, but what are wrought on the Sampler". Earle's female hypocrite is represented in a series of stereotypes relating to both femininity and piety. Modesty in dress signifies false pride, and disguises the corruption underneath; she is "a Nonconformist in a close Stomacher and Ruffle of Geneva Print, and her puritie consists much in her Linen". Her chastity is questionable; she "rayles at the Whore of Babylon for a naughty woman", but she "marries in her tribe without a ring", goes miles to hear her favourite preachers, and thinks adultery a lesser sin than swearing. She ill-treats her maidservants while quoting scripture, resents not being allowed to preach, and is greedy – "what shee cannot at the Church, shee do's at the Table, where she prattles more then any against sense and *Antichrist*, till a Capon wing silence her" (Earle [1628] 1811, 94–9). Vain, overbearing, and driven by bodily appetites, she represents the performance of virtue with none of the substance.

She is also a durable figure, recurring in books of characters on and off over the next century (many of which echo Earle's), and strikingly consistent in her sins. By 1708 the "Female Hypocrite, or Devil in Disguise" wears the best silk and linen, but "rails at the Women of the World as Damn'd, for Wearing Fringes on their Petticoats; and Wears her own Plain, that she may take 'em up with lesser Trouble and Inconvenience." Sexual incontinence is foregrounded here as her primary vice:

> wearing *Lace* is a greater Sin in her Esteem, than Fornication, or Adultery... in *Company*, she's as Demure as a Saint; but take her

> Alone, she's as Gamesom as [a li]ttle *Cat* in a *Corner*, and will
> *Tee-Hee* at a Smutty Jest, and be as Brisk and Obliging, as the
> Rankest Sinner.
>
> (Anon. 1708, 7–9)

Women, for these satirists, are all about unseemly appetites, which they are experts in concealing; and religion for them is a useful disguise. As Robert Burton remarks, bad wives are "saints in shew, so cunningly can they dissemble, they will not so much as look on another man in his presence, so chaste, so religious, and so devout... Many of them seem to be precise and holy forsooth" (Burton [1621] 1926, 317–18). Sexual and spiritual untrustworthiness are figured as versions of one another.

Hypocrisy in early modern culture is a pervasive but unstable preoccupation. It ties into a set of wider cultural anxieties about dissimulation and pretence, which are particularly insistent at this period; courtiers, clergymen, actors, women, all generate disquiet about how the self may be performed rather than authentic. And as Earle's female hypocrite suggests, the deceitfulness of women is a natural match for the deceitfulness of puritans in popular satire. The seventeenth century gives a particular spin to the ancient trope of feminine falsehood by attaching it to ostentatious religiosity. Stereotypical puritans are by no means always female, and nor are stereotypical hypocrites; the lengthy and intense discussions of how to tell if one is a hypocrite in early modern spiritual literature do not focus their attention particularly on women. Nonetheless, femininity is a significant element in these discussions. The long-established misogynist tradition that sees women as natural dissimulators, whose outsides are charming but insides repulsive, is readily borrowed by devotional writers, both as description and metaphor: analyses of hypocrisy as a gap between inside and outside lean heavily on the imagery of feminine deceitfulness. The woman's body figures hypocrisy whether in its fraudulent seductiveness, or in its equally deceptive appearance of piety.

Hypocrisy interrupts the relation between inner and outer: the person you see on the surface is not what you get on the inside. The gap that opens here is a crucial one for religious thinkers of the early modern period. Across two centuries and many different shades of religion, writers of devotional texts, sermons, polemics and autobiographies wrestle with the unresolvable question of how to be sure that what appears to be is the same as what is; that outward virtue is genuinely an index of inward grace. And hypocrisy from a religious perspective has another, still more destabilising meaning, referring not only to those who pretended to piety, but those who mistakenly believed in their own faith, supposing themselves to be elect when in fact they were not. This makes it a peculiarly anxious, indeed agonising, topic for the many writers in doubt about whether they had true faith (Stachniewski 1991, 91–3). The secrets of the heart, self-examination, self-knowledge, true prayer, true

Abject Hypocrisy 121

repentance – all these are endlessly debated. Where inner and outer fail to correspond, the reason is hypocrisy.

The uneasy relation between inner and outer also recalls Julia Kristeva's association of hypocrisy with abjection. Abjection in her account is a psychic mode which signifies a disturbance at the boundary between inside and outside, something which troublingly belongs in both places and in neither, something hard to classify. It is also specifically about transgressions of the boundaries of the body: things that move between the surface of the body and its inside are experienced as abject, pushed away (a meaning also active in early modern spiritual writing, where to be abject from the Lord is to be cast off and excluded, as well as cast down and abased). More broadly, abjection is concerned with the clean and the unclean; with law, prohibition, and the sacred; with the maternal, and the constitution of the subject (Kristeva 1982).

Kristeva's elaboration of the concept highlights the ambiguity of hypocrisy, both in its performance of discontinuity between inner and outer, and as it is implicated in both body and mind, in ways which resonate with early modern preoccupations. Religious hypocrisy is in one sense a sin of the imagination, comparable to committing the sin against the Holy Ghost, or witchcraft; it exists in the mind of the person who is or who fears to be a hypocrite. But it is also inescapably an embodied sin. It is about clothes, deportment, gestures, eyes, as well as hidden appetites and secret sins of the flesh; and all these are insistently present in early modern discussions.

For the godly, hypocrisy is a recurrent and complex anxiety. Devotional writers repudiate the identification of religious fervour with hypocrisy, while simultaneously demanding that believers engage in intense self-interrogation to ensure that they are not unwitting hypocrites. Spiritual autobiographers worry over their own failures of sincerity, or identify their earlier religious professions as hypocritical; they attack the hypocrisy of others; they vehemently contradict those who accuse them of it. Anxieties over hypocrisy and dissimulation perhaps have a particular resonance for women. The ideal of the godly woman, offered in devotional texts as a pattern of female virtue, is at the same time unsettled by her association with dissimulation, and women's innate deceitfulness is often exemplified by their ostentatious religiosity; hypocrisy itself, too, is regularly personified as female. A woman writing an account of her spiritual life is potentially shadowed by association with hypocrisy, both as woman and as religious.

This chapter explores some of the ways in which hypocrisy is imagined, embodied, and gendered in early modern spiritual writing. In drawing on a range of devotional and autobiographical writings from across the seventeenth century, I have inevitably tended to flatten out and simplify difference, both across time and across confessional boundaries. There are important shifts in the course of the century, in emphasis

122 *Katharine Hodgkin*

and interpretation, in doctrine, and in the specific meanings of the term. Nonetheless, throughout the period hypocrisy, representing that which is cast out from God and the self, remains a destabilising force lurking at the heart of what should be a pure and solid interior, and a perennial reminder of the unknowability of the subject, whether self or other.

Hypocrites by Nature: Women and Puritans

The assumption that dissimulation is pre-eminently and archetypally a woman's vice, all too familiar in early modern culture (and indeed for many centuries before), is construed as a gap between inside and outside. Women are never what they appear to be; they weep to get their own way; their pretended love deceives silly helpless men into docility; their pretended virtue tricks the same men into marriage, only to discover too late that they have married a fiend. As Joseph Swetnam describes it in his *Arraignment of Lewd Idle Froward and Unconstant Women* (1615):

> a woman that hath a fair face it is ever matched with a cruell heart, and hir heavenly looks with hellish thoughts, their modest countenance with merciless minds, for women can both smooth and sooth... they beare two tongues in one mouth like *Judas*, and two hearts in one breast ... and all to deceive the simple and plaine meaning men.
>
> (Swetnam 1615, 4–5)

And the imagery here highlights how the body itself encodes deceit: beauty and smoothness conceal the two tongues in the mouth, the two hearts in the breast.

The association of women with dissimulation is also pervasive in less openly misogynist texts, not least because (also notoriously) women are very keen on outward display. The decoration of the body is seen as their overriding concern, and the identification of dress with deceit and with women's vices is universal. As Thomas Wright observes, "apparrell of the bodie, declareth well the apparrell of the mind":

> Much might be said here concerning the newfangle madnesse, or lascivious pride, or vaine superfluities, of womens pointing, painting, adorning, and fantasticall disguising: but I must say this vice in them to be remedilesse, because it hath bene in every age, ever cried against, and never amended.
>
> (Wright 1604, 137–8)

Dress encodes many anxieties. Vanity in costume may provoke lust; it may lead to confusion about status, as both men and women put on furs, silks, and velvets unsuited to their rank; it may lead even more alarmingly to gender confusion, as men turn effeminate and women wear doublets and hats.

Abject Hypocrisy   123

Too much attention to the outside will lead to a neglect of the inside, as Richard Brathwait reminds his readers in *The English Gentlewoman*: "Miserable is the condition of that Creature, who, so her skin be sleake, cares not if her soule be rough. So her outward habit be pure and without blemish, values little her inward garnish" (Brathwait 1641, 277). More seriously, it implies not merely neglecting that inward garnish, but actively concealing the true self: "you are to be *really*, what you appeare *outwardly*", he insists (1641, 330). And as the full title of the book suggests (*The English Gentlewoman, set out to the full body...*), it is specifically the body that declares the soul. Brathwait highlights the problem of correspondence between inside and outside, between the adornment of the body and the corruption of the heart:

> Many desire to appeare most to the *eye*, what they are least in *heart*. They have learned artfully to gull the world with apparances; and deceive ... with vizards and semblances. These can enforce a smile, to perswade you of their affability; counterfeit a blush, to paint out their modesty; walke alone, to expresse their love to privacy ... Their speech is minced, their pace measured, their whole posture so cunningly composed, as one would imagine them terrestriall Saints at least, whereas they are nothing less than what they most appear.
> (1641, 335)

The reference to saints is significant; for it is particularly in relation to godliness that Brathwait expects to find deception, as well as where it is most reprehensible. Women's insincerity is written on their bodies, whether by their inability to resist fine clothes, which proclaims their vanity, or conversely by the inner corruption which is concealed by an embodied performance of virtue.

Saintly behaviour masking a devil within is a contrast with a more or less proverbial status. Swetnam refers to women who are "like a Saint abroad but a Devill at home"; Brathwait to those "who are Saints in their tongues, but Divels in their lives" (Brathwait 1641, 384; Swetnam 1615, 63). However, the phrase is not restricted to women. Joseph Hall uses the same expression to characterise the pious hypocrite, who is "an Angell abroad, a Devill at home; and worse when an Angell, than when a Devill". This underlines the point that if dissimulation is the vice of women, hypocrisy is the vice of the godly (Hall 1634, 170). That the excessively pious were untrustworthy hypocrites is a standard satirical and theatrical assumption; Malvolio in Shakespeare's *Twelfth Night* and Zeal-of-the-land Busy in Jonson's *Bartholomew Fair* are amongst a troop of self-seeking, greedy, avaricious puritans on the early modern stage (Collinson 1995). If for the godly, holy behaviour was a mark of purity within and of separation from the vices of the world, for their critics it was a veil drawn over inner corruption. Beneath an illusory

124 *Katharine Hodgkin*

goodness, puritans were self-seeking and deceitful, full of hate, greed, and lust that they hid from the world, but would happily indulge in secret.

Hypocrisy in Devotional Literature: The Inside and the Outside

The popular stereotype of the hypocritical puritan was thus one that the pious expected to encounter. The Nonconformist minister Richard Baxter warns,

> Christians, you must not only *be sincere*, but patiently expect to be *accounted hypocrites*, and pointed at as the only dissemblers in the world: You must not only *be honest*, but patiently expect to be *accounted dishonest*.... You must not only *be chaste and temperate*; but also patiently expect to be defamed as incontinent and licentious.
> (Baxter 1660, 254–5)

Samuel Torshell, in *The Hypocrite Discovered and Cured*, worries that his book may feed the prejudices of those who scorn religion: "I know that all speech of and against Hypocrisie is acceptable to prophane men", he comments, "who... doe account every *Professour* to be an *Hypocrite*, and doe hate the godly under this pretence, that they are Hypocrites" (Torshell 1644, 2). And Samuel Crook, in his massive tome on hypocrisy *Ta Diapheronta*, bitterly resents the eagerness with which the ungodly seize on reports of hypocrisy:

> Hence those malicious out-cries, veiled over with a seeming sorrow and amazement at the report; *Wot you what? would you think it? such an one* (I heare) *swore an oath*, or *was taken in a false tale: O! these pure ones; are the vilest people alive; under a shew of sanctity, they commit any wickednesse in the dark, &c.*
> (Crook 1658, 137)

The contested meanings of godliness in this period are played out in terms of a conflict between surface and inner truth. The principle that holiness is internal, depending on faith rather than deeds, is of course at the heart of the Protestant Reformation. But in practice there is still a widespread expectation that goodness should be realised in good deeds, rather than in good words alone. Inward faith should show itself to the world by shaping outward behaviour; but behaviour in turn must be the index of inner virtue, rather than mere performance. In the absence of visible virtues – charity, benevolence, continence – how could someone be supposed truly elect? But if good deeds were taken as evidence of election, then how could one distinguish between the person who appeared virtuous for hypocritical motives, and the person who truly was so? Hypocrisy is a problem not least because it destabilises the possibility of knowing what your neighbour is really like: the self is not transparent, and the heart (as countless writers note) is only known to God.

The spiritual self is ideally a single and consistent whole, in contrast to the hypocrite's duplicity. "Sincerity", declares Thomas Fuller in *The Holy State*, "is an entire thing in it self: Hypocrisie consists of several pieces cunningly closed together" (Fuller 1652, 374). Inconsistency is the mark of the hypocrite. "He is not the same privately, that publikely; betwixt God and himselfe, that before others; at home and abroad ...", according to Whately. "But the true Christian, he is fixed and constant, always the same, rooted, grounded, established, and doth not give himselfe over to changes and alteration" (Whately 1619, 30). The imagery of deceit dwells insistently on gaps and discontinuities: this person is not the same before God and before other people, at home and abroad, internally and externally. "[I]n the *carnal religion* of the Hypocrite", says Baxter, "the *outside*, which should be the *ornament* and *attendant* of the *inward spiritual* part, hath got the *Mastery*" (Baxter 1660, 69–70). The "inward Cells" of those who falsely pretend virtue, according to Brathwait, "like corrupt Charnell-houses, afford nothing but filthiness" (Brathwait 1641, 362). For Thomas Adams the very body of the hypocrite is composed of contradiction:

> A man of great Profession, little Devotion, is like a bodie so repugnantly composed, that he hath a hot liver, and a cold stomacke: that which cools the liver, ouerheats the stomacke ... zeale burnes in his tongue, but come neare this gloeworme, and he is cold, darke, squallid.
>
> (Adams 1613, 33)

The metaphors through which hypocrisy is explained articulate this discontinuity by opposing the visible with the hidden. A popular image contrasts the outside and the inside of physical spaces – rooms, houses, shops. "Yea, well may the Hypocrite afford gaudy facing, who cares not for any lining; brave it in the shop, that hath nothing in the ware-house", declares Fuller (1652, 374). The hypocrite's inner world is an unclean room, as William Whately explains (*Gods Husbandry*, 1619):

> dissemblers looke altogether to their outward or open actions and speeches, not regarding the thoughts and corruptions of their hearts.... So then the hypocrite hath little to doe with his heart ... hee takes small paines to resist and oppose, the secret and darke disorders of his soule. But the true Christian finds himselfe to haue a world of labour within.... A hypocrite (like a slothfull or sluttish seruants) leaues the nooks and corners vnswept, and vncleaned; the

126   *Katharine Hodgkin*

true Christian, (as a true louer of cleanlinesse, is carefull to ransacke, and purge euery corner of his soule).

(Whately 1619, 32–3)

Such metaphors recur in many accounts: "we white and parget the walles of our profession, but the rubbish and cobwebs of sin hang in the corners of our consciences", confirms Thomas Adams (Adams 1613, 33).

By some way the commonest metaphor for hypocrisy, though, is appearance, explicitly juxtaposing the outside and inside of the body. Hypocrites appear like the virtuous, but they do so to mislead. "The hypocrite is neat and curious in his religious out-side, but the linings of his conscience are *filthy and polluted rags*", says Adams, quoting Isaiah 64.6 (1613, 32). For Crook, it is "dishonourable and damnable to put on the external fashion and habit of sober, grave and devout Christians, without the inward substance and vertue". But, he continues, all too common, so long as a reputation for virtue is based on appearance:

never an harlot in the world shall be more disguised, nor more curiously pranked in a religious dresse ... then this smooth-boots in his looks, vesture and gesture, to seem honest, religious, wise, grave, and what not, but what he is? He covers a fowle heart under a fair face; an ulcerous soul under neat cloaths, a wanton heart under a modest habit, and a world of spiritual wickednesse under an affected gravity of carriage and behaviour.

(Crook 1658, 62)

And as Crook's reference to the harlot suggests, of course, it is in the context of harlots and Jezebels that this metaphor is most forcefully expressed. The foul, ulcerous, wanton interior evokes sexual licence alongside disease to underline the corrupt reality.

Repeatedly, devotional writers articulate the idea of hypocrisy through the image of the painted woman, whose decorated face conceals a rotten inside. For Baxter, "Hypocrisie as the Harlots paint, is but a base and borrowed beauty, that will vanish away when you draw neer the fire" (1660, 116). Evil, for Crook, "as an old *Jezabel* fills up her wrinkles with artificial dawbery"; he contrasts "true vertues, as the army of Christ marching in holy beauty", with "hypocrisie the devils *Jezabel* with her painted visage" (1658, 3, 5). The hypocrite's self-presentation as demure and pious is identified with the harlot's self-presentation as more beautiful than nature has made her: a disguise that aims to entice, indicating a wanton and lustful soul. "The *chastest* woman will *wash* her face", according to Baxter, "but it's the *harlot*, or *wanton*, or *deformed*, that will paint it... a *curious dress*, and *excessive care*, doth signifie a *crooked* or *deformed body*, or a filthy skin, or which is worse, an *empty soul*" (1660, 68–9).

Abject Hypocrisy 127

What is also significant about this popular image, of course, is that it reiterates the association of female dissimulation with hypocrisy more generally. Devotional books tend to take the male reader for granted, and the analyses and typologies of hypocrisy accordingly focus on the hypocritical man, although there are occasional references to female frailty (hypocrisy, notes Torshell, is "most naturall to women", though "the lesson of both Sexes... all ages, and conditions"; 1644, 8). But the insistently feminine figurations – the painted jezebels covering up corruption, the harlots disguising themselves as modest matrons – assimilate hypocrites to women in their use of the outside of the body (dress, gesture, speech) to disguise the sinful inside. Women's hypocrisy consists in falsely pretending to beauty, as well as to virtue. "If thou beest faire," demands Stubbes in the *Anatomie of Abuses*, citing St Ambrose, "why paintest thou thy selfe to seeme fairer? and if thou bee not faire, why doest thou hypocritically desire to seeme faire ...?" (Stubbes [1595] 2002, 109–10).

Along with duplicity and inconstancy, an excessive attention to the outside of the body with the aim of disguising the inside (whether by suggesting more than one's true beauty, or more than one's true piety) is thus a connecting thread between hypocrisy and femininity. The destabilising end point of this, of course, is that in the end the appearance of modesty itself becomes proof of its opposite:

> whores in old time [Gen. 38.14] did *put on vails*, covering their shamelesnesse with a more then ordinary semblance of shamefac'tnesse, and by that affected modesty were commonly discovered and reputed to be immodest and light.
>
> (Crook 1658, 62)

The more a woman's body displays the marks of virtue, in effect, the more sceptical the onlookers should be. Stubbes attacks women's dress and behaviour not only for vanity but even for attempting to appear modest:

> when they have attired themselves thus, in the midst of their pride, it is a world to consider their coynesse in gestures, their minsednes in words and speeches, their gingerlynesse in tripping on toes like young Goates, their demure nicitie, and babishnesse, and withall their haughty stomacks.
>
> (Stubbes [1595] 2002, 124)

The smooth-boots in neat clothes, the terrestrial saints with blushes and mincing walk, the soberly dressed matrons, all undermine the possibility of reading religion through dress: the codes that ought to identify

128 *Katharine Hodgkin*

a person's allegiances and piety have become unreadable. Godliness, supposedly legible on the body, connotes hypocrisy to the outsider; but even amongst the pious, where preachers urge their congregations to dress with sobriety, it is easy to be mistaken. "All sober Christians are friends to *outward decency* and *order*", Baxter reminds his listeners, but he knows that this friendship is easily faked. "For my part", he concludes,

> I shall pronounce no one of you personally to be an hypocrite, as knowing that hypocrisie is a sin of the heart, which in it self is seen by none but God and him that hath it: But my business is only to help such to know and judge themselves.
>
> (1660, 144–5)

Self-Knowledge and Its Problems

"To know and judge themselves": how is this to be achieved? For the godly, accusations of hypocrisy in the sense of wilful deception were less troubling than the agonising possibility that one might be the other kind of hypocrite – the kind that doesn't know it. As Richard Baxter points out, "besides the *gross* Hypocrite that knoweth he doth *dissemble*, and only deceiveth others, there are also *close* Hypocrites, that know not they are hypocrites, but deceive themselves" (1660, 49). Is godly conduct actually self-flattery, wishing to appear good in the eyes of others or even oneself, rather than evidence of true faith? The dizzying downward spirals of self-analysis generated by such questions are part of the preoccupation with truth and inwardness that characterises the autobiographical writings of the seventeenth century. How to know that one is truly what one claims and wishes to be is a complex matter.

Devotional writers throughout the century thus warn of the dangers of over-confidence amongst those who "know not themselves to be Hypocrites, but think themselves in a good estate and sound enough", as Torshell describes them (1644, 7). Self-satisfaction is perilous:

> There are a number of professors of religion in the Church, of whom all that know them, have a very good opinion: supposing them to be most worthy Christians; yea, which in their owne hearts doe verily thinke of themselves, that they be indeede the sonnes and daughters of God, and that they serve him, and not themselves; when as in very deed, they doe nothing else but couson themselves, and the whole world; for within, they also are very rottennesse, and serve themselves alone, and not the Lord Jesus Christ.
>
> (Whately 1619, 22)

Crook similarly warns of the fatal possibilities of error:

> it concerneth every man to know his own estate and not to hood wink himself through wilful blindnesse... thinking and presuming that he hath faith, and hath believed in God ever since he could remember.... Such even while they believe are Infidels. They be not the men they take themselves to be, they do not the thing which they suppose they do, as shal anon appear.
>
> (1658, 281)

"They be not the men they take themselves to be, they do not the thing which they suppose they do" – this is surely a fundamental challenge to the possibility of self-knowledge.

The differences between the hypocrite and the sincere Christian are extraordinarily hard to detect, because they are inward rather than outward. Thus Timothy Rogers explains, "In all outward actions, as Prayer, Hearing, Giving to the Poor, and the like, there may be a very great resemblance between a true Christian and an Hypocrite" (Rogers 1691, 294). Thomas Cooper opens *The Estates of the Hypocrite and Syncere Christian* with a dissection of the similarities between the two, which seems to suggest that the hypocrite will look not just convincing, but possibly more convincing than the real thing. The hypocrite not only "*In shew...* hath whatsoever the regenerate possesseth; nay he many times in shew goeth *beyond him*", but also "*In substance* hee hath much common with the regenerate, as first, communion of outward meanes of religion, the *Word, Sacrament, conference, example, &c.* Secondly, use of outward means, for this life in an outward manner, and for externall ends." On top of this he has "*Faith temporarie*", which gives him a misleading security, and even "In *Substance* he hath some graces, even beyond the Elect. As he may do *Miracles*, and have extraordinarie knowledge of manie mysteries" (1613, 6–8):

> Yea, he may *live* all his daies in prosperitie; that so hee may the rather flatter himselfe in the worth of his profession: and he may *die* in a glorious carnall peace, to the great stumbling of the world, and abusing of his vaine heart...
>
> (1613, 13)

Readers took such reminders to heart; in the British Library copy an early reader has underlined the final phrase in this passage.

The solution Cooper offers, classically, is self-examination and self-knowledge. "Labour wee, *sound and perticular knowledge of our estate*, and measure, by daily *viewing* our selves in the glasse of the word, and *examining our hearts*, and privie corruptions" he urges (1613, 44). The hypocrite who fails to recognise his condition, explains Whately, does so "because out of his abundant selfe-love... hee is loath

130 Katharine Hodgkin

to bestow paines, in searching and examining his owne heart" (1619, 23–4). The Baptist Jane Turner advises pursuing true inner knowledge as a guard against hypocrisy, recommending "meditation, self-watching, self-judging, self-humbling and prayer, which are indeed such duties, as no hypocrite can do" (Turner 1653, 185). Self-knowledge, in principle, should be the means to uproot one's own hypocrisy; it must be possible to find out that one is a hypocrite. "There is no hypocrite so cunning as to hide himself absolutely from himself", asserts Crook (1658, 9):

> Neither man, woman, nor devil can deceive thee with danger to thy soul, unless thine own heart be in the plot. Only by this a man becomes a seducer, a devil to himself...
>
> (1658, 12)

But how to identify the heart's complicity remains a problem. Given the impossibly blurred boundary between the two conditions, it is no wonder that professors struggled over the question of their own status. If one could live in prosperity, following religious duties, believing in one's own salvation, and eventually "die in a glorious carnall peace", how was anyone to know with any confidence whether their own faith was well founded, or whether the traces of sin and hypocrisy that they inevitably detected were in fact fatal?

The books that attempted reassurance on this subject were often anything but reassuring. The signs of religion may themselves be signs of hypocrisy; a self-examination that fails to find anything wrong is simply a self-examination that has not gone far enough. "[W]ho will totally clear himselfe? let me tell thee, if thou doest, thou art the worst hypocrite", declares Thomas Adams, in his 1612 sermon *The White Devil, or the Hypocrite Uncased*; "... he that sayes, he hath not sinned in hypocrisie, is the rankest hypocrite" (1613, 28). Adams does concede that not everyone who sins in hypocrisy is in fact a hypocrite, but still this is not a rhetoric calculated to comfort the anxious. Even those whose actions are entirely virtuous may still be hypocrites; everyone must acknowledge in themselves "the stinking guzzle of original sin" (Whately 1619, 50), and their unworthiness to be saved. Uncleanness is pervasive:

> the hypocrite... imagines, that no more evill abideth within, than shewes it selfe without... Now the true Christian... knowing the loathsome fouleness of his owne heart, and being well acquainted with the bottomlesse quagmire of his owne originall corruption, is still humble and base in his owne eyes.
>
> (Whately 1619, 60)

The hypocrite does not know himself as internally filthy – as abject, indeed; and abject also from God.

Whately's conclusion highlights once again the difficulty of preserving a balance between confidence and fear, and the limitations of self-knowledge:

> ... be jealous over your selves, feare much, suspect much, enquire much, and prevent the evill of securitie. I doe not wish you always to stand in suspence of your selves, and still to bee doubtfull, whether you bee true Christians or dissemblers; it is no part of my meaning, to drive you unto this uncomfortable uncertaintie. But I wish you not to make too much haste, to thinke your selves certaine, for feare your certaintie should prove but a certaine delusion.
>
> (1619, 85)

For many it seems likely that uncomfortable uncertainty was the best they could hope for. To be secure, in this theology, is never a good thing.

Hypocrisy in Spiritual Autobiography

How do the godly deal with these problems of self-knowledge and uncertainty? In particular, how do godly women, doubly identified with deceit, position themselves in relation to the idea of hypocrisy? While devotional writers focus on what might be called the technical meaning of hypocrisy, involving unwitting self-deceit, the common understanding of the hypocrite as someone wilfully performing virtue while covertly pursuing their own interests remains prominent, adding to the negative weight of the word. So it is perhaps not surprising that the identification of the self as hypocrite seems to be relatively unusual. To confess to hypocrisy is a fundamental attack on the integrity of the self and the truth of one's religious profession; and for the writers of spiritual autobiography, integrity, and sincerity are crucial. If the hostile ungodly world accuses saints of hypocrisy, the task of spiritual autobiography is to demonstrate the eventual coherence of inner and outer. Spiritual autobiographers emphasise their manifold imperfections and spiritual struggles, but ultimately the narrative must demonstrate that the writer has achieved true faith, and writes from a place of certainty. Hypocrisy is thus located somewhere else: in the past, in the world, in demonic temptation. Any uncomfortable uncertainties are narratively positioned as overcome.

In the progressive narrative of spiritual autobiography, often characterised by a series of supposed conversions, which turn out to be mistakes, earlier versions of the godly self may eventually be recognised as hypocritical. Bunyan, after his first reformation of manners, amazes his neighbours with his "great conversion", but it is not genuine: "But, oh!... I was nothing but a poor painted hypocrite" (Bunyan [1666] 2008, 13). Anna Trapnel, in the grip of "spirituall idolatry", was much

132 *Katharine Hodgkin*

attached to forms and duties, and "delighted in the thunderings of the Law", before recognising that she had been "as full of heart hypocrisie as I could hold" (Trapnel 1654, 4, 7). In a more reserved identification of the self as hypocritical, others place it as something they worried about, but (implicitly) did not need to. Katherine Sutton evidently spent some time studying contemporary writers on the topic. "I was much stirred up to mind," she recounts,

> *how far an Hypocrite might go in Religion:* And I began to consider, whether I had gone any further than such a one might go, for I saw plainly that a person might go very far, and yet be in a sad state, though they may be enlightened and tast of the heavenly gift, and be partakers of the holy Spirit... and also hear the best Preachers gladly... and yet be but almost a Christian.

As she exclaims, "Oh, what a knotty place was I to work upon!" (Sutton [1663] 2001, 3–4).

The devil plays an active part here; it is often suggested that he was behind anxiety over hypocrisy. Sarah Davy describes how Satan "would often persuade me I was a *hypocrite*, and that I was fallen from grace", but God helps her overcome this belief (Davy 1670, 9). Satan similarly told Vavasor Powell "that I was a Reprobate, and let me profess what I would, my Damnation was sure, and my hypocrisie, and sinnes under profession, would be worse than any other sinnes" (Powell 1671, 9). Hannah Allen, convinced throughout her long period of melancholy that she has always been a hypocrite, with hindsight explains her self-accusation as a result of satanic suggestion. Hypocrisy in her narrative is always associated with the devil, and frequently with delusion. Allen's recovery depends on her acknowledging not that she is a hypocrite and must move on to a truer faith, but that she is (at least implicitly) amongst the elect, and need not attend to devilish delusions. She has imagined a discontinuity between her inner corruption and her outward behaviour, which is not in fact there. When she assures her friends that she is "given up to work all manner of wickedness with greediness", both she and they imagine the nature of her sin as a question of what is internal and what is external:

> *We see no such thing in you*, would some say; I would Answer, Aye, but it is in my heart; *Why doth it not break out in Act?* say they, It will do ere long; said I.
>
> (Allen 1683, 50)

Instead, however, the queasy horror at what lurks inside waiting to break out is eventually defeated by her recovery from melancholy. Satan's role here is to bring hypocrisy, or the fear of hypocrisy, inside the self; the sufferer must then find a way of getting rid of it.

Abject Hypocrisy 133

Another way of displacing hypocrisy beyond the borders of the self is to locate it as the vice of others, and particularly in the communities of the profane. For the godly, hypocrisy is a mark of worldliness. The Quaker Susannah Blandford describes herself as one "not loving Hypocricy, nor a feigned imitation whereby I might deceive others, in what I was not truly to God"; Elizabeth Stirredge attributes hypocrisy more comprehensively to everything that she as a Quaker wants to separate herself from, believing "that the Lord would *Redeem* a People out of the *World*, and its *Ways*, and *Customs*, *Language*, *Marriage*, and *Burying*, and *All* the *World's* Hypocrisy" (Blandford 1698, 11; Stirredge 1711, 19).

An intriguing example of such distancing is to be found in the writings of the Anabaptist Anne Wentworth, who in the 1670s published a series of prophetic and autobiographical texts. In the first of her published works, *A true account of Anne Wentworths Being cruelly, unjustly and unchristianly dealt with by some of those people called Anabaptists* (1676), Wentworth inverts the association between women and deceit. Identifying hypocrisy implicitly with her husband (whom she had left), and explicitly with the male elders of her church, she locates herself as a pure and truthful person beset by dissemblers. Her husband, she claims in language that invokes the imagery of the clean outside and the polluted inside, is no true Christian:

> I know no gross sin that he is addicted too, nor never heard he was before he took up that form of Religion, to wash his body in water, the outside of the cup and platter, which stood in the least need, when his soul was never yet washed from the filth of his inbred natural corruption... I dare be bold to affirm that he never yet knew the new birth, the life of the new man; nor they must needs be no Saints or Christians in deed and in truth, nor know the new birth themselves, if they take him to be one that is born again, and examine but his carriage to a Wife this 23 years, not his carriage to the World before men, for that is fair enough; but what is it in secret, that God hath seen all along, and is angry at.
>
> (1676, 7)

The distinction between public and private self is portrayed as an embodied performance of virtue – cleansing the outside with the "form of Religion", but leaving the soul in filth. By contrast what speaks in Wentworth's own behaviour is her inward truth. "I am not a woman spending my time in the pleasures and vanities of the World," she declares, "and what my manner of life and conversation is, that is seen and known" (1676, 11). Truth also speaks in her body's external collapse. Twenty years of "being a dark, blind, formal professor", who "yet thought I was as zealous, and strong ... as any", left her both

134   *Katharine Hodgkin*

metaphorically and literally wrecked: her "dry, barren soul… eat up with blind zeal, and my soul starve for hunger" (1676, 14) literalised itself in the heat and aridity of fever:

> [I] was consumed to skin and bone, a forlorn sad spectacle to be seen, unlike a woman; for my days had been spent with sighing, and my years with crying, for day and night the hand of the Lord was heavy upon me, and my moisture was turned into the drought of Summer. *When I kept silence my bones waxed old through my roaring all the day long,* having an Hectiff Fever, which came through so great oppression, and sorrow of heart; and wanting vent, and smothering it so long in my own brest, grew so hot, and burnt so strong, that I was past all cure of man.
>
> (1676, 9)

This depiction of the body merges spiritual and humoural languages. Psalm 32.3–4 (which she quotes here) corresponds to the bodily experience by which the passions determine bodily health, and hectic fever is the result of sorrow. Weeping out her grief over many years, Wentworth is dried and heated into a fever; as a woman, too, constitutionally moist and cool, it is her female flesh that is consumed, leaving her "unlike a woman".

Wentworth's illness enacts precisely the correspondence in her of inner and outer, of soul and body: her embodiment of spiritual desolation demonstrates the truth and coherence of her entire being, in contrast to her husband's clean outside that in no way reflects his interior. The church elders, who are allied with this inwardly filthy husband, are similarly excluded from knowledge of true religion. In their attacks on her, she declares sarcastically, "there was either the truest piece of Christianity acted towards me, or else the greatest piece of Hypocrisie, Formality, and Idolatry". God's anger has been kindled, "and ere long he will blow it up into a Flame, so as all Formalitie and Hypocrisie shall tast and feel". Sensual experience will enforce a recognition of the distance that has grown between the inside and the outside, so that like her the elders will experience integrity (or its absence) as knowledge in the flesh (1676, 17).

For Wentworth, moreover, the conflict between her and these formal hypocrites is explicitly a gendered one. Her church, dominated by men, refuses to accept the justness of her cause, because of her sex:

> … I know no Man that is willing that God should Plead my cause, or that the Lord should discover Proud, Impious, hard hearted Men, and lay open Hypocrisie and formality, and look upon a poor weak despised Woman, that is trampled under the feet of men … they would rather have her Soul and Body lost and damned to all Eternity, as they have proved it themselves in what they have done to me.
>
> (1676, 19–20)

And in reiterating her own integrity she underlines further the nature of this opposition:

> this doth not come to the view of the World with eloquence of speech, nor any artificial dress, but in plainness of speech, in its own Mothers tongue, not set forth and adorned with the wisdom of men.
>
> (1676, 21–2)

Here she echoes the repeated association of hypocrisy with artifice and adornment, only to turn it on its head. Eloquence and decorative flourish is the wisdom of men; but she, the woman, will speak with simplicity, with (in a move that would surely have pleased Kristeva) her own mother's tongue refuting the words of men.

Hypocrisy as a spiritual sin is closely entangled with the feminine, both as a set of shared qualities – duplicity, dissembling, attention to the sleek outside of the body rather than its inner cleanliness – and as a rhetorical trope which highlights the discontinuity of the body's inside and outside through the metaphor of the painted woman. But it is also an unknowable condition; relegated to the body's inside, as a sin of the imagination, it is a constant threat to the integrity of the self. Once again Kristeva's characterisation of the place of sin is evocative:

> evil, displaced into the subject, will not cease tormenting him from within, no longer as a polluting or defiling substance, but as the ineradicable repulsion of his henceforth divided and contradictory being.
>
> (Kristeva 1982, 116)

This is about the shift from Old to New Testament, and sin replacing defilement. But the sense of defilement and pollution still attaches to sin, in the texts I have been discussing, precisely in the context of hypocrisy: the unclean inner space which unsettles the subject, refusing it knowledge of itself or of others. The hypocritical subject is not only divided and contradictory; he is ignorant of the extent of his division; he does not know that there are parts of himself he does not know about. Hypocrisy is where the great project of self-knowledge that drives so much spiritual autobiography collapses, as Samuel Crook's formulation makes clear ("he is not the man he thinks himself to be"); it is, in a perverse and abject way, a precursor of the unconscious. Hypocrisy, "crooked, selfe-covering and selfe-consuming", as Whately describes it, masks the self from the self (1619, 14).

Hypocrisy, I suggested earlier, is a sin of both mind and body; one that is paradoxically invisible, and focused above all on appearance. For early modern women in particular, it offers an ambiguous and problematic language to speak about the self. If, in certain ways, women were vulnerable

136 *Katharine Hodgkin*

to the figure of the hypocrite as dissimulator, its opposite could also offer a route out of conventional negative views of the feminine. The language of the true-hearted and sincere Christian, refocusing the gaze on inward truth, allows godly women to disown and distance themselves from the duplicitous feminine body that belongs to the hypocrite, as they distance themselves from bodily adornment in favour of plainness. Indeed, as with figures like the Whore of Babylon or the women who must not speak in church, reinterpreted within the sects as symbolising corruption in established religion, the dissembling woman is repudiated by actual women in favour of an assertion of integrity. If Wentworth is a lone voice in the explicitness with which she reinscribes the tropes of hypocrisy onto the masculine, she nonetheless speaks for many in asserting her integrity, and claiming to speak as subject rather than abject. Whether flesh and devil – the abject, as it were – can be so unconditionally pushed away, however, is another matter.

Works Cited

Adams, Thomas. 1613. *The White Devil, or the Hypocrite Vncased: in a sermon preached at Pauls Crosse, March 7 1612*. London: Melchisedech Bradwood for Ralph Mab.

Allen, Hannah. 1683. *A Narrative of Gods Gracious Dealings with that Choice Christian Mrs Hannah Allen*. London: John Wallis

Anon. 1708. *The True Characters of, viz. a Deceitful Petty-Fogger, Vulgarly Call'd Attorney. A Know-All Astrological Quack, or, Feigned Physician. A Female Hypocrite, or, Devil in Disguise. A Low-Churchman, or, Ecclesiastical Bisarius. A Trimmer, or, Jack of All Sides, &c*. London: J. Jones, near Fleet-Street.

Baxter, Richard. 1660. *The Vain Religion of the Formal Hypocrite, and the Mischief of an Unbridled Tongue (As against Religion, Rulers or Dissenters) Described, in Several Sermons Preached at the Abby in Westminster, before Many Members of the Honourable House of Commons*. London: R. W. [R. White] for F. Tyton; Kedderminster: N. Simmons.

Blandford, Susannah 1698. *A Small Account Given Forth by One that Hath Been a Traveller for These 40 Years in the Good Old Way*. London: s.n.

Brathwait, Richard. 1641. *The English Gentleman; and the English Gentlewoman; Both in One Volume Couched, and in One Modell Portrayed*. London: John Dawson.

Bunyan, John. [1666] 2008. *Grace Abounding, with Other Spiritual Autobiographies*, edited by John Stachniewski and Anita Pacheco. Oxford: Oxford University Press.

Burton, Robert. [1621] 1926. *The Anatomy of Melancholy*, edited by Arthur Richard Shilleto. London: G. Bell & Sons.

Collinson, Patrick. 1995. "Ecclesiastical Vitriol: Religious Satire in the 1590s and the Invention of Puritanism". In *The Reign of Elizabeth I: Court and Culture in the Last Decade*, edited by John Guy. Cambridge: Cambridge University Press.

Cooper, Thomas. 1613. *The Estates of the Hypocrite and Syncere Christian. Containing, Certaine Lively Differences, between Synceritie and Hypocrisie;*

Very necessarie, for the Tryall of our Estates in Grace. London: Thomas Creede for Arthur Johnson.

Crook, Samuel. 1658. *Ta Diapheronta, or Divine Characters in Two Parts, Acutely Distinguishing the more Secret and Undiscerned Differences between 1. The Hypocrite in His Best Dresse of Seeming Virtues and Formal Duties. And the True Christian in His Real Graces and Sincere Obedience...* London: C.B. and W.G., for A.B.

Davy, Sarah. 1670. *Heaven Realiz'd or the Holy Pleasure of Daily Intimate Communion with God.* London: A.P.

Earle, John [1628] 1811. *Micro-cosmographie, or, a Peece of the World Discovered, in Essayes and Characters*, edited by Philip Bliss. London: White and Cochrane.

Fuller, Thomas. 1652. *The Holy State.* London, R.D. for John Williams.

Hall, Joseph. 1634. *Characters of Vertues and Vices: in Two Bookes.* In The *Works of Joseph Hall, B. of Exeter. With a Table Now Added to the Same.* London. Nathaniel Butter.

Kristeva, Julia. 1982. *Powers of Horror: An Essay on Abjection*, translated by Leon Roudiez. New York: Columbia University Press.

Powell, Vavasor. 1671. *The Life and Death of Mr. Vavasor Powell.* [London?].

Rogers, Timothy. 1691. *A Discourse Concerning Trouble of Mind and the Disease of Melancholy.* London: T. Parkhurst and T. Cockerill.

Stachniewski, John. 1991. *The Persecutory Imagination: English Puritanism and the Literature of Religious Despair.* Oxford: Oxford University Press.

Stirredge, Elizabeth. 1711. *Strength in Weakness Manifest: in the Life, Various Trials, and Christian Testimony of that Faithful Servant and Handmaid of the Lord Elizabeth Stirredge.* London: Jane Sowle.

Stubbes, Philip. [1595, 1st ed. 1583] 2002. *The Anatomie of Abuses*, edited by Margaret Kidnie. Tempe, AZ: Renaissance Text Society.

Sutton, Katherine. [1663] 2001. *A Christian Womans Experiences.* Edited (extracts) in Elizabeth Skerpan Wheeler, *Life Writings I.* Aldershot: Ashgate.

Swetnam, Joseph. 1615. *The Arraignment of Lewd, Idle, Froward and Unconstant Women.* London: George Purslowe for Thomas Archer.

Torshell, Samuel. 1644. *The Hypocrite Discovered and Cured. A Discourse Furnished with Much Variety of Experimentall and Historicall Observations, and Most Seasonable for These Times of Happy Designe for Reformation. In two Bookes.* London: G.M. for John Bellamy.

Trapnel, Anna. 1654. *A Legacy for Saints; Being Several Experiences of the Dealings of God with Anna Trapnel, In, and after Her Conversion....* London: T. Brewster.

Turner, Jane. 1653. *Choice Experiences of the Kind Dealings of God, before, in, and after Conversion.* London: s.n.

Wentworth, Anne. 1676. *A True Account of Anne Wentworths Being Cruelly, Unjustly and Unchristianly Dealt with by Some of Those People Called Anabaptists.* [London].

Whately, William. 1619. *Gods Husbandry: The First Part. Tending to Shew the Difference Betwixt the Hypocrite and the True-Hearted Christian.* London: Felix Kyngston for Thomas Man.

Wright, Thomas. 1604. *The Passions of the Minde in General.* London: Valentine Simms for W. Burre.

8 Henry Hills and the Tailor's Wife

Adultery and Hypocrisy in the Archive

Michael Durrant

I

The printer-publisher, Henry Hills (*c*.1625–89), gained notoriety in large part because he worked for a variety of masters, serving as official printer to the New Model Army, Oliver Cromwell, his son Richard, Charles II, and finally James II. In doing so, Hills found himself labelled a *"Hypocrite"* (*A View* 1684), since many of his contemporaries saw Hills' willingness to jump ideological ship as an indication of his broader capacity to perform different roles while concealing his true intentions. This depiction stems not only from the fact that Hills worked "for a number of conflicting enterprises" (Stone Peters 1990, 53), but also because he spent much of his lifetime journeying between churches, starting off as a printer-preacher for the Particular Baptists in the 1650s and 1660s, and ending up a devout Catholic by 1685 via an alleged flirtation with the Church of England. Hills' confessional flexibility was of such notorious a variety that in 1932 J. G. Muddiman, the historian, declared (and not without some degree of admiration) that Hills is best described as "[t]he typographical vicar of Bray" (5): a real-world embodiment of the satirical Berkshire clergyman who, in order to retain his employment, hypocritically championed contrary beliefs in line with the various regime changes of the long seventeenth century.

Evidence related to Hills' sex life has traditionally reinforced the idea that his turncoatism was a symptom of his opportunistic disposition, rather than a situational response to the politico-religious vacillations that punctuated the period. The story goes that, in about 1650, Hills entered into a "scandalously open living arrangement" (Lynch 2007, 305) with "the wife of Thomas Hams, a Blackfriars tailor" (Walsh 2013, 109), and he is even said to have confessed to his adultery in a 1651 confession-cum-conversion account, *The Prodigal Returned to His Father's House*. The contents of this text, and the illicit circumstances under which it was composed, have often buoyed commentators' efforts to throw back the metaphorical "cloak" (*Revolution Politicks* 1733, 37) of his strategic mendacity, and to expose him for what he really was: that is, an "unpleasant and unreliable character" (Blagden 1960, 168).

Henry Hills and the Tailor's Wife 139

This chapter considers the possible origins of the story of Hills' adultery with the tailor's wife, and the way in which that act of sexual dishonesty has been treated, by his contemporaries and some later scholars, as an example in miniature of Hills' duplicitous nature, and as a means by which we can shorten the gap between what Hills seemed to be and what he really was. By redirecting questions of authenticity and consistency, which have historically been levelled against Hills's identity, towards the archival materials we use to biographically reconstruct him, and to narrativise his status as, amongst other things, a hypocrite, I will raise methodological questions about the complexities of textual production and the referential stability of printed texts. In doing so, the tailor's wife anecdote will not serve to validate claims to Hills' hypocrisy in sexual, religious, or political terms. Instead, my emphasis falls on problems of reliability associated with archival evidence rather than with an historical identity, with the so-called "intransparency" (Bos 2002, 65) of hypocritical behaviour serving as a useful metaphor for ambiguities associated with the documentary evidence.

Claims that Hills "enticed away the wife of ... a tailor in Blackfriars, and lived with her" (Whitley 1932–3, 215) are based on a number of textual sources, in particular a religious self-narrative and a biographical broadside, both of which I discuss in more detail below. The story these texts tell has occasionally triggered readings that somehow simplify, and therefore assert some form of control over, the extremely "volatile" nature of Hills' life and career (Mendle 2001, 127). A discreet example of this can be found in Amos Tubb's otherwise excellent 2013 study of the political identities of mid-seventeenth century printers, in which he suggests that the shape of Hills' print output "defies all categorization" (293). Tubb notes, as an example, that although Hills fought on the Parliamentarian side at the battle of Edgehill and the battle of Worcester, and despite the fact that he worked as printer to the New Model Army, as well as representing Cromwell as official printer to the Commonwealth, that did not stop him from printing at least two editions of the Royalist bestseller, *Eikon Basilike*, in 1649 (ibid.). We might add to Tubb's description that, although Hills is known to have printed copies of the King James Bible, a text over which he held sole publishing rights (1656–7 and 1659–60), this did not stop him from simultaneously issuing publications that contained "violent abuse[s] of all the reformers, and particularly of the translators of the Bible" (Lee et al. 1826, 82), an incongruity that one nineteenth century publisher, writing on the history of English printing privileges, found particularly "mortifying" and "monstrous" (ibid.). Elsewhere, we find Hills' insignia appearing on Dissenter and anti-Dissenter pamphlets, on Royalist and Republican propaganda, as well as on anti-Catholic and pro-Catholic materials. Perhaps it is no wonder, then, that Tubb concludes his own biographical snapshot by saying that "it is difficult to know if Hills, who was openly

140 *Michael Durrant*

living with another man's wife, had an ideological viewpoint or just enjoyed causing controversy" (293).

This desire to uncover or expose Hills' "ideological viewpoint" can be located as part of a recent turn within the field of book history and print culture studies, one in which scholars have become increasingly attentive to the "activities" (Gadd 2003, 196) of the "living human agents" (McDonald and Suarez 2002, 86) who worked in the early modern book trade. Interpretive energy is now being focused on the "human personalities" who utilised technologies of book production (McDowell 2007, 126); those side-lined figures that Elizabeth Eisenstein subsequently acknowledged as the "true protagonists" of her highly influential 1979 work, *The Printing Press as an Agent of Change* (1979, xv). Previous studies by Peter Isaac and Barry McKay (1999), Lois G. Schwoerer (2001), Paul Baines and Pat Rogers (2007), and Molly O'Hagan Hardy (2012) indicate this growing and persistent interest in biography of book-trade professionals in the period. Scholars have been encouraged to reclaim human lives from "the scene of textual creation" (Maruca 2008, 18), and attempts have been made to perform an archival "excavation" (Smith 2012, 6), recovering the "makers and movers" (ibid.) responsible for printed texts. These calls to reclaim and remember can be viewed as an ethical injunction, in that a turn to the materials that make up a life can recalibrate our understandings of the creative capacities of printers, publishers, and booksellers, and in turn "challenge the enduring trend of characterizing early-modern producers as a crafty, profit-hungry, and even dishonest group" (Erickson 2007, 10).

Tubb's interest in establishing Hills' "ideological viewpoint" may therefore be discretely situated as being part of this biographical trend within the field of book history and literary-bibliographical studies more broadly. However, his inability to place a fix on Hills' thoughts, his beliefs, even his motivations, may indicate the limits of efforts to retrieve an historical identity from "publication records" (Tubb 2013, 293). In the binary formulated by Tubb, Hills is "difficult" because, unlike other "stalwart" printers and booksellers of the period, his publications do not offer up evidence of a "consistent" political stance (294). Indeed, the diversity of Hills' print output raises difficult questions regarding his allegiances and, by extension, the authenticity of his identity. The near-1000 print works that bear Hills' insignia in its variant forms – 'H.H.', 'H. Hills', 'H. Hill', or 'Henry Hill' – collectively express a radical kind of pluralism and flexibility, which together strongly resist those recent calls for a return of the human agents into bibliography and the history of the book, and to reclaim human "motivation" (Raven 2007, 3) from scene of textual creation.

But what if Tubb's embedded reference to the fact that Hills "was openly living with another man's wife" serves to construct specific meanings about his identity that his print work fails to provide? His aside towards Hills' domestic life substitutes open-endedness for meaning, in that it generates a particular impression of Hills as having lived a life defined by immorality and sin. In this context, Hills no longer "defies categorization"; in fact, in elaborating his adultery, Tubb reifies an issue to which Hills' contemporaries were particularly attuned: that is, the way in which "the language of politics slides into the language of ... adultery", and how tales of sexual infidelity could be called upon to "expose" – and, we might imagine, to make sense of – "the hypocrisy of a sudden switch of allegiance" (Helgerson 2000, 105). That accusations of sexual duplicity in the domestic sphere may have carried broader political resonances is a particularly important acknowledgement in relation to the world occupied by many early modern Stationers. As Adrian Johns points out, the trade was highly "dependent on ties of kinship and marriage", and many Stationer's houses were hybrid spaces including both sites of textual production and domestic accommodation for a printer and his or her family (1998, 76). The close association between domestic space and business premises meant that attacks on a "Stationer's domestic morality", particularly "allegations of sexual impropriety" (77), often doubled as a means by which many commentators, both within and outside the trade, could stage attacks on not only a stationer's character, but also on the value of their print output.

II

There is every possibility that the story of Hills' adultery, when read in the contexts from which it first emerged, is bound up with specific forms of royalist satire, in which "sexual depravity" (Adlington 2013, 455) functioned as shorthand for the "political hypocrisy and tergiversation" (ibid., 457) of Cromwell's republican cohorts. As the following sections show, a closer look at the evidence that remains to detail Hills' relationship with the tailor's wife might even reveal the extent to which the story rests on missing, or even fabricated, texts.

Our major sources for the story of Hills' adultery are the anonymous broadside of 1684 entitled, *A View of Part of the many Traiterous, Disloyal, and Turn-about Actions of H.H.*, and an interrelated pamphlet of 1688 entitled *The Life of H.H.*, which claims on its title page to be a "Relation at large of what passed betwixt [Hills] and the Taylors Wife in *Black-friars*, according to the Original". Together, these publications tell us that Hills was already married, and an established member of the Devonshire Square branch of the Particular Baptist Church, when he entered into a relationship with the tailor's wife. They also tell us that, as a result, Hills was cast out by his fellow Baptist Saints, sued by the tailor for £250, and imprisoned in the Fleet on account of his inability to pay the damages awarded against him. It is from this location that Hills is thought to have composed his confession-cum-conversion

142 *Michael Durrant*

account, *The Prodigal Returned*. This text was reportedly printed by Giles Calvert (*bap.* 1612, *d.* 1663), London's foremost radical publisher and bookseller, and sold from his "shop of poysons" (Baxter 1653, 39) at the sign of the Black-Spread-Eagle in 1651. Subsequently, it is said that Hills gained "re-admission to church fellowship" (Holden Pike 1870, 31–2), which may in fact be true, as within a year of *The Prodigal's* publication his insignia was appearing on major works for the Baptists, including Jane Turner's conversion narrative, *Choice Experiences* (1653).

An original version of *The Prodigal* is not known to have survived. This is why *The Life of H.H.* has been considered "the more important" (Kreitzer 2012, 47–8), because alongside a reprint of the 1684 biographical broadside, *A View*, it contains "the text of Hills' original confession from 1651" (ibid.). If this is the case, then we know that in that confession Hills figuratively aligned himself with, and adopted the voice of, the Prodigal Son (Luke 15, 11–32, King James Bible) in order to allegorise his departure from and return to godliness. The text also appears to have included paratextual materials, including a copy of the letter Hills sent to Hams in which he pleaded for leniency and forgiveness, as well as two epistles by leading Baptists, William Kiffen, and Daniel King. But in the absence of an original version of *The Prodigal*, what is it that we are reading when we read *The Life of H.H.*? As suggested, appended to the 1688 reprint of these documents is a reprint of *A View* of 1684. This revelatory biography has been described as a "sarcastic commentary" (Loveman 2008, 37), interpolated into *The Life* package as a rival narrative to the documents that purport to make up Hills' 1651 confession. By reading *A View* alongside Hills' admission of adultery, *The Life's* readers are called on to locate radical disjunctures between different versions of Hills by reading between texts.

Hence in one part of *The Life*, Hills asserts that his confession "is not a fiction or imagination ... but the truth" (xvi); Kiffin signs off his own epistle "hoping" Hills' confession is "reality and truth" (ii), while King asserts that Hills' "repentance is real" (v). This collaborative claim to "authentic faith", so "crucial" in puritan conversion accounts (Baker 2005, xviii), is compromised by evidence provided in the concluding document of *A View*, which bookends *The Life* by telling us that "this conversion of our Saint" was just another example of Hills' dissembling nature, "[r]eligion he [made] use of upon all changes" (49; 54). We are told that Hills only "writ this Book" to procure his "Re-admittance" into the Particular Baptist congregation, and by this "apostasy, and his hearty Pennance for that Crime", he became a "printer" to the congregation (49). To reinforce the idea that Hills was driven by mercenary motives and that his textual self is not to be trusted, it is also claimed that he became a preacher amongst the Baptists, and that he "Thump'd the Tub" with such enthusiasm that "he caus'd the Congregation to Deposite a very considerable sum of Money" into a Particular

Henry Hills and the Tailor's Wife 143

Baptist fund. Hills then absconded with the money in 1659, leaving the Devonshire Square Baptists to "shift for a new *Teacher*" (50). There is no evidence to support this claim, but by presenting an alternative account of Hills' dealings with the Baptists, the author-editor of *The Life* package attempts to convince us that, despite Hills' claims to the contrary, this godly performance of repentance really is a work of fiction.

To expose an individual as a hypocrite one must point towards "a discontinuity between motive and action" (Davidson 2004, 1), highlighting the gap "between the mask and the person behind the mask, between what they say now and what they once did" (Runciman 2008, 3). We might see this as the driving principle behind the republication of *The Prodigal*. The documents are recast and therefore rewritten, not as an example of "*Gods* great *grace* and goodness to a soul exceedingly declined and *Apostatized* from him" (i), or as the product of Hills' overwhelming sense of "duty" (xvi), but as a bid to cajole the Baptists into accepting him back into their inner circles, which is presented as having neatly doubled as a productive career move. Also, *The Life*'s provocative claim in its title to be a "Relation at large of what passed betwixt [Hills] and the Taylors Wife in *Black-friars*" functions as a wholesale revision of the documents of Hills' 1651 confession, paratextually placing them within the contexts not only of careerism, but of sexual hypocrisy, too.

However, there is an interesting sleight of hand at work here, not least because in the documents that purport to make up Hills' confession of 1651 Thomas Hams' profession is not mentioned. In fact, although Hams' profession and Hills' adultery appear to have been central to *The Life*'s pitch for readers' attention, it is a topic on which the "Original" documents it contains remain silent. In his confession, for example, Hills promises to "bring to open view" his "hidden works of darkness" (43); however, the text repeatedly defers autobiographical revelation around the circumstances of his adultery, Hills devoting much more narrative space to an extended exegetic reading of the prodigal parable than to his life. This might mean that, in telling us where Hills is from ("*Kent*"), and what his father did ("*a Ropemaker*" [47]), the editor of *The Life* package was actively filling in biographical gaps that the original documents of his confession stoutly refused to fill.

We can move this idea forward by pointing out that *The Life*'s appended biography contains significant editorial additions and amendments that do not appear in the 1684 version. So for example, "he writ his *Prodigal Return'd*" in *A View* becomes "he writ this Book the *Prodigal Return'd*" in *The Life* (49), the 1684 broadsheet pointing to the existence of an original outside of itself, while the 1688 reprint points to the text we have already encountered while reading *The Life* package. Interpolated passages not included in the 1684 broadsheet include the suggestion that in 1659 Hills had an unnamed royalist printer taken into custody for printing material in support of Charles II's restoration,

144 *Michael Durrant*

and it quotes him as "saying, *What Print in Right of the King, sure we have had King enough already*" (52). The author-editor of *The Life* has also integrated a new conclusion into the document of *A View*, stating that "the Publisher will prove to *H.H.*'s face" the accusations the work presents against him, but only "if he hath the confidence to deny any of them" (54). By goading Hills into a face-to-face encounter, the editor's final interpolated words suggest that this is not only an ongoing story, but potentially the beginning of a new one.

This would indicate that the story of adultery *The Life* package promises to reveal is elastic rather than prescriptive, which simultaneously makes the claim that the documents of *The Prodigal* were reprinted "[w]ithout comment or amplification" (Lynch 2007, 305) a difficult one to sustain. Historically, however, rather than focusing on a sense of the work's ephemerality, assumptions of typographical fixity have stabilised readings that damn Hills as an "obsequious flatterer" (Phelps Morand 1969, 41) and a "strained and unconvincing" spiritual autobiographer (Watkins 1972, 49). Hills' "extraordinary" confession of 1651 has been described as being so "full of unctuous hypocrisy", and "so obviously insincere", that it hardly merits serious critical attention (Smart 1925, 386). Even in the absence of an "Original" to which *The Life*'s title page confidently gestures, *The Prodigal* has sanctioned readings of its author as "shameless" and therefore morally corrupt (Haffenden 2009, 141). But to use *The Prodigal* as a means of exposing Hills' hypocrisy, or even to reveal the limits of his creative abilities as an author, would be to derive a conclusion from something that is potentially lost, while also assuming a degree of impartiality on the part of *The Life*'s "less than trusty" editorial persona (Loveman 2008, 37).

In the last three decades, scholars have become increasingly aware that printed accounts of early modern lives were "contested, retold, and re-worked" (Chartier 1994, 46). First-person texts like *The Prodigal* could take on "implications or symbolism that stretched far beyond the person involved and their immediate circle" (Farness 1996, 21). The material "instabilities and multiplicities" (Sharpe 2008, 239) that characterise early modern lives often meant that authorial identities could be "appropriated and fictionalised" (Raymond 2003, 97). Indeed, as Frances Dolan reminds us, if we were to read *The Life of H.H.* in terms of the way the text marketed itself – that is, as a "Relation" – then the problem of the trustworthiness of the evidence would become even more acute. "[T]he designation of a text as a relation", writes Dolan, "announced its particular claim on the reader's trust or belief" (2013, 2–4). Author-editors of true relations would often support their truth claims by listing living witnesses, or alternative narratives, to the events they describe. Such texts assure the reader of their authenticity through their claims to accurately reproduce original documentation. These authors "assemble a kind of archive to substantiate truth claims" (ibid.) and in doing so the textual relation becomes evidence of its own claims to authenticity.

The Life of H.H. package works in broadly similar terms: it refers to "Mr. *William Kiffin* and Mr. *Daniel King*" as "living [...] Witnesses" to Hills' adultery with the tailor's wife, both having "written an Epistle" before his confession (49); as discussed above, its title page promises an "Original", too. But such affirmations "cannot be verified" but rather "stand in for the proofs toward which they gesture" (Dolan 2013, 4). For example, the fact that Hills was fined "250 *l.*", that his confession was called *The Prodigal* and that it was printed by "*Giles Calvert*" in "1651", are details found only within the biographical document of *A View* and its subsequent reprint in *The Life* (49). Further, given that there is an absence of an original version of *The Prodigal*, *The Life* becomes the only evidence that Hills' confession ever existed in the form that we have it now, and even this works "on the assumption that it was actually printed" (Loveman 2008, n. 78, 37). But we cannot really know this, since there is nothing outside of this document to challenge *The Life*'s own claims to textual authenticity, and this includes its seemingly axiomatic assertion that in 1651 Hills publicly confessed to having committed adultery with the wife of a Blackfriars tailor.

III

The earliest surviving references to Hills' adultery appear in mock-query pamphlets, satirical ghost dialogues, and satirical mock-book catalogues, which have been described as "[s]poof inventories" of imaginary texts that "formed a staple part of royalist propaganda" (Adlington 2013, 455, 459–60) in the 1650s and 1660s. The first reference appears in the anonymous *Bibliotheca Parliamenti* of 1653, which includes a list of thirty-eight fictitious books and edicts related to Parliamentarian "Rebels" (2). The counterfeit titles often circulate around a sense of the world as having been "metamorphosed" (7), with one "Act for the speedy suppressing all Plays, the Fools being all turned Commanders or Parliament men" (5). Another serves up a low blow related to Cromwell's physical ugliness: "21. Whether Cromwell be not an absolute hater of Images, since he hath defaced Gods in his own countenance" (ibid.). Attacks are also made on the perceived sexual hypocrisy of politico-religious radicals: the politician and regicide, Henry Marten, for example, is represented as a lowly pimp, keeping a "Regiment of Whores" (5). In a similar vein, there is a book composed by the "Printer", Hills: "26. The art of multiplying, proving it lawful for one man to entice away another mans wife" (3).

In May 1653, Hills had just been nominated as an official printer to the Cromwellian government, and he would serve in this capacity until 1659, producing at least 400 works, 268 of which would bear the imprint, "Printer to his Highness, the Lord Protector" (Kreitzer 2012, 35). This promotion provides the immediate historical context and stimulus for

146 *Michael Durrant*

Hills' appearance in *Bibliotheca Parliamenti*, but his rise to become Cromwell's printer-in-chief also gives the joke its edge. Indeed, that the man responsible for producing Cromwellian acts and ordinances was a known adulterer must have seemed striking, especially given that the regime he represented in his print output had spent much of the early 1650s passing legislation that made adultery, amongst other sexual misdemeanours, a capital offence (Dabhoiwala 2012, 47–8). Thus from a royalist perspective the title of Hills' fictive book captures the awful irony of republican hypocrisy: the regime may hark on about standards of decency and godliness, even threatening to enforce the most severe form of corporeal punishment on those who erred in marriage, but they did not apply those same standards themselves, and, indeed, the implication is that Cromwell allowed known adulterers like Hills to make a profit out of this outrageous double-standard.

"The art of multiplying" invokes stereotypes of printing as an elitist craft, and "the press as a God-given instrument" (Eisenstein 2011, 34), but notions of the high are brought into contact with the low by the use of the word "multiplying", which registers an equation between "sexual and textual reproduction" that was well-established by 1660 (Brooks 2006, 224). Indeed, the linkage between the loss of civil order, illicit sexuality, and printing as a mass technology was something to which royalist polemicists were "particularly attuned" (Mowry 2004, 33) during the Interregnum period. Print technologies had aided the "the antimonarchists' cause", and printers like "the radical Henry Hills" were "blamed for their role in validating the sense of political entitlement" (ibid.) that royalists felt had been unleashed by the republican press.

Conspicuous by their absence in *Bibliotheca Parliamenti*'s mock title is the tailor, Hams, and his unnamed wife; moreover, no reference is made to Hills' published confession of 1651, *The Prodigal Returned*. Surely this seems odd: why bother inventing a title that captures a sense of Hills' adulterous behaviour when a real one had been published not long before, one that must have been circulating, in one form or another, amongst Hills' contemporaries? We cannot know the answer, but it is interesting that the 'real' material evidence of Hills' adultery – his *Prodigal Returned* – is here being substituted for one of *Bibliotheca Parliamenti*'s "nonbooks" (Brown 2008, 856), listed amongst a set of texts that have "names but no bodies" (Lake Prescott 1998, 175). "The art of multiplying" is in this context an imagined material enactment and validation of Hills' sexual immorality, simulacra that was no more available to Hills' contemporaries as Hills' now lost confession is to us today.

After the fall of Richard's Protectorate and the Rump, royalist satirists again returned to the representation of Hills as an adulterer, and again the form in which they did so in explicitly imaginative contexts. For instance, printed in March 1659–60, the anonymous mock-query pamphlet, *Fanatique Queries*, asked whether Hills' familiarity with the "crime

Henry Hills and the Tailor's Wife   147

of Polygamy" – here and only here is Hills described as a polygamist – made him especially suitable in the role of "the States Printer" (4). As such, polygamy emerges as a metaphor for the divided loyalties that one might expect of a republican book-trade professional negotiating the return of a monarchical regime. More generally, captured within that term "Polygamy" appears to be a deeply politicised anxiety about plurality and radical dividedness, where his involvement with multiple wives makes the reader sceptically review his submission to multiple masters.

Further reference to Hills' adultery exists in another anti-republican mock-book catalogue, *Bibliotheca Fanatica, or, the Fanatick Library* (1660). Here we find fictive titles that attack not a republic that is just finding its feet, but one that is in "Ruines" (2), written and published in the wake of the "utter destruction of the Rotten RUMP of a Parliamentary *Junto*" (3). Fictive books include the "paraphrastical meditations upon the Rumps Lamentations" (4), and one entitled "the Ulcer of the Rump; wherein is shown, that there is no better way to cure such distempers, then a burning, or cauterising" (5). A cast of "Fanatick" characters (3), newly set adrift by the collapse of the commonwealth, are listed and ridiculed: the author and politician, Sir Henry Vane the younger, for, perhaps a little unimaginatively, his vanity; again, we find Henry Marten, mocked for thinking it better to be "hung like a Stallion" than to have "virtue" (5); Hills' Devonshire Square Particular Baptist pastor, "*William Kiffin*", in an abhorrent bastardisation of scripture, is derided as having produced a book that proved that "*Gain is great godliness*" (5). As with *Bibliotheca Parliamenti*, Hills' adultery is once again invoked to encapsulate a sense of his characteristic licentiousness, only here he is constructed as the author of a book entitled "*De antiqueitate Typographa*", published "to shew, that Printing or Pressing was as ancient as Grandfather *Adams*, learnedly put home by *Henry Hills*, Printer, to the Taylors wife in Black-Friers" (3).

The "ancient" art of "Printing or Pressing" is flagged up to the reader, but those terms are deliberately unstable. The "or" clause may in fact indicate a comic vexation at the whole process of defining the act of printing; but then it also opens up a sense of "Pressing" as an alternative idea to "Printing", and vice versa. Buried within "Pressing" is a link between the pressing of paper and sexual intercourse. This is the most obvious reading available given that, as Margareta de Grazia points out, the printing press was "sexually gendered" (1996, 83). It was, she states, an apparatus comprising of various pieces that were anthropomorphised as "mechanical counterparts" to human "sexual organs" (ibid.). Together these "copulating parts" operated only "when the force of the press and the press-man bore down on the forme ... to imprint the absorbent and retentive page" (ibid.). The image of Hills bearing down on the tailor's wife thus takes on the representational force of a press-man applying his weight to a mounted sheet. But "Pressing" may have an even more

148   *Michael Durrant*

protean quality, since it was a technical term related not only to the making of books but of clothes: clothes presses and pressing irons were crucial tools in tailor's shops, and stitching, cutting, binding, as well as pressing, were common to both professions.

A wide range of literatures from the sixteenth and seventeenth centuries attest to the fact that, like the printer's hand-press, the trappings related to professional tailoring were similarly sexualised. For example, in England and elsewhere in early modern Europe, the comparison between the image of "open scissors and open female legs" signified illicit, and potentially a castrating, form of female sexuality, as well as the threat of marital infidelity (Santesso 1999, 505). More generally, the tailor's shop was represented as a space of "suspect transactions" (Ellinghausen 2004, 302) where not only clothes but identities could be fabricated, or "patcht" together from "new" and "old" "shreds" (Parsons 1612, 445), the "tailor-idol" assembling man-made humans out of man-made "fabric" (Lamb 2011, xxiii).

These early modern representations of the tailor's shop provide a curious parallel to the issues generated in modern discourses around the printing house. Helen Smith describes this place of book production as a space in which books, rather than bodies, "could change" (2012, 87). In fact, with scholarly criticism often viewing the printing house as a "strange little world" (Grafton 1980, 106) that had a "corrupting influence" on the textual "originals" that passed through them (Massai 2005, 104), both the printing house and the tailor's shop are, at different ends of the historical spectrum, being considered as places where people manufactured and marketed deceptions. This might help to underscore a discursive overlap between the construction of clothes and books that *Bibliotheca Fanatica*'s use of the word "Pressing" may also be galvanising.

Of course, we should notice what *Bibliotheca Fanatica*'s mock title wants us to notice: "the Taylors wife". It is her first surviving appearance in the story of Hills' adultery, and it appears to be the last time she appears within explicitly comic and imaginative contexts. All other references to Hills' adultery post-1660 are pretty straight-faced and decidedly un-comical, and we might include within that description Hills' revised appearance in the *Oxford Dictionary of National Biography* in 2004 (Gadd).

IV

As Mark Jenner reminds us, in the spirit of carnival that appears to have greeted Charles's immanent restoration in London, anti-republican satirists appealed to festive imagery of shitting, drinking, and feasting, and they characterised commonwealthmen by means of "a wide range of stock satirical tropes" (2002, 94). Prominent republicans were

Henry Hills and the Tailor's Wife 149

discursively sketched in terms of the bestial, the diabolic, the monstrous, and through imagery linked to comic inversion. In this way "familiarity" (ibid.) was key to textual denigrations of high-profile republicans and parliamentarians at this time. These texts did not set out to represent real people in realistic ways, since their authors "drew heavily and self-consciously upon literary models" (110).

With this in mind, it is worth pointing out that the figure of the tailor and his adulterous wife were "common objects of humour" on the early modern stage and in popular print, anxious metonyms for "sexual ambiguity" and "potential corruption" (Sanders 2002, paragraph 21, 13, and 4). The literary figure of the tailor's wife was widely "mocked as the essence of common behaviour"; she was "akin to a fishwife" and was frequently, and mercilessly, "the butt of jokes and stereotypes" (Sanders, paragraph 21). In general tailors were represented as "comic figures": "gossips and cheats" (Shepherd 2008, 19) who had a "reputation for thieving, malice, and degeneracy" (Santesso 1999, 505). But the tailor's generic malevolence is often counterbalanced by a concurrent sense of his effeminacy, and his wife's sexual rapaciousness.

Broadside ballads from the period often represent the tailor figure as his wife's enabler, providing her with the fashions in which she can attract, and sometimes dupe, other men. The tailor husband assists his wife's sartorial cravings alongside those of his other patrons, dressing them all up in the fancy clothes that have the potential to conceal their true identities, while he simultaneously makes a profit from doing so. As Simon Shepherd puts it, in contemporary ideology, tailors "assisted in and benefited from the illegitimate activities involved in social climbing (and the expanding market for consumer luxuries); they ministered to 'excess'" (2008, 18). *Bibliotheca Fanatica*'s reference to Hills' adultery appears to be activating, and drawing on, this tension. Indeed, one can see how the tailor's wife and Hills were well matched, both figures represented as having been driven by a disregard to formal hierarchy and codes of decency, and both are linked to transformations that conceal the true self. Access to "rich attire" could allow a tailor's wife to pass for a "Maid" even though she is a "Begger-wench" (*The Treppan'd Taylor*, 1674–79?); Hills, too, is a figure who continues to be defined in terms of his dynamic "flexibility" (Zwicker 2006, 445), and his knack for "reinvention" (ibid.).

Hills and the tailor's wife also appear in *O. Cromwell Thankes to the Lord Generall*, printed anonymously in May 1660, the same month that Charles II was received back into London. This text tells of a conversation between the ghost of Cromwell and his preacher, Hugh Peters, in St James's Park. Cromwell's ghost makes an earnest request "for sending severall persons to him" in hell. Peters reports that "Harry Hills" will not be long in joining Cromwell in the afterlife; indeed, sex with the "Taylors wife in Black-friers" had left Hills in need of "a better head

150   *Michael Durrant*

piece, or a steel cap to keep in his Brains" (6), a line that plays off a double sense of "head piece" as a human skull and a printed ornament at the top of a page. As with *Bibliotheca Fanatica*, this reference to Hills' adultery suggests that the story of the "Taylors wife" was still intimately bound up with specific forms of royalist satire that, while pulling on "conventions of news reporting" were marketed as "transparently fictional" (Raymond 2003, 252) exaggerations or grotesquery. However, this would not remain the case.

In sharp contradistinction to the previously discussed works, *The London Printers Lamentation* (1660), has its tongue firmly out of its cheek when its anonymous author flags up Hills' adultery (twice) to the reader:

> that libidinous & professed Adulterer *H. Hills* in *Aldersgate-street*, one that for his Heresie in Religion (being an Anabaptist,) and his luxury in conversation (having hypo-critically confessed his fact in Print, and been imprisoned for his Adultery with a Taylors Wife in *Black-friers*,) would scandalize a good Christian and an honest man to be in his company.
>
> (7)

The tone is altogether serious, the extract seguing from adultery, through religious heresy, via the weirdly paradoxical notion of a hypocritical confession, and looping back to adultery by way of the "Taylors Wife". Although *The London Printers Lamentation* retains a sense of uncontrollable proliferation that marks earlier representations of Hills' adultery – the author notes that "[i]n one dayes time a Printer will Print more, / Than one man Write could in a Year before" (2) – imaginary books have been superseded with a reference to real-life material evidence circulating "in Print", indicating to the reader that Hills' adultery is to be understood as anything but a joke. This is because the "Adulterer *H. Hills*" is a real-world embodiment of a group of opportunistic printers who set up unregistered printing houses during the tumult of the civil wars, advanced by senior military figures outside of the formal hierarchies of the Stationers' Company (Blagden 1960, 3–17). Hills is represented as having had the ability to "creep" into positions of "trust and "profit" (*London Printers Lamentation*, 7) by means of simulation, a metaphor that, perhaps paradoxically, relegates a printer who was pushing texts into the light to a world of secrecy and shadows. Marital infidelity here serves a metonymic function, signifying what for this author was seen as a wider form of adulteration within the trade:

> [n]ever was there such an honourable, ingenious and profitable Mystery and Science in the world so basely intruded upon, and disesteemed; so carelesly regarded, so unworthily subjected to

Henry Hills and the Tailor's Wife 151

infamy and disgrace, by being made so common, as Printing hath been since 1640s.

(3)

The above-mentioned biographical broadside, *A View*, was next to make a seemingly straight-faced reference to Hills' adultery with "a Taylors Wife in *Black-friers*", a statement that would be reiterated when *A View* was reprinted in 1688 alongside the documents of *The Prodigal* in *The Life of H.H.* (49). As discussed, *The Life* package even references Hills' adultery on its title page. Indeed, its frontispiece markets the text as a "Relation at large of what passed betwixt him and the Taylors Wife ... according to the Original". One of the things the "Original" does not tell us is that Hills conducted an affair with the wife of a tailor – this, it appears, is a biographical fact that may have an origin in royalist satire from the early years of the Restoration, and one that the author-editor of *The Life* has subsequently reiterated when he reprinted *A View* alongside *The Prodigal*.

In what appears to be a process of journalistic snowballing, the tailor's wife's appearance in accounts of Hills' life story become less obviously satirical over time, less obviously fictional, culminating in that insistent association of Hills with "the Taylors Wife" which brands the title page of *The Life of H.H.* in 1688. As I have suggested, that text, and the reprinted biographical broadside which it contains, have been used by later historians of the press as evidence of Hills' adultery with a tailor's wife, but it could just as easily be read as an example of significant tensions between the assumed facts and the possible fictions of the case.

We get a real sense of this strain in an anecdote provided by the author-editor(s) of *A View* and *The Life*, where it is claimed that in 1659 Hills printed some "pocket *Bibles*" in which he "corrupted the Commandments, and made it, *Thou shalt commit Adultery*; remembering probably how delightfully he had liv'd with honest *Thomas Ham*'s the Taylor's Wife" (*The Life of H.H.*, 51). This infamous misprint actually appeared in Robert Barker's (d. 1645) so-called 'Wicked Bible' of 1631. As Kate Loveman writes, "when this 'wicked bible' was published Hills was about six years old: it was an amusing charge but not a true one" (2008, 37). Nevertheless, what we see here is the way his reputation as a sexual hypocrite, coupled with his reputation amongst members of the print trade for printing Bibles which contained errors, allows for the emergence of new stories about Hills. But like the mock title which first referenced Hills' sexual reputation in 1653, the claim that Hills left a trace of his adultery in an edition of the Bible is a fiction. Those early references to Hills' adultery in *Bibliotheca Parliamenti* and *Bibliotheca Fanatica*, which together pulled on satirical traditions of "[d]isembodied books", offer their readers, both then and now, "the fantasy of knowledge" (Brown 2008, 836). *The Life of H.H.*'s promise to be a story of

152 *Michael Durrant*

Hills' adultery with a tailor's wife might be understood in similar terms, throwing very different light on an anecdote that currently features heavily in biographical accounts of Hills' life, and is seen to, in some way, capture a sense of his hypocritical identity.

V

The theme of hypocrisy is said to generate questions about "authenticity" and the "integrity" of identity (Grant 1997, 162), and these issues anxiously preoccupied polemicists on all sides in the Stuart period. Although early moderns often propounded the ideal that outer appearances should correlate with a person's inner qualities, that same assumption was often radically undermined by the psychological pressures of day-to-day experience, particularly during times of political and religious experimentation, upheaval, and crisis. Seventeenth-century English culture was "deeply interested" (Hodgkin 2007, 56) in the relationship between the inner and outer self, and in response literatures of the period scrutinised occasions where that assumed connection was seen to fail or be somehow insufficient. Those literatures which took as their subject examples of hypocrisy and dissimulation were often linked to anti-Catholic and anti-puritan polemic; but they were also emerging out of a broader set of societal anxieties about the "tension between appearance and reality" (Dodd 2015, 136).

Similar epistemological questions still underpin modern philosophical interactions with the theme of hypocrisy, which, as a concept and a practice, calls into question the extent to which one can "expose the hypocrite's true self" (Davidson 2004, 1), especially if that hypocrite is a "sophisticated" one (ibid.). Interestingly, the language of authenticity, and the limits of exposure, can also be seen to underscore scholarly vocabularies associated with the archive and the way in which scholars use archival sources. Rather than offering up "documentary truth" (Summit 2008, 13), archives and the evidence they contain have increasingly become "subject to question" (Blouin and Rosenberg 2007, 9), with "rumor, disputation, missing documents, [and] contested authority" (Dolan 2013, 381) coming to sublimate discourses that privilege archives "as a source of historical truth" (Starn 2002, 388). Much like the figure of the hypocrite, archival evidence can be understood as potentially double, at least in terms of the fact that the evidence might not tell us "the plain truth, the whole truth" (Belsey 2009, 206), and neither is the evidence always to be treated as "transparent" (ibid.).

So, when, in the second volume of Donald McKenzie and Maureen Bell's monumental resource, *A Chronology and Calendar of Documents Related to the London Book Trade* (2006), we find the inclusion in its topic index an entry for "tailor's wife, stationer's adultery with", should we not question, rather than accept, the assumed transparency of the link being

Henry Hills and the Tailor's Wife 153

established between the indexed biographical anecdote and the life lived? As this chapter has fleetingly shown, if we do raise the question, then the story of Hills' adultery with the tailor's wife in Blackfriars becomes not a means by which we can access or expose Hills' character, but a story about other texts, texts that, like *The Prodigal Returned*, are now lost, or, like that mock-book title, "*De antiquetate Typographa*", may never have existed.

Works Cited

Adlington, Hugh. 2013. "'The *State*'s Book-man'?: References to Milton in Satirical Book Catalogues of the Interregnum". *The Seventeenth Century* 27: 454–76.

Anon. 1653. *Bibliotheca Parliamenti, libri, Theologici, Politici, Historici, qui Prostant voenales in vico vulgò vocato Little-Britain*. London.

———. 1659–60. *Fanatique Queries, Propos'd to the Present Assertors of the Good Old Cause*. London.

———. 1660. *Bibliotheca Fanatica, or, the Fanatick Library*. London.

———. 1660. *O. Cromwell Thankes to the Lord Generall*. London.

———. 1660. *The London Printers Lamentation, or, the Press Opprest and Overprest*. London.

———. 1674–79. *The Treppan'd Taylor*. London.

———. 1684–85. *A View of Part of the many Traiterous, Disloyal, and Turn-about Actions of H.H. Senior*. London.

———. 1688. *The Life of H.H. With the Relation at Large of What Passed Betwixt Him and the Taylors Wife in Black-friars, According to the Original*. London.

———. 1733. *Revolution Politicks: Being a Compleat Collection of All the Reports, Lyes, and Stories, which were the Fore-Runners of the Great Revolution in 1688*. London.

Baines, Paul, and Pat Rogers. 2007. *Edmund Curll, Bookseller*. Oxford: Oxford University Press.

Baker, Naomi. 2005. *Scripture Women: Rose Thurgood, 'A Lecture of Repentance' and Cicely Johnson, 'Fanatical Reveries'*. Nottingham: Trent Editions.

Baxter, Richard. 1653. *The Worchester-shire Petition to the Parliament for the Ministry of England Defended*. London.

Belsey, Catherine. 2009. "The Death of the Reader". *Textual Practice* 23: 201–14.

Blagden, Cyprian. 1960. *The Stationers' Company: A History, 1403–1959*. Stanford, CA: Stanford University Press.

Blouin, Francis X., and William G. Rosenberg. 2007. *Archives, Documentation, and Institutions of Social Memory: Essays from the Sawyer Seminar*. Ann Arbor: University of Michigan Press.

Bos, Jacques. 2002. "The Hidden Self of the Hypocrite". In *On the Edge of Truth and Honesty: Principles and Strategies of Fraud and Deceit in the Early Modern Period*, edited by Toon van Houdt, Jan L. Jong, Zoran Kwak, Marijke Spies, and Marc van Vaeck, 65–84. Leiden: Brill.

Brooks, Douglas A. 2006. "Inky Kin: Reading in the Age of Gutenberg Paternity". In *The Book of the Play: Playwrights, Stationers, and Readers in*

154 *Michael Durrant*

Early Modern England, edited by Marta Straznicky. Amherst and Boston: University of Massachusetts Press.

Brown, Piers. 2008. "'Hac ex consilio meo via progredieris': Courtly Reading and Secretarial Mediation in Donne's *The Courtier's Library*". *Renaissance Quarterly* 61: 833–66.

Chartier, Roger. 1994. *The Order of Books*. Stanford, CA: Stanford University Press.

Dabhoiwala, Faramerz. 2012. *The Origins of Sex: A History of the First Sexual Revolution*. London: Allen Lane.

Davidson, Jenny. 2004. *Hypocrisy and the Politics of Politeness: Manners and Morals from Locke to Austen*. Cambridge: Cambridge University Press.

de Grazia, Maria. 1996. "Imprints: Shakespeare, Gutenberg and Decartes". In *Alternative Shakespeares, Volume II*, edited by Terrance Hawkes, 63–94. London: Routledge.

Dodd, Elizabeth S. 2015. *Boundless Innocence in Thomas Traherne's Poetic Theology*. Oxon: Routledge.

Dolan, Frances E. 2013. *True Relations: Literature and Evidence in Seventeenth-Century England*. Philadelphia: University of Pennsylvania Press.

Eisenstein, Elizabeth. 1979. *The Printing Press as an Agent of Change*. Cambridge: Cambridge University Press.

———. 2011. *Divine Art, Infernal Machine: The Reception of Printing in the West from First Impressions to the Sense of an Ending*. Philadelphia: University of Pennsylvania Press.

Ellinghausen, Laurie. 2004. "Black Acts: Textual Labor and Commercial Deceit in Dekker's *Lantern and Candlelight*". In *Rogues and Early Modern English Culture*, edited by Craig Dionne and Steve Mentz, 294–311. Ann Arbor: The University of Michigan Press.

Erickson, Stacy L. 2007. "Collaboration in the Marketplace: Writers, Publishers, and Printers in Early Modern London". PhD diss., University of Iowa.

Farness, Jay. 1996. "Disenchanted Elves: Biography in the Text of *Faerie Queene* V". In *Spencer's Life and the Subject of Biography*, edited by Judith H. Anderson, Donald Cheney, and David A. Richardson, 18–30. Amherst: University of Massachusetts Press.

Gadd, Ian. 2003. "Hunting Down John Wolfe for the New *DNB*". In *Lives in Print: Biography and the Book Trade from the Middle Ages to the 21st Century*, edited by Robin Myers, Michael Harris, and Giles Mandelbrote, 193–202. New Castle: Oak Knoll Press.

———. 2004. 'Henry Hills, Senior (*c*.1625–1688/9)'. *ODNB*. doi:10.1093/ref:odnb/13322.

Grafton, Anthony T. 1980. "The Importance of Being Printed". *Journal of Interdisciplinary History* 11: 265–86.

Grant, Ruth W. 1997. *Hypocrisy and Integrity: Machiavelli, Rousseau, and the Ethics of Politics*. Chicago, IL: University of Chicago Press.

Haffenden, John. 2009. "William Empson: The Milton Controversy". *Literary Imagination* 11: 136–53.

Helgerson, Richard. 2000. *Adulterous Alliances: Home, State, and History in Early Modern European Drama and Painting*. Chicago, IL: University of Chicago Press.

Hodgkin, Katharine. 2007. *Madness in Seventeenth Century Autobiography*. Basingstoke: Palgrave.

Henry Hills and the Tailor's Wife 155

Holden Pike, Godfrey. 1870. *Ancient Meeting Houses: Or, Memorial Pictures of Non-conformity in Old London.* London: S.W. Partridge.

Isaac, Peter, and Barry McKay. 1999. *The Human Face of the Book Trade: Print Culture and Its Creators.* Winchester: Oak Knoll Press.

Jenner, Mark. 2002. "The Roasting of the Rump: Scatology and the Body Politic in Restoration England". *Past and Present* 177: 84–120.

Johns, Adrian. 1998. *The Nature of the Book: Print and Knowledge in the Making.* Chicago, IL and London: University of Chicago Press.

King James Bible. 1613. *The Holy Bible Containing the Old Testament, and the New: Newly Translated Out of the Original Tongues... by His Majesties Speciall Commandement.* London: Robert Parker.

Kreitzer, Larry J. 2012. *William Kiffen and his World (Part 2).* Oxford: Regent's Park College.

Lake Prescott, Anne. 1998. *Imagining Rebelais in Renaissance England.* New Haven, CT: Yale University Press.

Lamb, Jonathan. 2011. *The Things Things Say.* Princeton, NJ: Princeton University Press.

Lee, John, John Bruce, George Buchan, and David Hunter Blair. 1826. *Additional Memorial on Printing and Importing Bibles.* Edinburgh: A. Belfour and Co.

Loveman, Kate. 2008. *Reading Fictions, 1660–1740: Deception in English Literary and Political Culture.* Farnham: Ashgate.

Lynch, Katherine. 2007. "Religious Identity, Stationers' Company Politics, and Three Printers of the *Eikon Basilike*". *The Papers of the Bibliographical Society of America* 101: 287–312.

Maruca, Lisa. 2008. *The Work of Print: Authorship and the English Text Trades, 1660–1760.* Seattle: University of Washington Press.

Massai, Sonia. 2005. "John Wolfe and the Impact of Exemplary Go-Betweens on Early Modern Print Culture". In *Renaissance Go-Betweens: Cultural Exchange in Early Modern Europe*, edited by Andreas Höfele and Werner von Koppenfels, 104–20. Berlin: Walter de Gruyter.

McDonald, Peter D., and Michael F. Suarez. 2002. Introduction to *Making Meaning: "Printers of the Mind" and Other Essays*, by Donald F. McKenzie, 13. Amherst: University of Massachusetts Press.

McDowell, Paula. 2007. "'On the Behalf of Printers': A Late Stuart Printer-Author and Her Causes". In *Agent of Change: Print Culture Studies after Elizabeth L. Eisenstein*, edited by Sabrina Alcorn Baron, Eric N. Lindquist, and Eleanor F. Shevlin, 125–39. Amherst: University of Massachusetts Press.

McKenzie, Donald, and Maureen Bell. 2006. *A Chronology and Calendar of Documents Relating to the London Book Trade.* Oxford: Oxford University Press.

Mendle, Michael. 2001. *The Putney Debates of 1647: The Army, the Levellers, and the English State.* Cambridge: Cambridge University Press.

Mowry, Melissa M. 2004. *The Bawdy Politic in Stuart England, 1660–1714: Political Pornography and Prostitution.* Farnham: Ashgate.

Muddiman, Joseph G. 1932. "Henry Hills, Sen. Printer to Cromwell and to James II". *Notes & Queries* 163: 5–7.

O'Hagan Hardy, Molly. 2012. "Literary Pirates as Agents of Change: Jonathan Swift and the Dublin Printing Pirates of the Eighteenth Century". *LATCH* 5: 120–40.

156 Michael Durrant

Parsons, Robert. 1612. *A Discussion of the Answers of M. William Barlow*. London.

Phelps Morand, Paul. 1969. *The Effects of his Political Life upon John Milton*. London: Folcroft.

Raven, James. 2007. *The Business of Books: Booksellers and the English Book Trade, 1450–1850*. New Haven, CT: Yale University Press.

Raymond, Joad. 2003. *Pamphlets and Pamphleteering in Early Modern Britain*. Cambridge: Cambridge University Press.

Runciman, David. 2008. *Political Hypocrisy: The Mask of Power, from Hobbes to Orwell and Beyond*. Princeton, NJ: Princeton University Press.

Sanders, Julie. 2002. "'Wardrobe Stuffe': Clothes, Costume and the Politics of Dress in Ben Jonson's *The New Inn*". *Renaissance Forum* 6. Available online at www.hull.ac.uk/renforum/v6no1/sanders.htm (accessed 6 June 2017).

Santesso, Aaron. 1999. "William Hogarth and the Tradition of Sexual Scissors". *Studies in English Literature, 1500–1900* 39: 499–521.

Schwoerer, Lois G. 2001. *The Ingenious Mr. Henry Care, Restoration Publicist*. Baltimore, MD: The Johns Hopkins University Press.

Sharpe, Kevin. 2008. "Whose Life is it Anyway?: Writing Early Modern Monarchs and the 'Life' of James II". In *Writing Lives: Biography and Textuality, Identity and Representation in Early Modern England*, edited by Kevin Sharpe and Steve Zwicker, 233–54. Oxford: Oxford University Press.

Shepherd, Simon. 2008. "What's So Funny about Ladies' Tailors? A Survey of Some Male (Homo)Social Types in the Renaissance". *Textual Practice* 6: 17–30.

Smart, John S. 1925. "Milton and the King's Prayer". *The Review of English Studies* 4: 385–91.

Smith, Helen. 2012. *Grossly Material Things: Women and Book Production in Early Modern England*. Oxford: Oxford University Press.

Starn, Randolph. 2002. "Truths of the Archives". *Common Knowledge* 8: 387–401.

Stone Peters, Julie. 1990. *Congreve, the Drama, and the Printed Word*. Stanford, CA: Stanford University Press.

Summit, Jennifer. 2008. *Memory's Library: Medieval Books in Early Modern England*. Chicago, IL: University of Chicago Press.

Tubb, Amos. 2013. "Independent Presses: The Politics of Print in England during the Late 1640s". *The Seventeenth Century* 27: 287–312.

Walsh, Marcus. 2013. "Swift's *Tale of a Tub* and the Mock Book". In *Jonathan Swift and the Eighteenth-Century Book*, edited by Paddy Bullard and James McLaverty, 101–18. Cambridge: Cambridge University Press.

Watkins, Owen C. 1972. *The Puritan Experience: Studies in Spiritual Autobiography*. New York: Schocken Books.

Whitley, William T. 1932–33. "Henry Hills, Official Printer". *Baptist Quarterly* 215–17. Available online at www.biblicalstudies.org.uk/pdf/bq/06-5_215.pdf (accessed 6 June 2017).

Zwicker, Steve. 2006. "Is There Such a Thing as Restoration Literature?" *Huntington Library Quarterly* 69: 425–50.

Notes on Contributors

Silvia Bigliazzi is Professor of English literature at Verona University (Italy). She has worked on literature and the visual arts (*Il colore del silenzio*, Marsilio 1998), textual and theatrical performance (*Sull'esecuzione testuale*, ETS 2001; *Theatre Translation in Performance*, Routledge 2013), Shakespeare (*Oltre il genere*, Edizioni dell'Orso 2001; *Nel prisma del nulla*, Liguori 2005; *Romeo e Giulietta*, Einaudi 2012; *Revisting The Tempest*, Palgrave 2014), and Donne (*Poesie*, Rizzoli 2009). She has translated Shakespeare for the stage (*Romeo and Juliet Q1*, 2016; *Macbeth* 2016). She is one of the Editors of *Skenè. Theatre and Drama Studies.*

Michael Durrant is Lecturer in Early Modern Literature at Bangor University. He has previously taught at the University of Manchester, Staffordshire University, and Hang Seng Management College, Hong Kong. He is currently working on his first monograph, *Writing and Rewriting Henry Hills, Printer (c. 1625–1688/9)*, under consideration with Manchester University Press.

Katharine Hodgkin is Professor of Cultural History at the University of East London, and UEL Director of the Raphael Samuel History Centre. Her research focuses on early modern English literature and culture, including autobiographical writing, gender, religious writing, and the history of madness. Publications relating to these themes include *Madness in Seventeenth-Century Autobiography* (Palgrave 2007), and an edition of an early seventeenth-century autobiographical manuscript, *Women, Madness and Sin: The Autobiographical Writings of Dionys Fitzherbert* (Ashgate 2010). More recently her work has focused on memory and subjectivity in early modern culture. Publications in this area include "Women, Memory and Family History in Seventeenth-Century England", in Erika Kuijpers and Judith Pollmann (eds), *Memory Before Modernity: Memory Cultures in Early Modern Europe* (Brill 2013); "Elizabeth Isham's Everlasting Library: Memory and Self in Early Modern Autobiography", in Sally Alexander and Barbara Taylor (eds), *History and Psyche: culture, psychoanalysis and the past* (Palgrave 2012); and an article for a journal special

158 *Notes on Contributors*

issue on early modern nostalgia, "Childhood and Loss in Early Modern Life Writing", *Parergon* 33.1, 2016. She is currently co-editing a special issue of the journal *Memory Studies* on early modern memory cultures.

Lucia Nigri is Lecturer in Early Modern English Literature at the University of Salford, Manchester. Her research interests focus on early modern literature with a particular emphasis on drama. She has written articles on intertextuality in John Webster's plays (*Il Confronto Letterario* 2007), maternal misrecognition in early modern tragedies (*Nuova Cultura* 2010), the notion of identity in Shakespeare and his contemporaries (Universitalia 2011), the question of authorship in Arden of Faversham (*Memoria di Shakespeare*, Bulzoni 2012), the relation between dominant and marginal languages in translating for the theatre (Routledge 2013), performativity in the Victorian adaptations of *The Tempest* (Palgrave 2014), on the natural and monumental body in *Romeo and Juliet* (Routledge 2016) and on Shakespearean narratives used in particular times of crisis in Italy (forthcoming). She has extensively written on the figure of the malcontent (*Notes and Queries* 2012 and ETS 2014), on intertextuality on stage (ETS 2014), and on scepticism and self in Elizabethan and Jacobean period (*English Literature*, 2014). She was awarded the Vice-Chancellor Early Career Research Scholarship (2015–2017) for her research project on 'Shakespeare in Manchester'.

Jacqueline Pearson is Professor Emeritus at the University of Manchester. She has published widely on Jacobean and Restoration drama, early modern and eighteenth-century women writers (including Aemilia Lanyer, Margaret Cavendish, Aphra Behn, Susanna Centlivre, Frances Burney, and Maria Edgeworth) and readers (*Women's Reading in Britain 1750–1834: A Dangerous Recreation*, Cambridge University Press 1999). She is currently editing two plays by Aphra Behn and contributing to The Cambridge Guide to the Eighteenth-Century Novel, and is also working on the seventeenth-century supernatural, her recent publications including '"Then she asked it, what were its Sisters names?": Reading between the Lines in Seventeenth-century Pamphlets of the Supernatural' (*Seventeenth Century* 28, 2013, 63–78) and 'The Ghost of Col. Bowen: 1655, 1691, 1941/2' (*Preternature* 5:1, 2016, 86–111).

Markku Peltonen is Professor of History and currently an Academy Professor at the University of Helsinki. His publications include *Classical Humanism and Republicanism in English Political Thought 1570–1640* (CUP 1995), *The Duel in Early Modern England: Civility, Politeness and Honour* (CUP 2003) and *Rhetoric, Politics and Popularity in Pre-Revolutionary England* (CUP 2013).

Notes on Contributors 159

Rossana Sebellin is Lecturer in English Literature at the University of Rome, Tor Vergata (Italy). Her field of research mainly focuses on early modern literature, bilingualism, and self-translation, Samuel Beckett, and contemporary theatre. She is the author of *"Prior to Godot"*: Eleutheria *di Samuel Beckett* (2006), *La doppia originalità di Samuel Beckett. Play / Comédie e* Not I */ Pas moi* (2008), and *Leggendo* Godot (2012). She is co-editor (with Daniela Guardamagna) of *The Tragic Comedy of Samuel Beckett* (2009). She has published on post-modernist rewritings of Shakespeare and on translation.

Naya Tsentourou is Lecturer in Early Modern Literature at the University of Exeter, Penryn. Her current project investigates the relationship between breath and emotions in sixteenth- and seventeenth-century England as represented in literary, religious, and medical texts. She also has research interests in the history of emotions, religious lyric, and material culture. She is the author of *Milton and the Early Modern Culture of Devotion: Bodies at Prayer,* forthcoming with Routledge.

Index

Abbott, George 102, 114
abject 12, 119, 121, 130, 135–6
Adams, Thomas 101–2, 114–5, 125–6, 130, 136
Adlington, Hugh 141, 145, 153
adultery 119, 138–9, 141–5
Aers, David and Gunther Kress 41–3
agency 7–9, 93, 101, 109, 112
air 7
allegory 35, 38–9, 50
Allen, Hannah 109, 111, 115, 132, 136
Anabaptists 20, 133, 150
Anderson, Judith 2, 13
anxiety 6, 46, 57, 69, 70, 91, 121, 132, 147
Aphthonius 24
Aquinas, Thomas 18
Aristotle 27, 35, 51
Ashton, Jane 111
Ashton, Thomas 103–4
audiences 10, 12–13, 26, 28–29, 58–9, 61–6, 68–9, 81, 83, 85
Augustine 9
authenticity 12, 61, 105–7, 109–10, 114, 120, 139–40, 144–5, 152
autobiography 10, 12, 131, 135

Bacon, Francis 19, 37, 52
Bailey, Michael 4, 13
Baines, Paul and Pat Rogers 140, 153
Baker, Naomi 142, 153
Ball, Robert 4, 13
Baptists 130, 138, 141–3, 147
Baring-Gould, Sabine 111, 115
Barrow, James 108, 113, 115
Bate, John 5, 13
Batman, Stephen 101, 115
Baxter, Richard 124–6, 128, 136, 142, 153

Beauregard, David 67
Beier, A. Lee 60
Belsey, Catherine 152–3
Berensmeyer, Ingo and Andrew Hadfield 7, 9, 13, 84, 86
Bigliazzi, Silvia 7, 10
Black, Joseph 94, 99
Blagden, Cyprian 138, 150, 153
Blandford, Susannah 133, 136
Blouin, Francis and William Rosenberg 152–3
Bodrugan, Nicholas 18
Bolton, Robert 59–60
Booy, David 101, 115
Bos, Jacques 8, 13, 139, 153
Bound, Fay 39
Bouwsma, William 15–6
Bower, Sarah 108
Brandolini, Aurelio 25
Brathwait, Richard 123, 125, 136
Breitenberg, Mark 114–5
Breton, Nicholas 39–40
Bridges, Grey 20
Brigges, Agnes 106
Brigges, Robert 106
Brooke, Arthur 67–8
Brooks, Douglas 146, 153
Brown, Cedric C. 41, 51
Brown, Piers 146, 151, 154
Bryn Roberts, S. 60
Bullinger, Heinrich 20
Bunyan, John 89, 131, 136
Burgiss, Elizabeth 111
Burke, Peter 36, 39, 52
Burke, Peter and Roy Porter 39
Burton, Robert 120, 136
Butler, Charles 25–6

Cable, Lana 88, 99
Calvert, Giles 142, 145

162 *Index*

Campbell, Gilbert 109, 110;
    Thomas 110
Carrington, John 104
Castiglione, Baldassarre 9, 36, 39,
    73, 76
Catholicism 11, 36, 57–70, 87, 91–2,
    96–7, 103–5, 107–8, 112, 138–9,
    152; *see* Roman Catholic Church
Cavaillé, Jean-Pierre 15
Charron, Pierre 19
Chartier, Roger 144, 154
Chaucer, Geoffrey 57–8
Church of England 103, 105,
    111, 138
Cicero, Marcus Tullius 26–8, 39
civic 7, 15, 29
Clark, Stuart 102, 112, 114, 115
Clarkson, Leslie 90, 93, 99
clothes 2, 65, 69, 72, 76–77, 79, 86,
    89, 93, 95, 97–8, 109, 121, 123,
    148–9; *see* clothing and garments
clothing 1–2, 7, 36, 63, 65, 69, 81, 88,
    89, 93–7; *see* clothes and garments
Collinson, Patrick 123, 136
community 6, 10, 28–9, 91, 109–110
confession 68, 107–8, 138,
    141–6, 150
conversion 108, 114, 131, 138, 141–2
Cooper, Margaret 111
Cooper, Thomas 129, 136
Corbin, Peter and Douglas Sedge 11,
    13, 72, 85, 86
courtesy books 28, 33
Cromwell, Oliver 138–9, 141,
    145–6, 149
Cromwell, Richard 138, 146
Crook, Samuel 124, 126–7, 129–30,
    135, 137
Crump, Hannah 113

Dabhoiwala, Faramerz 146, 154
Danielson, Dennis 89, 99
Darling, Thomas 106–8, 111, 114
Darrell, John 103–105, 107–8
Davenport, John 101, 115
Davidson, Jenny 9, 13, 143, 152, 154
Davy, Sarah 101, 115, 132, 137
Day, Angela 39
Daybell, James 39
deceit 12, 26, 75, 89, 122, 125,
    131, 133; deceitfulness 2, 63, 66,
    120, 121
decency 38, 90–1, 96–8, 128,
    146, 149

Derrida, Jacques 97, 99
devotion 4–6, 40, 47, 60–63, 65, 67,
    88–9, 95, 97–8
devotional writing 120–1, 124, 126–7
de Grazia, Margareta 147, 154
de Guevara, Antonio 19
demonic possession 12, 101–14,
Dini, Vittorio 17
disease 88, 92, 94–6, 101, 108, 111,
    126; *see also* illness
disguise 37, 39, 52, 60, 63, 65, 76, 81,
    83, 119–20, 126–7
display 11, 36, 42, 57, 62, 73–4,
    78–80, 82, 85, 87, 90, 93–4, 102,
    122, 127
Dissenters 103–5, 109, 113, 139
dissimulation 4, 7, 9, 10, 13, 15–29,
    37–9, 72–3, 76, 83, 85, 103, 107,
    120–3, 127, 152
Doelman, James 66
Dodd, Elizabeth 152, 154
Dolan, Alice 90, 99
Dolan, Frances 144–5, 152, 154
Drake, Joan 111
Dugdale, Richard 103–5
Donne, John 7, 11, 35, 40–51
duplicity 35–7, 40, 73–4, 125,
    127, 135
Durrant, Michael 7, 12
Dzelzainis, Martin 52

Earle, John 11, 119–20, 137
education 10, 15–29
Egan, James 94, 99
Eikon Basilike 95, 139
Eisenstein, Elizabeth 140, 146, 154
eloquence 20, 22, 135
Eliav-Feldon, Miriam 4, 7, 13–4,
    76, 86
Ellinghausen, Laurie 148, 154
Elyot, Thomas 18–9, 33–4
epistles/letters: verse epistles 33, 35,
    40, 45; letter-writing 39, 46–8
equivocation 7, 73, 84–5
Erasmus Roterodaus, Desiderius
    23, 39
Erickson, Stacy 140, 154

falsehood 9, 10, 12, 25, 85, 120; *see*
    falseness
falseness 11, 79, 82; *see* falsehood 9,
    10, 12
family 34, 107, 109–13, 141
Farness, Jay 144, 154

Index 163

Ferber, Susan 108, 111, 115
Fisher, Will 89, 99
flattery 11, 17, 20, 22, 72–3, 128;
   flatterers 21, 36, 73–81, 84, 86
Fletcher, Alan J. 57
Forker Charles R. 72
form 7–10
Foucault, Michel 39
Fowles, Susannah 106, 111
Foxe, John 69
friars 19, 62–3, 67, 69, 74;
   Franciscans 67–9
Fuller, Thomas 125, 137
Fulwood, William 39–40

G. Co. 103, 11, 116
Gadd, Ian 140, 148, 154
Gainsford, Thomas 20
garments 11, 62, 64–5, 69, 87–89,
   91–8 *see* clothing and clothes
Gauld, Alan, and Anthony Cornell
   110, 116
gender 12, 89, 111, 119–36, 147
ghost 96–8, 102, 149
Glover, Mary 111–3
godliness 8, 101, 112, 123–4, 128,
   142, 146–7
Goffman, Erving 9–10, 13
Grafton, Anthony 148, 154
Grant, Ruth W. 7, 13, 152, 154
gratitude 33–5, 45, 48–9
Greenblatt, Stephen 104, 116
Grierson, Herbert J. C. 45
Guazzo, Stefano 17, 20–3, 28–9, 76
Gunter, Anne 106
Gurr, Andrew 72
Gurr, Margaret 111

Haffended, John 144, 154
Hall, Joseph 11, 14, 18–9, 59, 70, 98,
   123, 137
Hams, Thomas 138, 142–3, 146
Handley, Sasha 98, 99
Hankins, James 23
Harmes, Marcus 89–90, 99
Harsnett, Samuel 103–10, 114, 116
Hartley, Edmond 112
Hathaway, Richard 102, 115
Hayward, Mary 90, 99
Helgerson, Richard 141, 154
Hentschell, Roze 89, 99
Herdt, Jennifer 15–6, 18
Herzig, Tamar and Miriam
   Eliav-Feldon 7, 76

Hills, Henry 12–13, 138–53
Hobbes, Thomas 52
Hodgkin, Katharine 7, 12, 109, 116,
   152, 154
Hogan, Patrick 6, 14
Holden Pike, Godfrey 142, 155
holiness 8, 18, 58–65, 91, 108, 124
Holland, Peter 67
Howson, Robert, 106, 111, 116
Hoxby, Blair 96, 99
Hug, Tobias B. 8, 14
Hwang, Su-kyung 1, 63, 65,
Hyland, Peter 60
hypocrisy 7–9, 15–21, 33, 35–6, 47,
   51, 57–8, 62–5, 69, 73, 76, 78, 82,
   85; as simulation of virtue 24, 65;
   hypocrisy and religious overtones
   19, 57; virtues of hypocrisy 39; *see*
   hypocrite
hypocrite 8–9, 11, 12, 18–9, 29, 39,
   51, 57–61, 65, 69; *see* hypocrisy

I.D. 103–4, 106, 116
identity 8, 11, 36, 61, 85, 101, 103,
   109–10, 139–40, 152; ungodly and
   godly 8
idolatry 87, 97, 132, 134
illness 108, 114, 134; *see also* disease
ingratitude 33–4, 40, 47
inwardness 8, 128
Isaac, Peter and Barry McKay 140, 155

Jack, Sibyl 90, 99
Jackson, Louise 110, 116
Jackson, MacDonald P. 72
Jenner, Mark 148, 155
Jessey, Henry 108, 116
Johns, Adrian 141, 154
Johnstone, Nathan 105, 116
Jollie, Thomas 104, 116
Jones, Ann and Peter Stallybrass, 2,
   14, 89, 98–9
Jonson, Ben 52, 72, 123
Jorden, Edward 108, 116

Kant 9
Kaula, David 87, 99
Kearney, James 87, 99
Kendrick, Christopher 96, 99
Kiffen, William 142, 145
King James Bible 4, 101, 102,
   139, 142
King, Daniel 142, 145
King, John 94, 99

164 *Index*

Kirby, Richard 108, 111, 116
Knights, Mark 8, 14
Kreitzer, Larry 142, 145, 155
Kristeva, Julia 121, 135, 137
Kronenfeld, Judy 89, 99
Kruger, Stephen 57

La Primaudaye, Pierre 33–4, 49
Lake, Peter 8, 14, 91, 100
Lake Prescott, Anne 146, 155
Lamb, Jonathan, 148, 155
Laud, William 87–92, 94–5, 100
Leishman, James Blair 41
Levy Peck, Linda 90, 100
linen 12, 87–98
Loveman, Kate 142, 144–5, 151, 155
Luckij, Christina 64–6
Lucy Harrington, Countess of Bedford
  35, 42–3, 49, 50
lying 9, 16–7, 36, 73
Lynch, Katherine 138, 144, 155

Machiavelli, Niccolò 9, 39, 73, 75;
  Machiavellian (figure) 7, 65
MacIntyre, Jean and Garrett P. J. Epp
  69, 79
Mack, Peter 23
Macropedius, Georgius 26
Malpas, Katharine 106
manners 10, 21, 36, 37, 82, 131
Marlowe, Christopher 69
Marotti, Arthur F. 35, 43, 46, 49
Marten, Henry 145, 147
Martin, John Jeffries 15–6
Martin, Randall 109, 117
Maruca, Lisa 140, 155
Marwood, Anthony 105
Massai, Sonia 148, 155
masking 8, 36, 123
materiality 2, 10, 88–9, 95, 97–8;
  material forms 7, 9, 10, 12, 62
Maurer, Margaret 43
Maus, Katharine Eisaman 8, 14,
  34, 55
Maxwell-Stuart, P.G. 110, 117
Mayo, Janet 90, 100
Mazzio, Carla 3, 14
McDonald, Peter and Michael Suarez
  140, 155
McDowell, Paula 13, 14, 140, 155
McKenzie, Donald and Maureen Bell
  152, 155
Memory 41, 45, 97
mendacity 9, 15, 17, 20, 23, 25, 27, 138

Mendle, Michael 139, 155
Milgate, Wesley 45
Milne, Kirsty 87, 100
Milton, John 12, 87–98; works
  Paradise Lost 89; *Samson Agonistes*
  89, *Of Reformation* 92, *The Reason
  of Church Government* 92; *An
  Apology against a Pamphlet* 94;
  Eikonoklastes 95; *Areopagitica* 95
Moberg, David 5, 14
Montaigne, Michel 33–4, 53:
  Essays 34
Montini, Donatella 72
More, George 106, 111–2, 117
Mowry, Melissa 146, 155
Mucci, Clara 39
Muddiman, Joseph 138, 155
Murdock, Graeme 90–1, 100
Muschamp, Margaret 113

New Model Army 138–9
New Testament 36, 58
Newbold, W. Webster 39
Newton, Hohn 105, 117
Nigri, Lucia 7, 11, 12
Nyndge, Alexander 101, 102
Nyndge, Edward 112, 117

O'Hagan Hardy, Molly 140, 155
Oldridge, Darren 111, 116
Overton, Richard 87, 92

Parsons, Robert 148, 156
Patterson, Angus 98, 100
patronage 10, 33–5, 40, 44–5, 47;
  structure of 40, 47; culture of 45;
  see patrons and patronesses
patrons and patronesses 33, 35, 41–2;
  see patronage
Peacham, Henry 22
Pearson, Jacqueline 7, 12
Pebworth, Ted-Larry 41
Peltonen, Markku 7, 10, 23–4, 28
Pemble, William 25–7
performance 9–13, 23, 41, 57–70, 79,
  93, 95, 101, 106, 109–114, 119,
  121, 123–4, 133, 143
Perry, Curtis 33
Perry, William ('The Boy of
  Bilson') 106
Peters, Hugh 149
Petto, Samuel 106, 108, 117
Pharisees 4–6, 58, 101
Phelps Morand, Paul 144, 156

Index 165

Pierce, Helen 94, 100
piety 17, 58, 60, 92, 119–20, 127–8
Pindar, Rachel 106
Poole, Kristen 89, 100
Porter, Roy 39
post-reformation 10, 15, 87, 90
Powell, Vavasor 132, 137
Pricket, Robert 18
print culture 7, 90, 96–7, 138–53
Proffitt, Michael 2, 7, 14
propaganda 60, 65, 107, 139
Prynne 76
Prynne, William 19
Puritans 57, 105, 107, 120, 122–4
Purkiss, Diane 109, 113, 117
Puttenham, George 37–8, 51, 53

Quintilian 25

R.B. 101, 107, 117
Raiswell, Richard 106, 117
Raven, James 140, 156
Raymond, Joad 144, 150, 156
readers 10, 28, 63, 96, 123, 129,
   142–3
Reformation 10, 15, 36, 87, 90, 92,
   95, 124
Restoration 12, 57, 105, 143,
   148, 151
rhetoric 10, 20, 23–5, 29, 88, 92, 95,
   97–8, 130, 135; rhetoric manuals/
   books 17, 26, 37; *ars rhetorica*
   23–5, 28; rhetorical strategies
   35, 94
Richards, Jennifer 8, 14, 28, 32, 76,
   86
Rider, John 19
Robbins, Rossell Hope 110, 117
Robinson, Hugh 24, 26
Robinson, John 19
Rogers, Timothy 129, 137
Roman Catholic Church 11, 57–8,
   65: protestant/Anglican *versus*
   Catholics 36, 60, 63, 65, 69; *see*
   Catholicism
Runciman, David 17, 32, 143, 156

Sanders, Julie 149, 156
Sands, Kathleen 106, 113, 117
Santesso, Aaaron 148–9, 156
satire 46, 87, 94, 120, 141, 150
Sawday, Jonathan 39
Sawdie, Thomas 111, 113
Seary, Peter 2, 14

Schneider, Gary 41
Schwoerer, Lois 140, 156
Sebellin Rossana 7, 11
self 12, 16; self-examination 120,
   129–30; self-fashioning 8, 11;
   self-knowledge 120, 128–31,
   135; self-representation 8, 58;
   prudential self 15; inner self 17;
   dissimulation of 73
Seneca 45
Shakespeare, William 7, 11, 69, 123;
   works *Hamlet* 1–2; *King Lear*
   80; *Measure for Measure* 63, 68;
   Richard II 75, 77, 79; *Richard III*
   61–2, 67, 69; *Romeo and Juliet* 67;
   Thomas of Woodstock (apocrypha)
   11, 72–6
Sharpe, James 106, 117
Sharpe, Kevin 144, 156
Shepherd, Simon 149, 156
sincerity 7, 36, 52, 64, 81, 105, 121,
   123, 125, 131
Sinclair, George 109–10, 118
Skinner, Quentin 23–4, 28
Smart, John 144, 156
Smith, Edward 106
Smith, Helen 140, 148, 156
Smith, Roger 39
Snyder, Jon R. 15–6
Somers, William 103–4, 106–7
space 62, 76, 125, 135, 141, 143, 148
Spatchet, Thomas 108
Speed, Samuel 5, 14
Stachniewski, John 12, 120, 137
Starkie children 111–2
Starn, Randolph 152, 156
Stearne, John 101, 115
Stirredge, Elizabeth 133, 137
Stirry, Thomas 94
Stone Peters, Julie 138, 156
Stretton, Jane 111
Strohm, Paul 7, 14
Stubbes, Philip 51–2, 55, 127, 137
Stubbs, John 43
Styles, John 90, 100
Summit, Jennifer 152, 156
Sutton, Anne 90, 100
Sutton, Katherine 132, 137
Swan, John 103, 111, 112, 118
Swetnam, Joseph 122–3, 137

Targoff, Ramie 76
Taylor, Zachary 103–5, 114, 118
Tertullian 36, 51

166 Index

textiles 12, 88, 90
theatre 10, 11, 19, 58, 60–1
theatricality 7, 11, 69, 79, 83, 104
Thomson, Patricia 51
Throckmorton children 106, 111
Tipton, Alzada 84
Torshell, Samuel 124, 127–8, 137
trade 2, 5, 11, 34, 87–8, 90, 93, 96, 98, 140–1, 147, 150
transgression 52, 111, 121
Trapnel, Anna 131–2, 137
truth 7–10, 19–25, 50, 65, 77–8, 80, 83–6, 89, 96, 105, 124, 128, 131, 133, 134, 136, 142, 144, 152; truthfulness 10, 73, 133
Tsentourou, Naya 7, 12
Tubb, Amos 139–41, 156
Turner, Jane 130, 137, 142
Turval, Jean l'Oiseau de 24
Tyndale, William 19

Ure, Peter 72

Valerius, Cornelius 24, 26
Van Dijkhuizen, Jan Frans 114, 118
Vane, Henry 147
vanity 58, 78, 122–3, 127, 147
vestments 2, 12, 65, 69, 88–91, 95–6, 98
Vicars, Thomas 26

Vickers, Brian 52, 58, 61
Villari, R. 15
Vincent, Susan J. 36
virtue 11, 18–9, 21–5, 119–127, 131, 133, 147; display of 79

Walsh, Brian 57
Watkins, Owen 109, 118, 144, 156
Webb, Mary 111
Webster, John 69, 77; works *The White Devil* 63–7
Weightman Stewart, Patricia 36
Wentworth, Anne 133–4, 136–7
Westaway, Jonathan and Richard Harrison 103, 105, 118
Whately, William 125–6, 128–31, 135, 137
Whitley, William 139, 156
Wikander, Matthew H. 62
Williamson, Elizabeth 62
Wilson, Robert 61
Wilson, Thomas 24
witchcraft 108, 110–1, 114, 121
Wolsey, Thomas 98
Wright, Katherine 112
Wright, Thomas 122, 137

Zagorin, Perez 4, 7, 14, 17, 32, 36, 56
Zwicker, Stephen 87, 100, 149, 156